D1081914

YOUR WORD IS TRUTH

YOUR WORD IS TRUTH

A Project of Evangelicals and Catholics Together

Edited by

Charles Colson and Richard John Neuhaus

WILLIAM B. EERDMANS PUBLISHING COMPANY
GRAND RAPIDS, MICHIGAN / CAMBRIDGE, U.K.

© 2002 Wm. B. Eerdmans Publishing Co.
All rights reserved

Wm. B. Eerdmans Publishing Co.
255 Jefferson Ave. S.E., Grand Rapids, Michigan 49503 /
P.O. Box 163, Cambridge CB3 9PU U.K.

Printed in the United States of America

07 06 05 04 03 02   7 6 5 4 3 2 1

ISBN 0-8028-0508-6

www.eerdmans.com

Contents

Introduction

On the long list of what might be called traditional disagreements between Evangelical Protestants and Roman Catholics is the relationship between Scripture and tradition. In fact, there are few disagreements on the list that have been more agitated over the centuries. Whatever else Evangelicals and Catholics may be able to agree about, it is commonly said, there is no way of getting over or around the fundamental difference on the very source of Christian teaching — Scripture alone *(sola scriptura)*, on the one hand, or Scripture and authoritative tradition, on the other.

The statement that is the centerpiece of this book, "Your Word Is Truth," is the result of intensive prayer, study, and uncompromisingly candid discussion among the Evangelicals and Catholics whose names are appended to it. We do not claim that this statement resolves all our differences about Scripture and tradition, and it should be evident that we resolutely reject any thought of getting around such differences. We believe the statement does go a long way toward recasting an old dispute in a new and promising way. It underscores the utter singularity of the authority of Scripture and, at the same time, the unavoidable necessity of discerning the right interpretation of Scripture in the history of Christian faith and life — a history that is rightly called tradition.

But we say no more here about the statement itself. We urge the reader to study "Your Word Is Truth" with the same prayerful care that produced it. And we strongly urge that the statement be read along with the papers especially prepared for this project and included as chapters in this book. Each chapter, written by a distinguished Evangelical or Catholic theologian, stands on its own as a valuable contribution to understanding Scripture and its interpretation, while together the chapters reflect the comprehensive nature of the inquiry that informed our discussion. They also provide a valuable context for understanding "Your Word Is Truth," addressing concerns that are reflected, but not treated explicitly, in the statement itself.

This statement and this book are part of the ongoing project known as "Evangelicals and Catholics Together," commonly called "ECT." The project began in 1992 with a conference occasioned by growing and often violent conflicts between Catholics and Evangelical Protestants in Latin America. In March 1994 we issued a statement, "Evangelicals and Catholics Together: The Christian Mission in the Third Millennium." In that statement we explained why it is necessary, as "brothers and sisters in Christ," to work with one another, and not against one another, in the great task of evangelization, and to support one another in facing up to the ominous moral and cultural threats of our time. The many signers of the statement pledged themselves to that Christian solidarity and, while this initiative has not been without its critics, both Evangelical and Catholic, we are greatly heartened by the thousands who have joined in that pledge.

Such solidarity, if it is to be true and enduring, must be grounded in nothing less than the gospel of Jesus Christ. This has been an insistent theme of ECT, reaffirmed every step of the way: The only unity that is pleasing to God, and therefore the only unity we can seek, is unity in truth. This theme was deepened and exemplified in the 1997 statement, "The Gift of Salvation." In that statement we together affirmed the way in which we understand justification by faith alone as a gift received by God's grace alone because of Christ alone. As with the present statement, and as we have at every step along the way, we also noted carefully the questions on which, as Evangelicals and Catholics, we continue to disagree.

We speak of steps along the way because ECT must be understood as a work in progress. We are convinced that this is a work of the Holy Spirit. This work was underway long before ECT was begun. In recent decades, Evangelicals and Catholics have encountered one another as brothers and sisters in Christ in many forums, and especially as they contend together for a culture of life that will protect the unborn, the aged, the handicapped, and others whom some deem to be expendable. These encounters and the patterns of cooperation they have produced are aptly described as "the ecumenism of the trenches." ECT can be understood as simply making explicit what was implicit: that our unity in action is the fruit of our unity in faith. Our unity in action and in faith is by no means perfect. If this is the work of the Holy Spirit, as we firmly believe, it will continue long after the present participants in ECT have gone to their eternal reward. We do not know how or when, but we do believe that the prayer of our Lord in John 17 will be answered, that his disciples will be one in a way that will lead the world to see and believe that he was sent by the Father.

Moreover, our historical circumstance makes our common witness increasingly urgent. Our circumstance is one of unremitting conflict between two distinct and antithetical worldviews, or understandings of reality. The lines of conflict are variously drawn and the combatants are variously defined, but the undeniable contention is between a militantly secular naturalism, on the one side, and, on the other, a biblical understanding of reality as the object of God's creating and redeeming work. Those who deny or ignore that understanding have met with considerable success in eliminating the influence and even the memory of Christianity from more and more aspects of our public life.

Evangelicals and Catholics together share, and must together contend for, that biblical worldview. Whatever differences there have been between us in the past, and whatever differences persist still today, we stand side by side in contending for the truth of that understanding of reality. Such solidarity is aptly called co-belligerency, and such co-belligerency is the more solid as it is more firmly grounded in the same Bible, the same creeds, and the same confession that Jesus Christ is Lord. With this book and related undertakings, we seek to deepen our understanding of the common faith that binds us that we might more effectively address the common tasks that claim us.

A century ago, the great Calvinist leader, Abraham Kuyper, recognized that the common defense of a biblical worldview made necessary precisely the kind of effort in which we are today engaged. In his Stone Lectures at Princeton, Kuyper argued that, when we understand Christianity also as a worldview, we "might be enabled once more to take our stand by the side of Romanism in opposition to modern pantheism." In a similar way, Catholic teaching officially and strongly encourages the fullest possible cooperation among Christians in contending for a culture of life and of truth against the encroaching culture of death and deceit. If then anyone asks about the purpose of this book and of the ongoing project of which it is part, the answer is clear: It is to evangelize more effectively, to convince the world that Jesus is the Lord and Savior sent by the Father, and to bring that great truth to bear on every dimension of life — just as we are commanded to do.

It only remains to be said that ECT is an unofficial initiative. We speak from and to the communities of which we are part, but we do not presume to speak for them. We wholeheartedly support the several official theological dialogues between Evangelicals and Catholics. ECT is a supplementary initiative, serving as a kind of advance scouting party to explore possibilities and, as such, has received much appreciated encouragement from official sources, both Evangelical and Catholic. We have no illusions that the centuries-long wounds of our divisions will be quickly or easily healed. We are convinced that ECT is part of a project that is God's before it is ours, and is only ours because it is God's. We offer this statement and this book in the spirit of the concluding words of our first statement in 1994: "This is a time of opportunity — and, if of opportunity then of responsibility — for Evangelicals and Catholics to be Christians together in a way that helps prepare the world for the coming of Him to whom belongs the kingdom, the power, and the glory forever. Amen."

January, 2002   CHARLES COLSON
                                                             RICHARD JOHN NEUHAUS

Your Word Is Truth

Our Lord and Savior Jesus Christ prayed for his disciples: "Sanctify them in the truth; your word is truth. . . . I do not pray for these only, but also for those who believe in me through their word, that they may all be one; even as you, Father, are in me, and I in you, that they also may be in us, so that the world may believe that you have sent me" (John 17:17, 20, 21).

We thank God for the years of prayer, study, and conversation in the project known as "Evangelicals and Catholics Together." Among the many blessings resulting from this cooperative effort, we note especially our common affirmation of the most central truths of Christian faith, including justification by faith, in the 1997 statement, "The Gift of Salvation." From the beginning of this venture, and at each step along the way, we have insisted that the only unity among Christians that can be pleasing to God is unity in truth. Therefore, we have understood it to be our duty to note, carefully and clearly, matters both of agreement and of disagreement between Evangelicals and Catholics.

Among matters of utmost importance, and involving both agreements and disagreements, is the question traditionally framed as the relationship between Scripture and tradition. As we have together explored this question, we have prayed for the guidance of the Holy Spirit, and we believe that prayer has been answered. We respectfully submit the following considerations and conclusions to the ecclesial communities and transdenominational fellowships of which we are part, with the hope that they will be received and examined as possible contributions to our better understanding of one another and our greater unity in Christ's truth.

From before the foundation of the world, God has desired a people to

1

share forever in his life and love (Eph. 1:4). To that end, God disclosed himself and his loving intention by a sequence of revelatory and redemptive acts that involved the uttering of verbal messages and the producing of written records (Heb. 1:1). He created a world that bears witness to his glory (Ps. 19:1-6), and when humanity sinfully rebelled against his purpose, he chose Israel to be instructed by word and deed in the ways of covenant fidelity in order to become a light to all the nations (Gen. 12:1-3; Deut. 4:1-8). To this people he promised a Savior, who is Jesus the Christ, the very Word of God who was in the beginning with God, and who is to be recognized and confessed as the Son of God (John 1:1-14). The God of Israel is the One whom Jesus calls Father and teaches us to call Father (John 17:1-5; Matt. 6:6-13). To his disciples, and to those who would become disciples through their word, he promised the Spirit to guide them into all truth. Thus the new Israel worshipped, obeyed, and proclaimed the one true God — Father, Son, and Holy Spirit — in faith-filled anticipation of participating in the divine life forever (Heb. 12:18-24; John 16:3; Acts 1:8). Already now, God's promised redemption is fulfilled in the mediatorial ministry of Jesus Christ that is centered in his cross, resurrection, ascension, present reign, and assured return in glory to establish his eternal kingdom (2 Cor. 1:19, 20).

God gives his people full and final knowledge of his plan of salvation through Jesus Christ. "In many and various ways God spoke of old to our fathers by the prophets; but in these last days he has spoken to us by a Son, whom he appointed the heir of all things, through whom also he created the world" (Heb. 1:1, 2). The Son sent and sends the Holy Spirit who, bestowing the gift of faith, creates the community of faith for whose unity Jesus prayed. Christ himself is the head and cornerstone of his church, which is built on the foundation of apostles and prophets. In its understanding, believing, celebrating, living, and proclaiming the gospel of Jesus Christ, the church is guided by the Holy Spirit (Eph. 2:19-22).

Both Evangelicals and Catholics affirm the one, holy, catholic and apostolic church, as set forth in the Nicene-Constantinopolitan Creed, but they define the church and its attributes in distinctive ways. Evangelicals stress the priority of the gospel over the church, whose primary mission is to herald the good news of God's salvation in Christ. For Evangelicals, the church, as the one body of Christ extending through space and time, includes all the redeemed of all the ages and all on earth in every era who have come to living faith in the body's living Head. Everyone who is personally united to Christ, having been justified by faith alone through his atoning death, belongs to his body and by the Spirit is united with every other true believer in Jesus. Evangelicals maintain that the one church becomes visible on earth in all local congregations that meet to do together the things that according to Scripture the church does.

Catholics hold that the church is the body of Christ, a sacramental and mystical communion in which Christ is truly and effectually present and through which his justifying and sanctifying grace is mediated. While Christ is the unique mediator of salvation for all humanity, the church of Jesus Christ "subsists in" and is most fully and rightly ordered in the Catholic Church, meaning the church governed by the bishops in communion with the bishop of Rome, the successor of Peter. Although there have been variations through history in the exercise of that governance, and may be further variations in order to accommodate a fuller expression of Christian unity, Catholics believe that Christ has endowed the church with a permanent apostolic structure and an infallible teaching office that will remain until the Kingdom is fully consummated.

While Catholics and Evangelicals have not been able to reconcile these different views of the church, with both communities finding serious aberrations in the ecclesial understanding of the other, as individual believers we do recognize in one another, when and where God so permits it, the evident reality of God's grace expressed by our trust in Jesus himself as Master and divine Savior. All who truly believe in Jesus Christ as Savior and Lord are brothers and sisters in the Lord even though they are not in full ecclesial fellowship.

In communion with the body of faithful Christians through the ages, we also affirm together that the entire teaching, worship, ministry, life, and mission of Christ's church is to be held accountable to the final authority of Holy Scripture which, for Evangelicals and Catholics alike, constitutes the word of God in written form (2 Tim. 3:15-17; 2 Pet. 1:21). We agree that the phrase "Word of God" refers preeminently to Jesus Christ (John 1:1, 14). It is also rightly said that the gospel of Jesus Christ is the word of God, as is the faithful preaching of the gospel (Acts 6:7; 8:4). Then the canon, the listed set of writings making up the Bible, is recognized by the community of faith as the written word of God, possessing final authority for faith and life. On the extent of the canon we do not entirely agree, though the sixty-six books of the Protestant canon are not in dispute. In every form — the gospel, the preaching of the gospel, and the Scriptures of the Old and New Testaments — the word of God is in service to Jesus Christ, the Word of God preeminent.

The divinely inspired writings of the New Testament convey the apostolic teaching, which is the authoritative interpretation of God's revelation in Christ. The early Christian community recognized the authority of the first apostles who planted local churches and urged them to be faithful to the teaching they had received. Still today we possess that apostolic teaching in the New Testament which, together with the Old Testament of which the New is the authoritative interpretation, is the written word of God. This entire process of the reception and transmission of God's revelation is the work of the Holy Spirit (John 14:26; 2 Tim. 3:15-17; 2 Pet. 1:20, 21).

Evangelicals and Catholics alike recognize the promised guidance of the Spirit in the elucidation and unfolding of apostolic teaching that took place as historic Christian orthodoxy emerged. This continuing work of the Spirit is evident in, for instance, the formulation of the Apostles', Nicene, and Athanasian creeds, and in the conciliar resolution of disputes regarding the two natures of Christ and the triune life of God. Such development of doctrine, typically in response to grave error and deviant traditions built upon such error, is to be understood not as an addition to the apostolic teaching contained in Holy Scripture but as Spirit-guided insight into the fullness of that teaching. In this way, the Lord has enabled faithful believers both to counter error and to make explicit what is implicit in the written word of God.

In the course of that same history, and in the context of crises posed by philosophical and cultural changes as well as manifest ecclesiastical corruptions, the question of how to determine authentic apostolic teaching came into intense dispute. The mainline Reformers of the sixteenth century posited what is called the "formal principle," which holds that the Scriptures are (in the words of the 2000 Amsterdam Declaration) "the inspired revelation of God . . . totally true and trustworthy, and the only infallible rule of faith and practice." The Reformers vigorously protested what they viewed as deviations from biblical teaching, but they never used Scripture to undermine the trinitarian and christological consensus of the early church embodied in the historic creeds that had come down from patristic times. The Reformers stoutly resisted the charge of innovation: they did not seek to found new churches but sought simply to reform the one, holy, catholic and apostolic church on the basis of the word of God.

We who are Evangelicals recognize the need to address the widespread misunderstanding in our community that *sola scriptura* (Scripture alone) means *nuda scriptura* (literally, Scripture unclothed, that is, denuded of and abstracted from its churchly context). The phrase *sola scriptura* refers to the primacy and sufficiency of Scripture as the theological norm — the only infallible rule of faith and practice — over all tradition rather than the mere rejection of tradition itself. The isolation of Scripture study from the believing community of faith *(nuda scriptura)* disregards the Holy Spirit's work in guiding the witness of the people of God to scriptural truths, and leaves the interpretation of that truth vulnerable to unfettered subjectivism. At the same time, we insist that all Christians should have open access to the Bible,

4

and should be encouraged to read and study the Scriptures, for in them all that is necessary for salvation is set forth so clearly that the simplest believer, no less than the wisest theologian, may arrive at a sufficient understanding of them.

We who are Catholics must likewise address the widespread misunderstanding in our community that tradition is an addition to Holy Scripture or a parallel and independent source of authoritative teaching. When Catholics say "Scripture and tradition," they intend to affirm that the lived experience (tradition) of the community of faith through time includes the ministry of faithful interpreters guided by the Holy Spirit in discerning and explicating the revealed truth contained in the written word of God, namely, Holy Scripture.

Together we affirm that Scripture is the divinely inspired and uniquely authoritative written revelation of God; as such it is normative for the teaching and life of the church. We also affirm that tradition, rightly understood as the proper reflection of biblical teaching, is the faithful transmission of the truth of the gospel from generation to generation through the power of the Holy Spirit. As Evangelicals and Catholics fully committed to our respective heritages, we affirm together the coinherence of Scripture and tradition: Tradition is not a second source of revelation alongside the Bible but must ever be corrected and informed by it, and Scripture itself is not understood in a vacuum apart from the historical existence and life of the community of faith. Faithful believers in every generation live by the memories and hopes of the *actus tradendi* of the Holy Spirit: this is true whenever and wherever the word of God is faithfully translated, sincerely believed, and truly preached.

We recognize that confessing a high doctrine of the nature and place of Scripture is insufficient without a firm commitment to the intense devotional, disciplined, and prayerful engagement with Scripture. We rejoice to note that in our communities, and in joint study involving people from both communities, such engagement is increasingly common. In this engagement with Scripture, Evangelicals and Catholics are learning from one another: Catholics from the Evangelical emphasis on group Bible study and commitment to the majestic and final authority of the written word of God; and Evangelicals from the Catholic emphasis on Scripture in the liturgical and devotional life, informed by the lived experience of Christ's church through the ages.

There always have been, and likely will be until our Lord returns in glory, disputes and disagreements about how rightly to discern the teaching of the word of God in Holy Scripture. We affirm that Scripture is to be read in company with the community of faith past and present. Individual ideas of what the Bible means must be brought to the bar of discussion and assessment by the wider fellowship.

"The church of the living God is the pillar and bulwark of the truth" (1 Tim. 3:15). Because Christ's church is the pillar and bulwark of truth, in disputes over conflicting interpretations of the word of God the church must be capable of discerning true teaching and setting it forth with clarity. This is necessary both in order to identify and reject heretical deviations from the truth of the gospel and also to provide sound instruction for passing on the faith intact to the rising generation.

Evangelicals and Catholics alike are concerned with these questions — What does the Bible authoritatively teach? And how does Christ's church apply this teaching authoritatively today? Catholics believe that this teaching authority is invested in the magisterium, namely, the bishop of Rome, who is the successor of Peter, and the bishops in communion with him. Some Evangelicals see the communal office of discerning and teaching the truth in the covenanted congregation of baptized believers, while others see it in a wider synodical or episcopal connection. In either case, however, Evangelicals believe that a true understanding of the Bible is achieved only through the illuminating action of the Holy Spirit. For this reason, all attempts at discernment and teaching must rely on prayerful attentiveness to the guidance of the Spirit in the study of Scripture.

While Catholics agree that the entire community of the faithful is engaged in the discernment of the truth *(sensus fidelium)*, they also believe the Evangelicals have an inadequate appreciation of certain elements of truth that, from the earliest centuries, Christians have understood Christ to have intended for his church; in particular, the Petrine and other apostolic ministries. While Evangelicals greatly respect the way in which the Catholic Church has defended many historic Christian teachings against relativizing and secularizing trends, and recognize the role of the present pontiff in that important task today, they believe that some aspects of Catholic doctrine are not biblically warranted, and they do not accept any claims of infallibility made for the magisterial teachings of popes or church councils.

With specific reference to the subject of the present statement, we are not agreed on the exercise of teaching authority in the life of Christ's church. To Evangelicals it appears that, in practice if not in theory, the Catholic understanding of magisterium, including infallibility, results in the Roman Catholic Church standing in judgment over Scripture, instead of vice versa. Catholics, in turn, teach that the magisterium exercised by the successors of the apostles — which they believe is intended by Christ, is guided by the Holy Spirit, and is in clear continuity with the orthodox tradition — enables the church to explicate the truth of Holy Scripture obediently and accurately. We both recognize that judgments must be made in the life of Christ's church as to what is and what is not scriptural truth. We are not agreed on how such judgments are to be made, nor can either group accept all the decisions that have resulted from what they regard as a flawed way of deciding.

Among the Catholic teachings that Evangelicals believe are not biblically warranted are the eucharistic sacrifice and transubstantiation of the elements, the doctrine of purgatory, the immaculate conception and bodily assumption of the Blessed Virgin Mary, and the claimed authority of the magisterium, including papal infallibility. Catholics, on the other hand, believe that Evangelicals are deficient in their understanding of, for instance, apostolically ordered ministry, the number and nature of the sacraments, the company and intercession of the saints, the Spirit-guided development of doctrine, and the continuing ministry of the Petrine office in the life of the church. On these and other questions of great importance, we are not agreed. Nor do we agree on how we view our differences. Catholics view Evangelicalism as an ecclesially deficient community that needs to be strengthened by the full complement of gifts that they believe Christ intends for his church. Evangelicals see Catholicism as centering upon an idea of the church that clouds the New Testament gospel, and so needs to be brought into greater conformity with biblical teaching. The contrast here is far-reaching, and goes deep.

At the same time, we recognize that, during the past five hundred years, the Holy Spirit, the Supreme Magisterium of God, has been faithfully at work among theologians and exegetes in both Catholic and Evangelical communities, bringing to light and enriching our understanding of important biblical truths in such matters as individual spiritual growth and development, the mission of Christ's church, Christian worldview thinking, and moral and social issues in today's world. We praise God for his faithful work within each community as he has provided instruction and guidance in these and other important areas of Christian faith and life.

As Evangelicals and Catholics we are agreed on what we have said together in the statement "The Gift of Salvation" and on what we have been able to say together in the present statement on Scripture and tradition. The theological disagreements that still separate us are serious and require prayerful reflection and sustained mutual engagement. But in the face of a society marked by unbelieving ideologies and the culture of death, we deem it all the more important to affirm together those foundational truths of historic Christian orthodoxy that we do share in common.

We are confident that the Lord is watching over his gospel and over those who have been called by the gospel, and we are sure that the forces of hell will not be able to thwart his divine purpose. By God's grace, we will continue to pray for one another, to seek greater mutual understanding in continuing conversations and, in accordance with our deeply-held convictions, to work together to bring the love and light of Christ to all persons everywhere. We earnestly invoke the Holy Spirit's continuing guidance in further establishing and making manifest our unity in the truth of Jesus Christ, so that the world may come to believe (John 17:21). In union with our Lord and Savior Jesus Christ, we together pray, "Sanctify us in the truth; Your word is truth" (John 17:17).

Dr. Harold O. J. Brown
Reformed Theological Seminary

Dr. James J. Buckley
Loyola College in Maryland

Mr. Charles Colson
Prison Fellowship

Avery Cardinal Dulles, S.J.
Fordham University

Dr. Timothy George
Beeson Divinity School

Father Thomas Guarino
Seton Hall University

Dr. Kent R. Hill
Eastern Nazarene College

Dr. Frank A. James
Reformed Theological Seminary

Dr. Cheryl Bridges Johns
Church of God School of
    Theology

Father Joseph T. Lienhard, S.J.
Fordham University

Father Francis Martin
John Paul II Institute for Studies
    on Marriage and Family

Dr. T. M. Moore
Cedar Springs Presbyterian
    Church

Father Richard John Neuhaus
Religion and Public Life

Father Edward Oakes, S.J.
Regis University

Dr. Thomas Oden
Drew University

Dr. James J. I. Packer
Regent College, British Columbia

Dr. Timothy R. Phillips
Wheaton Graduate School of
    Theology

Dr. Robert Louis Wilken
University of Virginia

Dr. John Woodbridge
Trinity Evangelical Divinity
    School

An Evangelical Reflection on Scripture and Tradition

TIMOTHY GEORGE

Paul Dudley was admitted as a freshman to Harvard College at age eleven and went on to become a leading jurist in pre-Revolutionary New England. At his death in 1751, he left to his alma mater funds to endow an annual lectureship "for the detecting and convicting and exposing the idolatry of the Romish church, their tyranny, usurpations, damnable heresies, fatal errors, abominable superstitions and other crying wickednesses in their high places; and finally, that the Church of Rome is that mystical Babylon, that man of sin, that apostate church, spoken of in the New Testament."[1] It would be possible, of course, to cite equally virulent anti-Protestant sentiments from post-Tridentine Catholic sources. Suffice it to note these papal expressions aimed at early Protestant Evangelical efforts to disseminate the Scriptures throughout the world: "perverse machinations," "a deadly spring dispensing poison," "plague," "poisonous pastures."[2]

These quotations remind us of the mutual suspicions and hostilities shared by the heirs of both Rome and the Reformation. They are monuments of the torn and tattered condition of the church for whose unity Jesus prayed. Today we can still hear echoes of the older rhetoric in the comments of some

1. Samuel H. Morrison, *A History of Harvard College* (Cambridge: Harvard University Press, 1936), 2:450; George H. Williams, *Harvard Divinity School* (Boston: Beacon Press, 1956), 39. The original statutes for the Dudleian Lecture are quoted in Heiko A. Oberman, *"Quo Vadis?:* Tradition from Irenaeus to *Humani Generis," Scottish Journal of Theology* 16 (1963): 225.

2. Quoted in Yves Congar, *The Meaning of Tradition* (New York: Hawthorn Books, 1964), 90 n. 16. These statements are drawn from the papal pronouncements of Pius VII (8 September 1816) and Leo XII (5 May 1824).

of our fellow Evangelicals and Catholics who regard collaboration in theological dialogue as a "betrayal of the gospel" or a "denial of the faith." As brothers and sisters in Christ who desire to speak the truth to one another in love, we cannot be deflected by such criticism. At the same time, we cannot brush off as trivial the serious differences which have divided us in the past and which still prevent us from sharing together the one Holy Supper of our Lord. We reject the old canard still touted by many mainline ecumenists that "theology divides but service unites." We are engaged in an ecumenism of conviction, not accommodation, and thus we dare to confront one another in love, as well as to learn from one another in humility. Cardinal Joseph Ratzinger speaks for all of us, Catholics and Evangelicals alike, when he observes that "our quarreling ancestors were in reality much closer to each other when in all their disputes they still knew that they could only be servants of one truth which must be acknowledged as being as great and as pure as it has been intended for us by God."[3]

"Evangelicals and Catholics Together: The Christian Mission in the Third Millennium" was released at the end of March 1994 with the promise that continuing theological conversations would be forthcoming. A second round of ECT discussions began with a conference on "The Gospel in the Church" but soon turned toward a more deliberate focus on soteriology. The original ECT statement declared that "all who accept Christ as Lord and Savior are brothers and sisters in Christ" and included the affirmation that "we are justified by grace through faith because of Christ."[4] The meaning of these statements was further explored in additional conversations resulting in a second joint declaration, "The Gift of Salvation," issued in December 1997 and jointly published in *First Things* and *Christianity Today*. Although misunderstood and attacked by some critics within both traditions, "The Gift of Salvation" continues to have an impact around the world. It has served as the basis for an important Catholic-Protestant reconciliation initiative in Ireland, and was recently translated into Chinese by a Catholic ecumenical worker in Hong Kong.

"The Gift of Salvation" represents a remarkable convergence on what has traditionally been called the material principle of the Reformation: the utter gratuity of salvation expressed, in classic Protestant terminology, as the doctrine of justification by grace alone, through faith alone, in Jesus Christ alone. At the same time, this document frankly acknowledges that there are other, necessarily interrelated, doctrinal differences which still remain to be re-

---

3. Joseph Ratzinger, *Church, Ecumenism, and Politics* (New York: Crossroad, 1988), 98.

4. Charles Colson and Richard John Neuhaus, eds., *Evangelicals and Catholics Together: Toward a Common Mission* (Dallas: Word Publishing, 1995), xviii.

solved. The fact that we are now turning to the theme of Scripture and Tradition does not mean that this task has been accomplished. Many of these issues, however, such as Marian devotion, sacramental theology, as well as teachings on purgatory, indulgences, and the saints involve diverse understandings of doctrinal development and ecclesial authority.

Our strategy in crafting "The Gift of Salvation" was to study the Bible together. All of us, Evangelicals and Catholics alike, acknowledge that the Bible is the divinely inspired book of the church and that it can be fully understood only in fellowship with the Brethren, and in communion with the Fathers, not forgetting the Sisters and the Mothers. But what does this mean and how does it relate to the historic debates on the relative importance of Scripture and Tradition? It would seem that we cannot proceed further along the soteriological axis until we have given *some* attention to the formal principle of the Reformation which holds, in the words of the Lausanne Covenant (1974), that the Scriptures are "the only written word of God . . . and the only infallible rule of faith and practice." Such a program of study was already presaged by the original ECT statement when it listed among the issues which had to be addressed more fully "the sole authority of Scripture *(sola scriptura)* or Scripture as authoritatively interpreted in the church."[5]

As an initial sounding in this theme, we shall look first at the disparagement of Tradition within recent Evangelicalism; second, at the Reformation corrective to this neglect in its own view of the coinherence of Scripture and Tradition; then we shall trace the trajectory of Tradition from the sixteenth to the twentieth century, with reference to the Second Vatican Council and the fourth World Conference on Faith and Order at Montreal in 1963; and finally, we shall list several items for further reflection and study.

The Tradition of Traditionless Evangelicalism

Nothing has been more characteristic of Evangelicalism than its emphasis on personal conversion. From John Wesley's heart-warming conversion at Aldersgate to Chuck Colson's born-again experience during Watergate, Evangelicals have preached the necessity of the new birth and have witnessed its radically transforming power in their lives.[6] In their focus on conversion,

---

5. Colson and Neuhaus, *Evangelicals and Catholics Together,* xxi.

6. Both Wesley and Colson are among those whose conversion stories are included in the anthology edited by Hugh T. Kerr and John M. Mulder, *Conversions: The Christian Experience* (Grand Rapids: Eerdmans, 1983).

Evangelicals can claim a heritage of piety deeply rooted in the Christian Tradition: Puritans such as John Bunyan, who described his own conversion in *Grace Abounding to the Chief of Sinners;* theologians such as Calvin, who claimed that through the Holy Spirit believers were united with Christ "more closely than are the limbs with the body"; Reformers such as Luther, who described his discovery of the gospel as his being "altogether born again" and his entering "paradise itself through open gates"; saints such as Teresa of Avila, who was converted, after twenty years of struggle, while reading Augustine's *Confessions;* and the Doctor of Grace himself, whose *tolle, lege* in the garden was the summons to a new life.

Today, however, many Evangelicals interpret their own conversion as the supreme act of individualism, a private response detached, if not divorced, from the corporate community of faith. William Abraham, among others, has argued that this pattern is a betrayal of the practice of the early church, where conversion was seen as a process of initiation into the Kingdom community rather than an act that stands on its own.[7] Without diminishing the call for personal repentance and faith, Evangelicals need to develop an authentic spirituality drawn from the riches of the whole Christian Tradition, a fuller life in God than the one evident in the pop-pietism of ditties such as this: "Me and Jesus, we've got a good thing going; me and Him, we've got it all worked out."

Some years ago Harvey Cox wrote a book entitled *Turning East,* in which he criticized the strategy of *ressourcement* in spiritual direction as naive and counter-productive.

> As late twentieth-century Christians trying to work out a viable spirituality, there are two principal historical sources to which we should look. They are the earliest period of our history and the most recent, the first Christian generations and the generation just before us. . . . The ransacking of other periods for help in working out a contemporary spirituality soon becomes either antiquarian or downright misleading.[8]

Perhaps we can claim Harvey Cox as at least a lapsed Evangelical since he began his ministerial career as a Baptist youth evangelist. In any event, his counsel against "ransacking" the past reflects an attitude common in American

---

7. William Abraham, *The Logic of Evangelism* (London: Hodder & Stoughton, 1989), esp. 117-39. Cf. the typically outrageous, but not nonsensical, statement by Stanley Hauerwas: "No task is more important than for the Church to take the Bible out of the hands of individual Christians in North America" (*Unleashing the Scripture: Freeing the Bible from Captivity to America* [Nashville: Abingdon, 1993], 15-16).

8. Harvey Cox, *Turning East* (New York: Simon & Schuster, 1977), 157.

culture and the Evangelicalism shaped by it. We may call this disparagement of Tradition the heresy of contemporaneity or, in less theological terms, the imperialism of the present. In the Middle Ages, everyone believed that the earth was at the center of reality, that all of the created cosmos was ordered in relation to what we now know, thanks to Copernicus, is a mere speck of dust among myriads of constellations and galaxies. While the Copernican revolution has radically altered our view of space, we have yet to experience the Copernican revolution with respect to time. Thus we arrogantly place ourselves, our values, our worldview at the center of history, relegating whole epochs to "the Dark Ages" or "pre-Enlightenment culture." For Evangelicals this has meant, and still too often means, that the Christian past is not so much something to be studied and appropriated as it is something to be overcome.

The statement by Harvey Cox stands in continuity with the liberal theology of Friedrich Schleiermacher, who defined religion as the feeling of absolute dependence and Scripture as a detailed expression of that faith which is present in a feeling of need.[9] Schleiermacher's displacement of the objectivity of divine revelation by the Christian self-consciousness allowed him to relativize the great doctrines of historic orthodoxy by, as he put it, "entrusting them to history for safekeeping."[10] It is not surprising that Schleiermacher's entire treatment of the doctrine of the Trinity is contained in a thirteen-page appendix to his nearly 800-page *Glaubenslehre.*

Most Evangelicals have never heard of Schleiermacher's misty theology, but the reductionism evident in his approach to faith has also taken its toll within a popular Evangelicalism shaped by the likes of Billy Sunday, who once boasted that he knew no more about theology than a jackrabbit knew about ping-pong! A higher level of discourse is carried on in the Evangelical Theological Society, but even this august group of scholars only very recently amended its annually subscribed statement of faith to include, in addition to the single affirmation of biblical inerrancy, a required belief of the doctrine of the Holy Trinity. If, in Tillich's terms, Protestant principle has swallowed up Catholic substance in much of contemporary Evangelicalism, this is because Evangelicals have paid too little attention to the sum total of the Christian heritage handed down from previous ages, a heritage shaped by the coinherence of Scripture and Tradition.

9. Friedrich Schleiermacher, *The Christian Faith* (New York: Harper & Row, 1963), 2:593.

10. See Jaroslav Pelikan, *Historical Theology: Continuity and Change in Christian Doctrine* (Philadelphia: Westminster, 1971), 160. See also Timothy George, "Dogma Beyond Anathema: Historical Theology in the Service of the Church," *Review & Expositor* 84 (1987): 691-707.

Sola Scriptura . . . Scriptura Numquam Sola

The renewal of the church in the sixteenth century was intimately connected with proper distinctions between Scripture and Tradition. "Scripture alone," said Luther, "is the true lord and master of all writings and doctrine on earth. If that is not granted, what is Scripture good for? The more we reject it, the more we become satisfied with men's books and human teachers."[11] Luther's breakthrough on the formal principle of the Reformation occurred during his debate with John Eck at Leipzig in 1519, an event of greater significance for the future course of events than either the Indulgence Controversy two years earlier, or the famous encounter at Worms ("My conscience is captive to the Word of God") two years later. At Leipzig Luther was cornered ("eckt") into admitting the fallibility of popes and councils: a simple layman, he asserted, armed with Scripture should be believed above a pope or a council without it.[12]

Drawing on romantic and idealistic notions of the Reformation (cf. Hegel's description of the Reformation as "the all-illuminating sun, which follows that day-break at the end of the Middle Ages"[13]), Luther emerges as the champion of private interpretation, freedom of conscience, and modern individualism. This popular stereotype of Luther, however, will not bear close scrutiny. For how then can we understand his concluding remark in the "Disputation Against Scholastic Theology," repeated in other settings: "In all I wanted to say, we believe we have said nothing that is not in agreement with the Catholic church and the teachers of the church"?[14] In fact, in making his astounding claim at Leipzig, Luther was not saying anything new. Writing nearly a century before, Nicholas de Tudeschis (d. 1445), archbishop of Palermo, had put forth a similar claim: "In matters of faith anyone armed with better reasons and authorities of the New and Old Testaments is to be

---

11. "Defense and Explanation of All the Articles Which Were Rejected by the Roman Bull" (1521), *WA* 7:317.1-9; *LW* 32:11-12.

12. Robert E. McNally, "Scripture and Tradition at the Beginning of the Reformation," in *Perspectives on Scripture and Tradition,* ed. Joseph F. Kelly (Notre Dame: Fides Publishers, 1976), 74-76. See also Scott H. Hendrix, *Luther and the Papacy* (Philadelphia: Fortress Press, 1981), esp. 71-94.

13. Georg Wilhelm Friedrich Hegel, *Sämtliche Werke,* ed. H. Glockner (Stuttgart-Bad Constatt, 1956-1965), 11:519. On Hegel as an interpreter of Luther, see Gerhard Ebeling, "Luther in the Beginning of the Modern Age," in *Luther in the Dawn of the Modern Era,* ed. Heiko A. Oberman (Leiden: E. J. Brill, 1974), 11-39.

14. *WA* 1:228; *LW* 32:16. See the exposition of this statement by Otto Hermann Pesch, "Luther and the Catholic Tradition," *Lutheran Theological Seminary Bulletin* (Winter 1984): 3-24. In 1519 Luther claimed that his denial of the inerrancy of general councils was in agreement with "all teachers of Scriptures and Law." *WA* Br1:472,257.

preferred even to the pope."[15] Even earlier, Henry of Ghent (d. 1293), in commenting on the *Sentences* of Peter Lombard, posed the question of whether Scripture or the church should be believed if they contradict one another. In this hypothetical cleavage, Henry sided with the Scriptures over against that community "which seems to be the church." The true church, he declared, may only be found "in a few just men."[16] During the multi-papacy of the Great Schism, the idea of the remnant church emerged as a major motif in late medieval ecclesiology. The Blessed Virgin Mary was seen as the archetype of the remnant church: her faithfulness alone kept the Catholic faith intact during Christ's passion on the cross. When all of the disciples (including Peter!) had fled in fear, Mary remained true to Christ and his word. Her fidelity under the cross showed that the true faith could be preserved in one sole individual, and thus Mary became the mother of the (true remnant) church.

The early Reformers retained a stronger degree of Marian devotion than their later followers: even Zwingli defended the use of the "Ave Maria." But it was Mary's submission to the Word of God and her fidelity to it *contra mundum* that reinforced their commitment to the primacy of Scripture. Only in this way can we understand Luther's appeal to the "simple layman" at Leipzig, or his audacious summary of the events of 1521: "At Worms I was the Church!" — a remark which must sound as jarring to Catholics as Pius IX's "I am Tradition!" does to Protestants. At both Leipzig and Worms Luther was arguing *against* tradition *from* tradition or, better put, he was arguing from a shallower tradition to a profounder one.

The principle of *sola scriptura* is found in all of the classic confessions of the Reformation, but nowhere is it more clearly stated than in the solemn *Protestation* (hence the word "Protestant," not in the sense of "protesters" but rather *pro-testantes*, those who bear witness on behalf of) set forth on behalf of the evangelical cause at the Diet of Speyer in 1529:

> There is, we affirm, no sure preaching or doctrine but that which abides by the Word of God. According to God's command, no other doctrine should be preached. Each text of the holy and divine Scriptures should be elucidated

15. The Latin text is cited in K. W. Noerr, ed., *Kirche und Konzil bei Nicolaus de Tudeschis* (Köln/Graz, 1964), 104-6. See also Hermann Schuessler, "Sacred Doctrine and the Authority of Scripture," in *Reform and Authority in the Medieval and Reformation Church*, ed. Guy F. Lytle (Washington: Catholic University of America Press, 1981), 55-68.

16. See George H. Tavard, *Holy Writ or Holy Church* (Westport, CT: Greenwood Press, 1978), 22-25. Tavard sees an adumbration of Reformation views in Henry's "ethereal conception of the Church. She is not necessarily identical with the community of believers. She can be embodied in a small remnant of orthodoxy within an all but universal heresy."

and explained by other texts. This holy book is in all things necessary for the Christian; it shines clearly in its own light, and is found to enlighten the darkness. We are determined by God's grace and aid to abide by God's Word alone, the Holy Gospel contained in the biblical books of the Old and New Testaments. This word alone should be preached, and nothing that is contrary to it. It is the only Truth. It is the sure rule of all Christian doctrine and conduct. It can never fail us or deceive us. Whosoever builds and abides on this foundation shall stand against all the gates of hell while all merely human additions and vanities set up against it must fall before the presence of God.[17]

An exposition of this text would require us to consider hermeneutical issues debated both between Rome and the Reformation and within each of these two communities: canonicity, biblical criticism, the perspicuity of Scripture and its relation to preaching, etc. At this point, however, we must ask whether the Reformation decision for *sola scriptura* must be understood only in an oppositional sense to Tradition, or whether we can also speak meaningfully of the coinherence of Scripture and Tradition in a genuine Evangelical sense.

The Reformers almost always used the word *traditio* in the plural to refer to those "human traditions *(Menschensatzungen),* instituted to placate God, to merit grace, and to make satisfaction for sins," as the Augsburg Confession puts it.[18] Zwingli was more radical than Luther in his liturgical prunings, eliminating holy days, incense, the burning of candles, the sprinkling of holy water, church art, and musical instruments — this "whole rubbish-heap of ceremonials" and "hodgepodge of human ordinances" which amounted to nothing but "tom-foolery."[19] In both cases, however, the pejorative use of *traditiones* referred to specific practices and acts believed to be departures from, or distortions of, true worship and sound piety. This negative attitude toward Tradition echoes the words of Jesus in Mark 7:8: "You have let go of the commands of God and are holding on to the traditions of men."

Overwhelmingly, however, the Reformers saw themselves as part of the ongoing Catholic tradition, indeed as the legitimate bearers of it. This was seen in numerous ways; here I shall mention only three: (1) their sense of continuity with the church of the preceding centuries; (2) their embrace of the ecumenical orthodoxy of the early church; (3) their desire to read the Bible in dialogue with the exegetical tradition of the church.

---

17. On the Diet of Speyer, see E. G. Léonard, *A History of Protestantism* (Indianapolis: Bobbs-Merrill Company, 1968), 122-28.

18. Philip Schaff, *Creeds of Christendom* (Grand Rapids: Baker Book House, 1977), 12.

19. See Timothy George, *Theology of the Reformers* (Nashville: Broadman & Holman, 1988), 131-32.

1. Ecclesial Continuity

In their efforts to restore what a noted Puritan of a later age called "the old glorious beautiful face of Christianity," many of the Anabaptists and radical reformers denounced the Catholic tradition entirely.[20] Caspar Schwenckfeld was among the most radical of this lot: he declared a *Stillstand* on the Lord's Supper, forbade baptism by water, and announced that the true church was no longer to be found on earth but had ascended to heaven in 1530![21] In writing against the errors of Schwenckfeld and other *Schwärmer,* Luther declared: "We do not act as fanatically as the sectarian spirits. We do not reject everything that is under the dominion of the Pope. For in that event we should also reject the Christian church. . . . Much Christian good, nay, all Christian good, is to be found in the papacy and from there it descended to us."[22] In his 1535 *Commentary on Galatians,* Luther further described the nature of this "descent." Although the Church of Rome is horribly deformed, Luther says, it still is holy because it retains baptism, the eucharist, "the voice and text of the Gospel, the sacred Scriptures, the ministries, the Name of Christ, and Name of God. . . . The treasure is still there."[23] Calvin, too, was willing to extend the word "church" to local congregations in Roman obedience so long as the gospel could be discerned in the preaching of the Scriptures and the celebration of the Lord's Supper. Thus, the Reformers affirmed the tradition of the living Word and believed they could discern it, albeit obscurely, even within the contemporary Church of Rome.

2. Ecumenical Orthodoxy

The Reformers embraced the trinitarian and christological consensus of the early church, set forth in the decrees of the first four ecumenical councils, as necessitated by, and congruent with, the teaching of Holy Scripture. Significantly, when Protestants published their own evangelical confessions in response to the exigencies of the sixteenth and seventeenth centuries, they did not, as it were, begin all over again with new statements and original reflections on the person of Christ or the reality of the Holy Trinity. Rather they accepted the Apostles' Creed, the Nicene Creed, and the Athanasian Creed "as

20. John Owen, *A Vindication of the Animadversions on Fiat Lux* (London, 1664), 207.
21. See George H. Williams, *The Radical Reformation* (Philadelphia: Westminster Press, 1962), 428-43.
22. *WA* 26:146.
23. *LW* 26:24.

the unanimous, Catholic, Christian faith," pledging themselves to uphold the doctrine set forth in these classic standards while rejecting "all heresies and teachings which have been introduced into the church of God contrary to them."[24]

This approach was true not only of Lutherans and Calvinists but also of Congregationalists and Baptists. Thus in 1679, long before they had taken up the slogan "no creed but the Bible," Baptists in England published a confession of faith in which they reprinted *en toto* the three historic creeds and commended them as something which "ought thoroughly to be received and believed."

> For we believe that they may be proved by most undoubted authority of Holy Scripture and are necessary to be understood of all Christians; and to be instructed in the knowledge of them by ministers of Christ, according to the analogy of faith, recorded in sacred Scriptures, upon which these creeds are grounded and catechistically opened and expounded in all Christian families for the edification of young and old which might be a means to prevent heresy in doctrine and practice, these creeds containing all things in a brief manner that are necessary to be known, fundamentally, in order to our salvation.[25]

As this Baptist statement shows, the early councils and creeds were embraced as witnesses and expositions of the faith, as accurate summaries of the teaching of Holy Scripture ("an abbreviated Word," to use the expression of John Cassian), not as independent authorities alongside or supplementary to the Bible.[26] While Scripture alone remained the only judge and touchstone by which all doctrines had to be understood and normed, the early creeds were not mere ad hoc statements which could be used or dispensed with willy nilly at the whim of an individual theologian or congregation. They belonged to the unfolding pattern of Christian truth and could be abandoned only at great peril.

In this sense Tradition served as a kind of guardrail on a dangerous mountain highway keeping the traveler focused on the goal of the journey by preventing precipitous calamities to the right and left. True enough, the Re-

---

24. This is from the opening paragraphs of the Formula of Concord. See T. G. Tappert, ed., *The Book of Concord* (Philadelphia: Fortress Press, 1959), 465.

25. Article 38 of "The Orthodox Creed" in Timothy and Denise George, eds., *Baptist Confessions, Covenants, and Catechisms* (Nashville: Broadman & Holman, 1996), 120-21.

26. John Cassian, *De Incarnatione Christi* 6,4 (PL 50, col 149A). Cited by George Tavard, "Scripture and Tradition," *Journal of Ecumenical Studies* 5 (1968): 315.

formers did not consider themselves irrevocably bound to the language and thought-forms of the early creeds and councils, as Luther made clear in his writing against Latomus in 1521: "Even if my soul hated this word *homoousios,* still I would not be a heretic, if I hold fast to the fact defined by the council on the basis of Scripture."[27] But when, in fact, Calvin tried to articulate the doctrine of the Trinity in biblical language alone, his thoughts were misinterpreted as a nascent form of anti-trinitarianism and he was forced, as Athanasius had been, to use non-biblical language precisely in order to be faithful to the biblical message itself.[28]

The Reformers believed justification by faith alone was the logical and necessary consequence of the ecumenical orthodoxy embraced by Catholics and Protestants alike. Melanchthon cited references to *sola fides* in patristic sources while others claimed to find the essence, if not the exact wording, of the Reformation doctrine of justification in the liturgy of the church and the prayers of the saints, especially those of Bernard of Clairvaux, a favorite writer of both Luther and Calvin. Jaroslav Pelikan has summarized this strong sense of doctrinal continuity on the material principle of the Reformation:

> If the Holy Trinity was as holy as the Trinitarian dogma taught; if original sin was as virulent as the Augustinian tradition said it was; and if Christ was as necessary as the Christological dogma implied — then the only way to treat justification in a manner faithful to the best of Catholic tradition was to teach justification by faith.[29]

27. *WA* 8:117-18; *LW* 32:244.

28. See John Calvin, *Institutes of the Christian Religion,* ed. J. T. McNeill and trans. F. L. Battles (Philadelphia: Westminster, 1960), 1:125-26 [1.13.5]: "If, therefore, these terms ["Trinity," "Person," etc.] were not rashly invented, we ought to beware lest by repudiating them we be accused of overweening rashness. Indeed, I could wish they were buried, if only among all men this faith were agreed on: that Father and Son and Spirit are one God, yet the Son is not the Father, nor the Spirit the Son, but that they are differentiated by a peculiar quality." On the Lutheran side Martin Chemnitz in his famous *Examen Consilii Tridentini* set forth eight different senses in which the word "tradition" could be used in theology. Chemnitz approves of the first seven of these senses, rejecting only the Tridentine statement about unwritten traditions. Among his "legitimate" definitions of tradition is this one: "What the fathers sometimes call those dogmas not set down in Scripture in so many words, but drawn from clear passages of Scripture by good, sure, firm, and clear reasoning." Quoted in Jaroslav Pelikan, *Obedient Rebels* (New York: Harper & Row, 1964), 50-51.

29. Pelikan, *Obedient Rebels,* 48. On Melanchthon, see Peter Fraenkel, *Testimonia Patrum: The Function of the Patristic Argument in the Theology of Philip Melanchthon* (Geneva: Droz, 1961).

3. Exegetical Polyphony

It is not coincidental that the Scripture principle in theology emerged historically at the same time as the biblical text was being restored (cf. Erasmus's
Greek New Testament of 1516), historical critical studies were being advanced
by humanist scholars, and the technology of printing was providing the basis
for a popular literate culture. The widespread distribution of the Bible in Europe contributed to an enormous revolution in sensibilities to which Thomas
Hobbes reacted with horror:

> After the Bible was translated, every man, nay, every boy and wench that
> could read English thought they spoke with God Almighty and understood
> what he said when by a certain number of chapters a day they had read the
> Scriptures once or twice over.[30]

The kind of "everyman theology" which so offended Hobbes is both a major
strength and a persistent challenge in the Evangelical tradition. Evangelicals
believe that the Scriptures in their essential message are sufficiently clear that
ordinary men and women, illumined by the Holy Spirit, may, "in a due use of
the ordinary means, attain unto a sufficient understanding of them."[31] Because Evangelicals are, as John Stott says, a Gospel people and Bible people,
the importance of the lay appropriation of Holy Scripture can hardly be exag-
gerated.

There is, nonetheless, a great danger in following the advice of Alexander
Campbell to "open the New Testament as if mortal man had never seen it before."[32] This kind of individualistic approach to *sola scriptura* results not in
exegetical polyphony but raucous cacophony. J. N. Darby, the founder of the
Plymouth Brethren, tried to eliminate all vestiges of the Catholic tradition,
including ministerial orders and the use of biblical commentaries. F. F. Bruce,
the great Evangelical New Testament scholar, relates a comment made about
Darby: "He only wanted men 'to submit their understanding *to God*,' that is,
to the Bible, that is, to his interpretation!"[33]

In their biblical commentaries, however, the Reformers of the sixteenth
century revealed an intimate familiarity with the preceding exegetical tradi-

30. Thomas Hobbes, *Works*, ed. William Molesworth (London, 1839-1845), 6:190.

31. This is from the chapter "Of the Holy Scripture" in the Westminster Confession of
Faith. *The Book of Confessions* (New York: General Assembly of the Presbyterian Church
USA, 1983), 6.007.

32. Cited in Nathan O. Hatch, *"Sola Scriptura* and *Novus Ordo Seclorum,"* in *The Bible
in America,* ed. Nathan Hatch and Mark Noll (New York: Oxford University Press, 1982), 72.

33. F. F. Bruce, *Tradition Old and New* (Exeter: Paternoster, 1970), 14.

tion, and they used it reverently as well as critically in their own expositions of the sacred text. The Scriptures were seen as the book given to the church, gathered and guided by the Holy Spirit. In his restatement of the Vincentian canon, Calvin defined the church as

> a society of all the saints, a society which, spread over the whole world, and existing in all ages, and bound together by the one doctrine and the one spirit of Christ, cultivates and observes unity of faith and brotherly concord. With this Church we deny that we have any disagreement. Nay, rather, as we revere her as our mother, so we desire to remain in her bosom.[34]

Defined thus, the church has a real, albeit relative and circumscribed, authority since, as Calvin admits, "We cannot fly without wings."[35] It was this instrumental authority of the church which Augustine had in mind when he remarked that he would not have believed the Bible unless he had been moved thereto by the church. The coinherence of Scripture and Tradition is thus understood as "a vertical descent of the Third Person upon the members of the Church, and a horizontal succession of kerygmatic transmission by which the Word is handed on."[36]

The Trajectory of Tradition

The two decades following World War II saw a veritable explosion of interest and writing about the problematic of Scripture and Tradition in both Protestant and Catholic circles. On the Protestant side, this interest was fueled by the theology of Karl Barth, who, for all his vigorous restatement of the principle of *sola scriptura,* demonstrated a remarkable knowledge of the church fathers and warmly embraced the "Catholic substance" of the Christian faith. Efforts at liturgical renewal, the rise of the biblical theology movement, and the formation of the World Council of Churches at Amsterdam in 1948 also contributed to this renewed emphasis on Tradition. At the Third World Conference on Faith and Order held at Lund in 1952, Methodist theologian Albert C. Outler proposed that a theological commission be established to explore more deeply "that common history which we have as Christians."[37] In 1961 this com-

34. John C. Olin, ed., *John Calvin and Jacopo Sadoleto: A Reformation Debate* (New York: Harper Torchbooks, 1966), 61-62.

35. Olin, *John Calvin and Jacopo Sadoleto,* 77.

36. Tavard, "Scripture and Tradition," 318.

37. Lukas Vischer, ed., *A Documentary History of the Faith and Order Movement 1927-1963* (St. Louis: Bethany, 1963), 96.

mission published an interim report, *The Old and the New in the Church,* which was followed by an official report on *Tradition and Traditions* in 1963. Then, at the Fourth World Conference on Faith and Order, held at Montreal in 1963, Scripture and Tradition was one of five major themes explored by the participants, the others being the church, the redemptive work of Christ, worship, and "the process of growing together."[38]

Montreal sought to reformulate the classic polarity between Catholics and Protestants on Scripture and Tradition by distinguishing several different meanings of the word *tradition:* Tradition (with a capital T), tradition (with a small t), and tradition*s.* Tradition in the first sense was defined as "the Gospel itself, transmitted from generation to generation in and by the Church, Christ himself present in the life of the Church."[39]

This definition was a definite improvement on the earlier statement of the Theological Commission: "The Tradition is the self-givenness of God in the self-giving of Jesus Christ." While few would quarrel with this affirmation, it hardly addresses the issue at hand, omitting reference both to Scripture and church. Scripture is still missing from the Montreal definition, although the report later refers to Scripture as "the Tradition in its written form," and also identifies Scripture as the source or criterion for rightly interpreting the Tradition.[40] The Montreal report also acknowledges the role of the Holy Spirit as the Lord and Giver of life who guides the church in rightly interpreting the Scriptures. No consensus was acknowledged on how the Spirit fulfills this function in the church, with various hermeneutical keys mentioned: a canon within the canon, the Fathers and Councils, the church's magisterium, etc. By tradition (with a small t) Montreal meant the traditionary process, that is, the actual means by which the gospel is conveyed from place to place and time to time: the creeds, the sacraments, the preaching of the Word, theological expositions of church doctrine, etc. Finally, by traditions (in the plural) Montreal referred to the diverse forms of expression and also to confessional families and cultural settings in which the Christian message may take on a specific contextual casting, e.g. the Anglican tradition, the North American tradition. While Montreal's threefold definition of Tradition/tradition/traditions is a helpful heuristic device, it has not been widely accepted in subsequent ecumenical discourse. The expansive meaning of Tradition in the first sense no

38. P. C. Rodger and Lukas Vischer, eds., *The Fourth World Conference on Faith and Order, Montreal 1963* (New York: Association Press, 1963). See also Joseph A. Burgess, "Montreal (1963): A Case Study," in *The Quadrilog: Tradition and the Future of Ecumenism,* ed. Kenneth Hagen (Collegeville, MN: The Liturgical Press, 1994), 270-86.

39. Rodger and Vischer, eds., *Montreal 1963,* 50.

40. Rodger and Vischer, eds., *Montreal 1963,* 53.

doubt reflected the presence of Orthodox participants, especially Georges Florvosky, in the Montreal deliberations. One of the few card-carrying Evangelicals to participate in the Montreal discussions, W. Stanford Reid, confessed that he found the debate "neither very enlightening nor conclusive." Reid objected to the destructively critical assumptions about the Bible, stemming from the thought of Rudolf Bultmann, which seemed to dominate the discussion.[41]

Catholic scholarship on Scripture and Tradition leading up to *Dei Verbum* at Vatican II (November 18, 1965) involved a significant and controversial reassessment of the language set forth in the fourth session of the Council of Trent (April 8, 1546). The Tridentine decree declared that the source of all saving truth and rule of conduct "are contained in the written books and unwritten traditions which have come down to us, having been received by the apostles from the mouth of Christ himself or from the apostles by the dictation of the Holy Spirit, and have been transmitted as it were from hand to hand." Trent further asserted that both Scripture and Tradition were to be received and venerated "with the same sense of loyalty and reverence" *(pari pietatis affectu ac reverentia suscipit et veneratur).*[42]

In the centuries following Trent, polemicists on both sides of the Reformation divide interpreted this decree to mean that there were two complementary sources of revelation, part of the truth being derived from Scripture and part from extrascriptural Tradition. The source of unwritten revelation was believed to derive from Jesus' personal communications to the apostles (cf. John 21:25) which, in turn, were passed down from generation to generation through an unbroken succession of bishops, chief among whom was the Holy Father. However, the publication of the Acts of the Council early in this century indicated that a vigorous debate on the wording of this decree had been carried on at Trent and that the first draft had been changed from "*partly* in written books, *partly* in unwritten traditions" to "in written books *and* unwritten traditions." The substitution of *et* for *partim . . . partim* seemed to allow for a belief in the material sufficiency of Scripture, a view much closer to that of the mainline Reformers than had been earlier supposed. The

---

41. W. Stanford Reid, *The Present Significance of Calvin's View of Tradition* (Redhill, Surrey: Sovereign Grace Union, 1966), 3-4: "Basing their thinking on the assumptions and premises of *formgeschichte* and demythologizing, this group held that the New Testament had its origins in the teaching or tradition of the early church. . . . Thus the Scriptures have lost their autonomous character and have become essentially a collection of traditions deriving from the early church."

42. J. Neuner and J. Dupuis, eds., *The Christian Faith* (New York: Alba House, 1996), 96.

comment of the Servite General, Agostino Bonuccio, made in the context of the Tridentine debate, seems to set forth the priority of Scripture in a way that is compatible with Reformation thinking: "Tradition is essentially an authoritative interpretation of Holy Writ, not its complement."[43] Jedin also reports an exchange at Trent between Bishop Nacchianti of Chioggia and Francisco de Navarra, the bishop of Badajoz. "It is ungodly *(impium),*" Nacchianti shouted, "to put Scripture and Tradition on the same level!" When Francisco de Navarra asked: "Are we an ungodly people?" he was answered harshly: "Yes, I repeat it! How can I accept the practice of praying eastward with the same reverence as St. John's gospel?"[44]

In 1956 the Tübingen theologian, Josef Rupert Geiselmann, reopened the debate over the proper interpretation of the Tridentine decree in an important article published in *Una Sancta.*[45] Geiselmann's criticism of the two-source interpretation of Trent was strongly challenged by Heinrich Lennerz on the Catholic side and Heiko Oberman on the Protestant side. But his views found support in the massive two-volume work by Yves Congar, *Tradition and Traditions* (originally published in 1960 and 1963), and the brilliant interpretive study by George Tavard, *Holy Writ or Holy Church: The Crisis of the Protestant Reformation,* published in 1959.

In describing the origin of *Dei Verbum,* Cardinal Ratzinger has identified three impulses which contributed to the formation of this historic document. The first was the new view of Tradition which had come to the fore in some of the literature just cited, but which in fact had been in the making for a century and a half. The concept of Tradition as a living process rather than a static transmission of specific information had been pioneered by the German Romantic theologian Johann Adam Möhler and by John Henry Newman, who interpreted the development of doctrine as the organic unfolding of a seminal idea inherent in the original deposit of faith. The revisionist interpretation of Trent, if we may call it that, left open at least the possibility of a Catholic version of *sola scriptura,* allowing Scripture to be defined as "the only place where the truly apostolic tradition is clearly and distinctly to be found."[46] The other two preparatory influences cited by Ratzinger were the emergence of a new approach to biblical studies among Catholic scholars,

---

43. Hubert Jedin, *A History of the Council of Trent* (New York: Nelson, 1961), 2:75.

44. Jedin, *Council of Trent,* 2:86-87. Quoted, McNally, "Scripture and Tradition at the Beginning of the Reformation," 78-79.

45. J. R. Geiselmann, "Das Missverständnis über das Verhältnis von Schrift und Tradition und seine Uberwindung in der katholischen Theologie," *Una Sancta* 11 (1956): 131-50.

46. Herbert Vorgrimler, ed., *Commentary on the Documents of Vatican II* (New York: Herder & Herder, 1967), 3:156.

triggered by the encyclical *Divino afflante* of Pius XII in 1943, and, *pari passu,* "a fundamentally new attitude to Scripture in large areas of Catholic Christendom." These latter two concerns would be reflected especially in chapters three to six of *Dei Verbum.*

The inner tensions within the Council and the prehistory of *Dei Verbum* are important for understanding the subsequent ecumenical dialogue on Scripture and Tradition. After working through several initial drafts, the preparatory Theological Commission, presided over by Cardinal Ottaviani, presented to the Council in 1962 a text entitled *Schema Constitutionis dogmaticae de fontibus Revelationis.* Cardinal Liénart, the bishop of Lille, spoke for many of his colleagues when he stated bluntly: "Hoc schema mihi non placet."[47] Eventually, nearly two-thirds of the Council fathers voted against moving forward with this proposal with its reiteration of the plural-sources motif. Pope Paul VI then removed this text from the agenda and appointed a new commission, chaired jointly by Cardinals Ottaviani and Bea, which reworked the original schema and ultimately proposed the text which was accepted by the Council and proclaimed by the pope in 1965. Had the original schema with its advocacy of multiple sources of revelation been adopted by the Council, Ratzinger avers that "the attempt to understand the idea of tradition in a new way, as well as a large part of the modern work on exegesis, would have been condemned."[48]

To summarize the developments leading up to Montreal in 1963, and *Dei Verbum* in 1965, we can say, speaking broadly, that Protestant theology was searching for a sturdier concept of Tradition than the one bequeathed to it by the legacies of liberalism, pietism, and individualism, while Catholic theology was struggling for a more liberated understanding of Tradition, one that could sidestep, without repudiating, the harsh polarities of the Tridentine formulation, providing in the meantime lots of breathing room for a fresh encounter with the sacred Scriptures themselves.

Further Explorations

In the light of the multiple meanings of Tradition set forth at Montreal, and the competing explanations of historic texts on Tradition in Catholic historiography, we might be tempted to embrace "a respectful skepticism" about

---

47. Vorgrimler, ed., *Commentary on Vatican II,* 3:160. See also Peter Van Leeuwen, "The Genesis of the Constitution on Divine Revelation," *Concilium* 1:3 (January 1967), 4,4-10.
48. Vorgrimler, ed., *Commentary on Vatican II,* 159.

further progress on this issue. After his extensive studies on Scripture and Tradition in the late Middle Ages, Dom Paul de Vooght seems to have reached just this conclusion: "If great theologians of the past could not arrive at a satisfactory conception of Tradition, we should not try to reach one: it may be that the process and the nature of Tradition do not belong to what has been revealed and must escape us forever."[49] Evangelical theologian David Wells, while not minimizing the difficulties, applauds the new attitude toward Tradition within Catholicism (that is, the one represented at Vatican II) as a possible point of contact for Catholic and Evangelical theology — "a bridge upon which the estranged parties might at least meet even if they do not journey on to the other side."[50] Wells's comment was made some ten years after the close of Vatican II, and the intervening decades have proved him correct. I have elsewhere described the Catholic-Evangelical alliance on moral and social values in our culture, especially the sanctity of human life, as an "ecumenism of the trenches." There is also an ecumenism of the library, the hymnbook, and the prayer bench. One need only look at syllabi from courses on spiritual formation in Evangelical seminaries, or read works of spiritual theology by Evangelical writers such as Richard Foster, Dallas Willard, and James Houston, to realize the way in which "the Catholic tradition" is being mined and appropriated for Evangelical purposes, sometimes even to the neglect of classic Protestant sources! On the other hand, some of the best scholarship on the Protestant reformers has come from Catholic historians and theologians (Wicks, Pesch, Ganoczy). The ECT process itself is a sign that we are moving beyond what Cardinal Cassidy has called "the dialogue of the deaf" in our efforts for greater mutual understanding.

Evangelicals have every reason to rejoice in the evident love for Christ and devotion to the Scriptures that shine through the lives and witness of so many Catholics. The statement of Vatican II that "easy access to sacred Scripture should be provided for all the Christian faithful" resonates with the

---

49. This is George Tavard's summary of De Vooght's views in John M. Todd, ed., *Problems of Authority* (Baltimore: The Helicon Press, 1962), 29.

50. David F. Wells, "Tradition: A Meeting Place for Catholic and Evangelical Theology?" *Christian Scholar's Review* 5 (1975): 50-61. Among other evangelical scholars who have looked seriously at the issue of Scripture and Tradition in the light of contemporary Roman Catholic/Evangelical relationships, see Norman L. Geisler and Ralph E. MacKenzie, *Roman Catholics and Evangelicals: Agreements and Differences* (Grand Rapids: Baker Books, 1995), 177-201, and especially the two articles by A. N. S. Lane: "Scripture, Tradition and Church: An Historical Survey," *Vox Evangelica* 9 (1975): 37-55, and "Sola Scriptura?: Making Sense of a Post-Reformation Slogan," in *A Pathway into Holy Scripture*, ed. P. E. Satterthwaite and D. F. Wright (Grand Rapids: Eerdmans, 1994), 297-327.

Evangelical passion for Bible reading and Bible study as mainstays of the devotional life (DV 22). Further, no Evangelical writer could extol the Bible and its role in the Christian community in more lyrical language than this from a Catholic theologian:

> Holy Scripture as the guardian of the Gospel is the dowry of the Holy Spirit to the Bride of Christ, the most precious jewel in which the *Spiritus creator* endowed her subsequent life with the word of Christ. The faith, prayer, and preaching of the Church are henceforward nourished and animated, as though by God's breath, by the Gospel which is announced by Christ the Church's Lord, preached by the apostles its foundation, and borne witness to by the Holy Spirit who caused it to be written down by the sacred writers. The Scriptures were given to the Church so that it could preserve the Gospel entrusted to it. "But continue in those things which thou hast learned and which have been committed to thee, knowing of whom thou hast learned them" (2 Timothy 3:14). They are also to lead the Church to its goal: "From childhood you have been acquainted with the sacred writings which are able to instruct you for salvation through faith in Jesus Christ" (2 Timothy 3:15). They are to serve the Church to enable it to fulfill its manifold tasks, for "all Scripture is inspired by God and profitable for teaching, for reproof, for correction and for training in righteousness" (2 Timothy 3:16). Holy Scripture is, therefore, the Church's "hearts blood, its very breath, its soul, its all."[51]

The "trend to the Bible" (von Balthasar) evident in this quotation and in many statements of Vatican II carries us very far along the hypothetical bridge of David Wells. Other matters, however, are more difficult and require further exploration, discussion, and study.

1. Canonicity

Catholics and Evangelicals differ on the extent of the biblical canon, reflecting confessional decisions of the sixteenth century. Luther's regrettable comments about the Epistle of James are well known, and Evangelicals disagree among themselves as to whether the canon is open or closed. Everyone agrees that the Bible's table of contents is not a part of the inspired text and that the process of canon formation required several centuries of controversy, debate, and assessment. Evangelicals do not regard this process as the church's cre-

---

51. Josef R. Geiselmann, *The Meaning of Tradition* (New York: Herder & Herder, 1966), 37-38. The final words in the last line are from J. A. Möhler.

ation of the canon but rather as its recognition and reception of the canon. This view seems to be in line with some recent Catholic views of canonicity as well. Tavard, for example, aptly describes the formation of the canon as "a self-manifestation of the Word in the church." He further characterizes the process of canon selection: "The Word spoke to them when they read or listened to some writings. He kept silent when others were read. The power of the Word imposed itself on the Christians."[52]

More important, perhaps, than the which-came-first-church-or-canon question is the actual function of the canon in the authority of the church. For Evangelicals, the canon of Holy Scripture embodies the prophetic-apostolic revelation of Jesus Christ: it is the means by which God continues to speak to the church by his Spirit through the witness of the apostles.[53] Bishops can be succeeded by other bishops, and presbyters by other presbyters, but the Apostle is unique in his historical proximity to the Incarnation and thus cannot be replaced in his function as the bearer of revelation for future generations. As Oscar Cullmann has said, "He must continue *himself* to fulfill his function in the church of today: *in* the church, not *by* the church, but by his word, *dia tou logou* (John 17:12); in other words, by his writings."[54]

That the early church, guided by the Spirit, recognized the canon in the first place is an indication that a clear line of demarcation was being drawn between the primordial *depositum fidei* and its subsequent exposition and proclamation (i.e., Tradition) in the ongoing life of the church. To elevate the teaching office of the church to the level of infallible interpreter, and to place Scripture and Tradition side by side as part of the "one sacred deposit of the Word of God" (DV 10), seems to relativize both the historicity of the Incarnation and the normativity of the apostolic witness to it. That church is apostolic which still listens to the voice of the apostles through which alone it hears the voice of its Shepherd, and not that of a stranger, calling, correcting, reforming, renewing, and judging (John 10:3-5).

---

52. Tavard, *Holy Writ or Holy Church*, 5, 8. See also this important statement by Yves Congar: "It is not that the Church and her Magisterium actually create the canon; even less do they endow Scripture with its authority as mistakenly rather than intentionally certain Catholic apologists have sometimes maintained. With this dogma, as with the others, Church and Magisterium simply recognize the truth established by God's action." *Meaning of Tradition*, 103-4.

53. I follow here the argument of Oscar Cullmann, "Scripture and Tradition," in Daniel J. Callahan et al., *Christianity Divided: Protestant and Roman Catholic Theological Issues* (New York: Sheed & Ward, 1963). See also Karl Barth, *Church Dogmatics* 1:2, 599: "The church can point us to the decision made in heaven in respect of the genuine Canon."

54. Cullmann, "Scripture and Tradition," 12.

Out of these differences between Catholics and Evangelicals arise not so much two views of Scripture as two conceptions of the church. From the perspective of Catholic ecclesiology, Congar has expressed the difference thus: "The Protestants want a Church ceaselessly renewing herself by a dramatic and precarious confrontation with the Word of God. Together with the Fathers we see the Church as the continuous communication, through space and time, of the mystical community born from the Lord's institution and Pentecost."[55]

2. Inerrancy

The historical critical study of the Bible is only tangentially related to the problem of Scripture and Tradition, but it suggests points of contact as well as divergences between Catholics and Evangelicals. Chapter three of *Dei Verbum* sets forth a high view of biblical inspiration, claiming that everything written by the inspired authors "must be held to be asserted by the Holy Spirit" (DV 11). Moreover, the Scriptures are acknowledged as "teaching solidly, faithfully, and without error that truth which God wanted put into the sacred writings for the sake of our salvation" (DV 11). In the light of intense, intra-Evangelical debates over the errorless character of Scripture, the statement of Vatican II prompts several questions: (1) How did the debates on inerrancy during the Council figure into the final wording of the decree? (2) According to Ratzinger, the earlier rejected draft "On the Sources of Revelation" had proposed a narrower interpretation of inerrancy *("in qualibet re religiose vel profana")*.[56] Was this earlier ecumenically-unfriendly text actually closer on this point to the views of Evangelicals who hold to biblical inerrancy? (3) Although more recent papal encyclicals have dealt with the freedom of scholarly inquiry and the role of biblical interpretation in the life of the church, how does Vatican II's commitment to the historicity of the Gospels and the decision to subject Scripture interpretation to the judgment of the church square with the fact that some Catholic exegetes seem to deny with impunity the miracles of Jesus, including the virgin birth and bodily resurrection? Put otherwise, does the teaching office in the Catholic Church really provide a better solution to theological vagrancy than judicatories in Protestant churches?

---

55. Congar, *Meaning of Tradition*, 104-5.
56. Vorgrimler, ed., *Commentary on Vatican II*, 159.

3. Proclamation

Chapter six of *Dei Verbum* is entitled "Sacred Scripture in the Life of the Church," and contains these two statements on the task of preaching: "Therefore, like the Christian religion itself, all the preaching of the Church must be nourished and regulated by the sacred Scripture" (DV 21); "By the same word of Scripture the ministry of the Word also, that is, pastoral preaching, catechetics and all Christian instruction, in which the liturgical homily must hold the foremost place, is nourished in a healthy way and flourishes in a holy way" (DV 24). Evangelicals can only rejoice in these statements asserting, as they do, the biblical basis of proclamation and its prominence ("in the foremost place") in the worship of the church.[57] Just as many Evangelicals are discovering that the celebration of the Lord's Table is more than a negligible appendage to the sermon, so too many Catholics are learning that the liturgy of the Word, including the sermon, is more than a dispensable preliminary to the eucharist. The correlation of Word and Sacrament is central to Reformation ecclesiology: where the Word is rightly preached, and the sacraments are duly administered, there is the true church. (Only later did the Reformed tradition add discipline as a third indispensable mark of the church.)

The place where the office of preaching intersects contrasting Catholic and Evangelical ecclesiologies is the doctrine of apostolic succession. Evangelicals understand this concept not in terms of an unbroken chain of ecclesiastical office holders going back through the centuries to Saint Peter, and last of all to Christ as the Founder of the church, but rather as the faithful preaching of the inscripturated apostolic witness. Some Evangelicals, such as the Landmark Baptists of the nineteenth century, have attempted to reconstruct the historical lineage of this faithful proclamation, a "trail of blood" meandering through various dissenting and sectarian movements, many of them quite heterodox, in church history. Such reconstructions, however, are as unnecessary as they are unconvincing. Evangelicals believe that the Lord has never left himself without a witness, albeit at times a lonely and hardly visible one *(ecclesia latens)*, and that Jesus' promise to protect the church against the incursion of infernal portals is alone sufficient to preserve the Word of God in both its written and proclaimed forms.

---

57. An earlier draft of this decree contained an even stronger expression of the normative function of Scripture in the preaching of the church: *"Semper respicere (scripturam) tamquam ad normam et auctoritatem quibus iudicantur et reguntur."* Vorgrimler, ed., *Commentary on Vatican II,* 264.

4. Development

The statement of *Dei Verbum* 8 that the apostolic tradition "develops" in the church with the help of the Holy Spirit, for "there is a growth in the understanding of the realities of the words which have been handed down" can certainly be understood in a proper Evangelical sense, especially when they are supplemented by the subsequent assertion (DV 10) that the teaching office is not above the Word of God, but rather serves the Word by listening to it devoutly and by explaining it faithfully with the Spirit's help. The principle of *sola scriptura,* rightly understood, does not preclude, but rather calls for, a bona fide theory of doctrinal development. When the New Testament kerygma moved from its original milieu into the Hellenistic context, it had to be recast in a different conceptual and linguistic framework, a process described by Bernard Lonergan as the move from an "undifferentiated to a differentiated consciousness."[58] When the disciples of John the Baptist inquired of Jesus' messianic identity, they did not receive the answer: "I am God of God, Light of light, very God of very God, begotten not made"! The language of Nicea was necessary, not merely for apologetic purposes, but precisely because of the inner logic and inexorable implications of Jesus' words and deeds. In this sense, Tradition is "the kerygma which in the act of being proclaimed receives new voice and life."[59]

But subsequent dogmatic developments in the Catholic tradition appear to Evangelicals to involve an accretion to, rather than an elucidation or growth in, the understanding of the primordial deposit of revelation, this despite the very clear statement of *Dei Verbum* that "we now await no further new public revelation" before the parousia of Christ in glory (DV 4). At one time, Catholic theologians seem to have taught that extrascriptural doctrines such as the Marian dogmas of 1854 and 1950 were passed down by word of mouth, from age to age, through the teaching office of the church. As I understand it, the more recent Catholic theology of tradition holds that such extrascriptural "truths" may never have been explicitly taught in either Scripture or Tradition, but that they may be held *(sola fide?)* to be implicitly present in Scripture. Thus, Congar does not explain the dogma of the Immaculate Conception or that of the corporal Assumption of Mary in the same way as he does the dogma of Nicea, i.e. the development of the latent qualities of an accepted idea or belief. He speaks instead of "the relationship and proportions existing between the different statements

58. Bernard Lonergan, *The Way to Nicea* (Philadelphia: Westminster, 1976).

59. E. Fleaseman-Van Leer, *Tradition and Scripture in the Early Church* (Assen: Van Gorcum, 1954), 186.

and articles that have been revealed," and cites as an example Leverrier's discovery of the planet Saturn which was identified by means of calculation without experimental or factual evidence.[60] Thus in presenting the doctrine of the Assumption, the Apostolic Constitution *Munificentissimus Deus* appeals to the unique consensus of the contemporary church rather than to specific arguments from either Scripture or Tradition.[61] Despite encouraging statements to the contrary, the three infallibly declared dogmas of post-Tridentine Catholicism seem to Evangelicals to require not one but three distinct, although related, sources of revelation: Scripture, Tradition, and magisterium.

5. The Teaching of "Equal Reverence"

Karl Barth was invited to participate in the final two sessions of Vatican II as a Protestant observer, but he was unable to do this because of ill health. However, in May 1966 he did travel to Rome as the guest of the Secretariat for Christian Unity to meet with Pope Paul VI and to discuss the work of the Council with Catholic theologians. His reflections on this encounter were published in his little book, *Ad Limina Apostolorum: An Appraisal of Vatican II.*[62] Barth's visit was made at a time when the Protestant ecumenical movement was moving away from the sounder instincts which had guided its work from Amsterdam to Montreal toward that loosening of Christian conviction epitomized in a slogan of the World Council of Churches during this time: "The world must set the agenda for the church." Aware of the slippage in his own tradition, Barth spoke in laudatory terms of the "dynamic recovery" he saw in Roman Catholicism:

> Might it not be a sound Christian rule to attribute a little more worth to others than to oneself and to be a little more critical of oneself than of others? Must not the Council . . . give us occasion to sweep away the dust before the door of our own church with a careful but nevertheless mighty broom?[63]

In his otherwise positive assessment of *Dei Verbum*, Barth identified the second chapter as "the great fit of weakness which befell the Council."[64]

60. Congar, *Meaning of Tradition*, 112-13.

61. Neuner and Dupuis, eds., *The Christian Faith*, 262-64.

62. Karl Barth, *Ad Limina Apostolorum: An Appraisal of Vatican II* (Richmond: John Knox Press, 1968).

63. Barth, *Ad Limina Apostolorum*, "Thoughts on the Second Vatican Council."

64. Barth, *Ad Limina Apostolorum*, 48.

By the way in which the holy tradition and, in 10, the teaching office of the church are also placed alongside the Holy Scriptures, this chapter obscures the unmistakable declaration of chapter one in reference to revelation itself and of chapters 3-6 in reference to Scripture, and thereby to some extent the intent of the whole document.[65]

There are three sentences in this chapter with which Evangelicals must struggle in a particular way. The first was inserted by intervention of Pope Paul VI and declares that "it is not from sacred Scripture alone that the Church draws her certainty about everything which has been revealed" (DV 9). While this sounds like a polemical thrust against the Protestant principle of *sola scriptura*, it can nonetheless be understood in a proper Evangelical sense, as Tony Lane has shown: "To deny that tradition, reason, or Christian experience can in any way strengthen our certainty about the Gospel would be an odd position to take."[66] As we have seen, *sola scriptura* does not mean *nuda scriptura* nor *scriptura solitaria!* It means instead that the word of God, as it is communicated to us in the Scriptures, remains the final judge *(norma normans)* of all teaching in the church. Hence it is always appropriate, and necessary, to submit every theological decision and formulation, whether of councils, popes, bishops, theologians, biblical scholars, Sunday school teachers, even angels (cf. Galatians 1:8 and the "revelations" of the Prophet Joseph Smith) to this infallible touchstone.

Many Evangelicals will also stumble over this sentence from the second chapter of *Dei Verbum:* "But the task of authentically interpreting the Word of God, whether written or handed on, has been entrusted exclusively to the living teaching office of the Church, whose authority is exercised in the Name of Jesus Christ" (DV 10). The difficulty here is with the word "exclusively," especially if it implies the infallibility and irreformability of any particular interpreter. Jesus Christ himself remains the Lord as well as the Center of Holy Scripture. But it does not follow from this axiom that there is no authoritative teaching office in the church, nor that this magisterium is exempt from saying *damnamus* as well as *credimus* in response to specific crises and deviations in the community of faith. Evangelicals and Catholics differ on the scope and locus of the magisterium but not on whether it exists as a necessary component in the ongoing life of the church.

The one sentence in the second chapter of *Dei Verbum* which, as far as I can see, does constitute an insuperable barrier between Catholics and Evan-

---

65. Barth, *Ad Limina Apostolorum.*
66. Lane, "Sola Scriptura," 317.

gelicals is this: "Therefore both sacred tradition and sacred Scripture are to be accepted and venerated with the same sense of loyalty and reverence" (DV 9). This, of course, is a verbatim quotation from the Council of Trent in whose footsteps the Fathers of Vatican II have declared their intention to follow (DV 1). At Trent itself the doctrine of equal reverence was hotly debated. Girolamo Seripando, among others, wanted to substitute "similar" for "equal."[67] In the end, one-third of the Fathers of Trent voted against the expression which was incorporated into the final text and reappropriated by Vatican II. From an Evangelical perspective, this language seems to imply at once a retreat from the "new theology" of Scripture and Tradition advanced prior to the Council and a reassertion of the two-source theory in all of its rigor. It would be interesting to know whether this expression was debated as vigorously at Vatican II as it had been at Trent. By repeating the exact wording of this controversial expression from the sixteenth century, was Vatican II moving forward in the footsteps of Trent, or simply standing still in the tracks of the earlier decision? Evangelicals can affirm the coinherence of sacred Scripture and sacred Tradition, but not their coequality. If I understand it correctly, no Evangelical can say that both Scripture and Tradition "are to be accepted and venerated with the same sense of loyalty and reverence" without becoming either Orthodox or Roman Catholic.

Conclusion

As Evangelicals and Catholics together, we know in part and we prophesy in part awaiting in common hope the final unveiling at the end of the ages. In the meantime, we remain "separated brothers" but, by God's grace, increasingly with more emphasis on our fraternity than our disjunction. We are confident that the Lord is watching over his Word and his church, and we live in the assurance that in the end God will save his people "in the intervals of sunshine between storm and storm . . . snatching them from the surge of evil, even when the waters rage most furiously."[68]

---

67. Giuseppe Alberigo, "Girolamo Seripando," *The Oxford Encyclopedia of the Reformation,* ed. Hans Hillerbrand (New York: Oxford University Press, 1996), 4:47-48.

68. This quotation is from John Henry Newman's *Via Media.* See Ian Ker, *John Henry Newman: A Biography* (New York: Oxford University Press, 1988), 144.

Revelation, Scripture, and Tradition

AVERY CARDINAL DULLES, S.J.

In writing this paper I have taken the liberty of incorporating materials from two previously published articles. The first of these was written for the dialogue between the Pontifical Council for Christian Unity and the World Evangelical Fellowship;[1] the second, for the Lutheran-Roman Catholic Dialogue in the United States.[2]

Since this paper is composed for an interconfessional exchange of views, I shall give primary attention to the official doctrine of the Catholic Church rather than to my personal theological opinions. My principal source will be *Dei Verbum*, the Dogmatic Constitution on Divine Revelation adopted by the Second Vatican Council on October 29, 1965. From this text I shall try to show, with the help of contemporary theologians, how the unity of Scripture and tradition is secured by their common basis in revelation, which they express in different ways. To accomplish this objective it will be important to begin with some reflections on the nature of revelation.

Genesis of the Vatican II Constitution

When the bishops assembled for the first session of Vatican II in October 1962, they were presented with several draft texts (or schemas) that had been

---

1. Avery Dulles, "Revelation as the Basis for Scripture and Tradition," *Evangelical Review of Theology* 21 (April 1997): 104-20.
2. Avery Dulles, "Tradition as a Theological Source," chapter 6 of Avery Dulles, *The Craft of Theology*, rev. ed. (New York: Crossroad, 1995), 87-104.

drawn up by the Preparatory Theological Commission, with Cardinal Alfredo Ottaviani as president and Sebastian Tromp, S.J., as secretary. The first of these schemas was a five-chapter draft of a dogmatic constitution to be entitled *De Fontibus Revelationis*. The first chapter depicted revelation as issuing from Scripture and tradition, rather than being the basis for them. It explained that the sources of revelation were two, since the entire revelation is contained not in Scripture alone but in Scripture and Tradition as in two sources, though in different ways.[3]

This schema was presented on November 14, 1962, by Cardinal Ottaviani and Monsignor Salvatore Garofalo, both of whom stressed the importance of condemning recent unsound opinions. But the schema did not fare well in the discussion. The first two speakers set the tone. Cardinal Achille Liénart of Lille, speaking first, faulted the schema for its failure to deal with the deeper source from which both Scripture and Tradition flow, namely the word of God. The entire tone of the schema, he objected, was too cold and Scholastic, since it failed to reflect love and gratitude for the mysterious ways in which God had manifested himself, especially through his incarnate Son. In this connection he remarked that the schema missed a splendid opportunity to inculcate reverence toward the word of God. "Our separated brothers, who have such a love and veneration for the word of God," should be given an occasion to see "that our devotion in this matter is not less than theirs." After several further observations on the polemical tone of the draft and on its neglect of the role of the Holy Spirit, the French cardinal concluded: "Our faith is not founded on Scholastic arguments but on every word that proceeds from the mouth of God. It is to be regretted that the decree on the sources of revelation has not been conceived according to such a principle, unhesitatingly admitted by all, and therefore I strongly urge that it be totally rewritten."[4]

The next speaker, Cardinal Joseph Frings of Cologne, spoke in similar terms.[5] The schema should be rejected, he held, first because of its tone and secondly because of two major doctrinal points. With regard to the tone, he asserted that the Council here spoke not with the voice of the Good Shep-

3. This approach in terms of two sources was not original with the 1962 schema. Pius IX in his letter *Inter gravissimas* (October 20, 1870) had declared that "Scripture and tradition are the sources of divine revelation" (*Acta Pii IX*, part 1, vol. 5, p. 259). Pius XII in the encyclical *Humani generis* (1950) followed the lead of Pius IX. See the excerpts from *Humani generis* in Denzinger-Schönmetzer, *Enchiridion symbolorum*, no. 3886. This anthology will henceforth be abbreviated DS.

4. *Acta Synodalia Sacrosancti Concilii Oecumenici Vaticani II*, vol. III, part 3 (Vatican City: Typis Polyglottis, 1974), 32-34. This collection will henceforth be abbreviated AS.

5. AS II/3, 34-36.

herd who calls his own by name but with that of the professor or judge who is eager to condemn. The schema lacked the pastoral tone for which John XXIII had called in his opening allocution at the Council. The first doctrine to which Frings objected was that of the two sources. This manner of speaking, he said, was alien to the fathers of the church, alien to the great Scholastics, including St. Thomas, and alien likewise to all the ecumenical councils. Although, in the order of discovery *(in ordine cognoscendi)*, one may speak of two sources being used by a scholar seeking to ascertain the doctrine of revelation, it should be recognized that in the order of being *(in ordine essendi)* there is only one source, the word of God. It would be particularly unfortunate, said the German cardinal, if the Council in its opening statement were to offend the separated brothers *(fratres separati)* by emphasizing a point that no longer has the same importance that it did four centuries ago.

The second doctrine to which Frings objected was the handling of inspiration and inerrancy. The schema, he said, embraced a rigid, deductive theory, according to which the inerrancy of the Bible in all details was deduced aprioristically from a certain concept of inspiration. Some Catholic theologians hold different theories of inspiration, based on the biblical texts as they stand. These other theories should not be rejected, because it is not customary for councils to settle debates among Catholic theologians or to anathematize particular schools, but only to condemn heresies and very dangerous errors.

A succession of other speakers followed, several, including Ernesto Ruffini and Giuseppe Siri, defending the schema. But the majority were opposed for substantially the reasons already mentioned. After a predominantly negative vote, Pope John XXIII ordered that the schema be withdrawn and that a new text be composed by a mixed commission that would be chaired jointly by Cardinal Alfredo Ottaviani of the Holy Office and Cardinal Augustin Bea of the Secretariat for Promoting Christian Unity.

The new text was circulated by mail in April 1963 and revised in the spring of 1964 on the basis of written comments from the bishops. On September 30, 1964, this revised text was discussed on the Council floor. Since there were disagreements within the drafting commission, it was decided to present both majority and minority reports. The majority view, defending the text as written, was presented by Archbishop Ermenegildo Florit of Florence. It dealt principally with the nature of revelation as the self-communication of God in Christ.[6] In his minority report, Bishop Franciso

6. AS III/3, 131-40.

Franič of Split, Yugoslavia, argued for the presence of certain revealed truths in tradition alone.[7]

Vatican II on the Bestowal of Revelation

The final text of *Dei Verbum* closely resembles the schema defended by Archbishop Florit in his majority report. In its first chapter it describes revelation primarily as an action or process originating from God. God, out of sheer love, emerges from his silence, and enters into conversation with human beings in order to bring them into fellowship with himself and make them sharers in his divine life (DV 2). Salvation is here depicted in terms of communion, though of course there are other aspects to be considered. Vatican II could take it for granted that, as the Council of Trent had taught, justification involves the remission of original and personal sin as well as the interior renewal by which we are made heirs of eternal life (Trent, Session 6, chap. 7, DS 1528).[8]

The same article (DV 2) mentions in general terms the means whereby God establishes this revelatory communication: words and deeds intrinsically connected with each other. On the one hand, the works that unfold in the history of salvation exemplify and confirm what the words declare. On the other hand, the words make the deeds known and elucidate the mystery contained in them. In other terms, revelation is not conferred through uninterpreted facts or through nonfactual interpretations, but through interpreted facts. The structure of word and deed is compared by Florit to that of the sacraments, in which words and actions are ordinarily joined together.

Revelation, of course, is not just a haphazard collection of revelatory words and deeds. Drawing on patristic authorities, the Council speaks of a unified plan of revelation and salvation: the economy. The teaching of Vatican II is at this point influenced by modern discussions of salvation history.

---

7. See AS III/3, 124-29.

8. A possible weakness of *Dei Verbum* is its failure to deal with the negative aspects of the human condition. As Joseph Ratzinger observes in commenting on article 3, "The whole vast subject of sin, law, and the anger of God is gathered together here in the one little word *lapsus (Post eorum lapsum . . .)* and thus is given neither its full weight nor is it taken seriously enough. The pastoral optimism of an age that is concerned with understanding and reconciliation seems to have somewhat blinded the Council to a not immaterial section of the testimony of Scripture." Ratzinger's commentary on chapters 1 and 2 of *Dei Verbum* may be found in *Commentary on the Documents of Vatican II,* ed. Herbert Vorgrimler, 5 vols. (New York: Herder & Herder, 1969), 3:155-98; quotation from 174.

The Council does not reduce the content of revelation to historical events, as some enthusiasts for salvation history have done. On the contrary, it holds that God himself, in his eternal reality, is the primary content or object of revelation. By his words and deeds in history God enables us to know him and his salvific intentions for his people.[9]

A further point is the role of Christ in the economy. In a closely packed sentence the Council declares that Christ is "the mediator and the fullness of all revelation." This sentence from *Dei Verbum* 2, further explained in no. 4, demands careful consideration. In what sense is Christ the revealer, the fullness of revelation, and the mediator of revelation?

As the eternal Word of God, Christ is identified with God the revealer. God reveals by means of his Word, the Logos, the reflection of his glory (Heb. 1:3). The Word, when he comes into the world, becomes the agent who makes the Father known (John 1:18). No one can know the Father except the Son and those to whom the Son reveals the Father (Matt. 11:27).

Christ is the fullness of revelation because he is the self-revealing truth, the expression of all that the Father has to say. Everything else is simply a preparation for, or a gloss upon, the essential message that God gives in his Son. At the Council one of the bishops (Archbishop P. Zoungrana of Ouagadougou, Upper Volta, speaking in the name of sixty-seven African bishops) declared that the very person of Jesus Christ is divine revelation. He supported this opinion by alluding to biblical texts such as 1 John 1:2-3, John 14:9-10, Col. 1:15, Heb. 1:3, and Matt. 17:5, as well as a famous passage from St. John of the Cross's *The Ascent of Mount Carmel* (Bk. II, chap. 22).[10] The great Spanish mystic, after quoting from Hebrews (1:1-2) the passage that God in these last days has spoken to us in his Son, goes on to say that if Christians were to ask God for visions and revelations, God could reply:

> I have already told you all things in my Word, my Son, and if I have no other word, what answer or revelation can I now make that would surpass this? Fasten your eyes on Him alone, because in Him I have spoken and revealed all, and in Him you shall discover even more than you ask for and desire.

John of the Cross then cites from Paul's letter to the Colossians that in Christ "are hidden all the treasures of the wisdom and knowledge of God" (Col. 2:3).[11]

---

9. See the first and last sentences of DV 2, which speak of God revealing himself.

10. AS III/3, 212-14.

11. St. John of the Cross, *The Ascent of Mount Carmel*, Book II, chap. 22, nos. 5-6; in *The Collected Works of St. John of the Cross*, trans. Kieran Kavanaugh and Otilio Rodriguez (Washington, D.C.: Institute of Carmelite Studies, 1973), 180-81.

Neither St. John of the Cross nor Vatican II intended to say that a passing glance at the man Jesus Christ is an adequate revelation of God's total plan of salvation. As the Constitution later explains, Christ reveals God by living among human beings, by speaking what the Fourth Gospel calls "the words of God" (John 3:34), by his symbolic acts and miracles, and especially by his death and resurrection, crowned by the sending of the Spirit of Truth (DV 4).

It is relatively easy, from the perspective of Christian faith, to acknowledge that Christ is both the revealer and the culminating revelation of God. More difficult, perhaps, is the thesis that Christ is the mediator of all revelation. In the perspectives of Vatican II there is only one economy of revelation. Every element in the economy finds its true revelatory meaning in relation to Christ, the center, who stands first in the order of the divine intention. The saving truth that is mediated through nature and history comes from him and finds its final significance in him. In the Old Testament Christ the Logos was at work giving anticipations of himself, preparing the way for his own advent in the flesh. The final verses of Romans, consistent with this outlook, declare that the gospel was "kept secret for long ages, but is now disclosed, and through the prophetic writings is made known to all the Gentiles" (Rom. 16:25-26; cf. 1 Cor. 10:1-11). The latent significance of all the types and prophecies of the Old Testament becomes manifest in the incarnate Son.[12] The total message of God, spread out in the history of salvation, appears in concentrated form in Christ, the *Verbum abbreviatum*.[13]

Dei Verbum 3 gives some indications of the ways in which revelation was given prior to the Incarnation. The paragraph begins by mentioning the function of the Word in the creation and conservation of the world. According to biblical texts such as Romans 1:19-20, God offers lasting testimony to himself in the works of creation. This general (or "cosmic") revelation appears to be something different from natural theology — the work of reason by which the human mind, so to speak, climbs up to God.[14] Rather, reference

12. Thus the Council can say in DV 16, echoing a passage from Augustine: "Thus God, the inspirer and author of the books of both Testaments, has in his wisdom arranged that the New Testament be hidden in the Old, and the Old be made manifest in the New (cf. Lk 22:20; 1 Cor 11:25)." In a footnote the text here refers to Augustine, *Quaest. in Hept.* 2:73; PL 34:623; CChr 33:106.

13. See Henri de Lubac, *La révélation divine*, 3d ed. (Paris: Cerf, 1983), 81-82.

14. Far from rejecting naturally acquired knowledge of God, Vatican II affirms this in DV 6, but makes it clear that achievement of reason falls short of the knowledge bestowed by revelation. In contrast to Vatican I, which spoke of natural knowledge before revelation and faith, Vatican II discusses the natural knowledge of God only after treating revealed knowledge and faith in DV 1-5.

is made to the activity of God who addresses the human spirit through the order of creation. The same idea seems to be conveyed by Paul in his speech at Lystra, in which he says that God "has not left himself without a witness in doing good — giving you rains from heaven and fruitful seasons, and filling you with good and your hearts with joy" (Acts 14:17). In its Pastoral Constitution, *Gaudium et spes,* Vatican II stresses the universal availability of cosmic revelation: "All believers of whatever religion have always heard his [God's] revealing voice in the discourse of creatures" (GS 36). Since the Word manifests aspects of himself in the whole work of creation (John 1:3; Col. 1:15-17; Heb. 1:3, 10; 11:3), revelation through nature is in its own way christological.

The next few sentences give a very brief summary of the course of salvation history. Although this history is not knowable to us today except with the help of Scripture, it is properly placed in chapter 1 of *Dei Verbum* because the patriarchs, Moses, and the prophets received revelation even before the Hebrew Scriptures, let alone the Christian Bible, existed.

The Completion of Revelation

When, if at all, does divine revelation come to a close? A decree of the Holy Office, in 1907, had condemned the modernist proposition that "the revelation that constitutes the object of Catholic faith was not complete with the apostles" (*Lamentabili sane,* prop. 21; DS 3421). Some Fathers at Vatican II, going even beyond this teaching about "the object of Catholic faith," wanted the Council to declare that revelation had ceased, or was closed, with the death of the apostles.[15]

As is evident from the texts quoted above, Vatican II preferred to avoid this negative manner of speaking and to concentrate on Christ himself as the consummation of revelation. According to Christian faith the supreme and unsurpassable revelation of God has been made in Christ, the incarnate Son. The Christ event, properly understood in its total context, teaches all that we can wish or hope to know by way of revelation. Against progressivists such as Joachim of Fiore and his disciples, the Catholic Church teaches that there will be no post-Christian dispensation of the Holy Spirit, since the Spirit can declare only the revelation given in Christ (John 16:12-15). *Dei Verbum* therefore preferred the positive formulation that "the Christian dispensation, as the new and definitive covenant, will never pass away. No new public revelation is to be expected before the glorious manifestation of our Lord Jesus Christ (cf.

---

15. See *relationes* of July 3, 1964, and Nov. 30, 1964; AS III/3, 77 and IV/1, 345.

1 Tim. 6:14 and Tit. 2:13)" (DV 4). In this final "manifestation" of the mystery of Christ the same revelation will be proffered in a new mode, that of glory, rather than, as at present, under the veil of faith. Because the eschatological revelation will clearly disclose what God has already attested in Christ, it will confirm the definitive character of the revelation we now possess.

Notwithstanding the centrality of the Paschal event, Christian revelation was not entirely complete with the Ascension and the day of Pentecost. The early church needed further interventions from the Holy Spirit so that it could rightly grasp the meaning of what God had disclosed in his Son and ascertain the essential structures and mission of the church itself. Karl Rahner makes this point persuasively:

> Theologically speaking, we certainly cannot hold that the Church was already complete on the day of Pentecost. The Church indeed had then visible existence as a community, a legal structure (at least in its basic traits) and the Holy Spirit. Still, she was not yet complete. There really existed, in the literal sense of Batiffol's term, an *église naissante,* the Church in the process of birth, and the process took a certain amount of time. In order to understand this point, we have only to recall that the Church, whose "only" mission, as it rightly said, is to conserve and interpret divine revelation, did not yet possess its complete being at Pentecost for the simple reason that there was further revelation after Pentecost (v.g. concerning the Canon of Scripture). The Apostolic Church had both more and less than the later Church's mission of conservation and interpretation; it had more because it was still [able] to receive new revelation, and it had less because it did not yet possess all the truths which the later Church was given to preserve, since they had not yet all been revealed.[16]

With the end of the apostolic period, which coincides approximately with the completion of the New Testament, the era of constitutive revelation came to a close. Nothing substantively new is added to "the faith which was once for all delivered to the saints" (Jude 3), the "deposit of faith" entrusted to the apostolic church (1 Tim. 6:20; 2 Tim. 1:14).

The completion of constitutive revelation should not be understood as the cessation of revelation itself. As we have seen, Vatican II taught that God's revealing voice is still heard in the discourse of creatures (GS 36). God continues to speak to his people when they gather to hear the Scriptures proclaimed

---

16. Karl Rahner, *Inspiration in the Bible,* revised translation (New York: Herder & Herder, 1964), 47-48; cf. German original, *Über die Schriftinspiration* (Freiburg: Herder, 1958), 53.

in the church (*Sacrosanctum concilium* [SC] 7; cf. DV 8, 21, etc). He speaks through the voice of conscience (GS 16) and through the "signs of the times," which are to be interpreted "under the light of the gospel" (GS 4, 11, 44). All these forms of "speaking" may be included under the category of revelation, provided that they are not seen as adding to the content of the definitive revelation given in the incarnate Son.[17]

In the four decades since *Dei Verbum* was composed, its teaching on the unsurpassability of God's revelation in Christ has taken on added relevance. Contemporary historical relativism inclines believers to deny that anything within history can be final or definitive. Against such tendencies the magisterium has considered it necessary to repeat with added emphasis the doctrine of Vatican II: "It must be *firmly believed* that, in the mystery of Christ, the Incarnate Son of God, who is 'the way, the truth, and the life' (Jn 14:6), the full revelation of divine truth is given."[18] But, we shall see, this does not mean that there can be no progress in the understanding of revelation.

Apostolic Tradition and Revelation

Emphasizing the permanent value of the apostolic deposit, *Dei Verbum* treats God's subsequent conversation with his people under the rubric of "The Transmission of Revelation," the title of its second chapter. This chapter, echoing in part the teaching of Vatican I, states that God in his providence saw to it that what he had revealed for the world's salvation would not be forgotten or corrupted (DV 7; cf. Vatican I, *Pastor aeternus,* DS 3050). What was to be preserved and handed down was nothing other than the gospel, which Vatican II, following Trent, described as God's revelation in Christ, promised in advance through the prophets and promulgated in its fullness by Christ (DV 7; cf. Trent, DS 1501). As we have already seen, Vatican II, under the prodding of cardinals such as Liénart and Frings, distanced itself from the rather bookish view, current in the nineteenth century, that Scripture and tradition were the sources of revelation. Like the Council of Trent, Vatican II characterized the gospel of Jesus Christ as "the source of all saving truth and moral discipline" (ibid.).

Dei Verbum gave a somewhat fuller description than did Trent of the

17. For a discussion of the problem of "continuing" or "dependent" revelation, see Gerald O'Collins, *Retrieving Fundamental Theology* (New York: Paulist, 1993), chap. 7, pp. 87-97.

18. Congregation for the Doctrine of the Faith, Declaration *Dominus Iesus: On the Unicity and Salvific Universality of Jesus Christ and the Church* (August 6, 2000), §5.

mode by which the apostles transmitted to others the revelation they had received. Whereas Trent concentrated primarily on the verbal element in the gospel and apostolic tradition, Vatican II mentioned also the nonverbal components:

> The apostles handed on, by their oral preaching, exemplary actions, and ordinances, what they had received from Christ's lips, his way of life or his works, or had learned by the prompting of the Holy Spirit. (DV 7)

Only after saying this did the Council mention the New Testament: "The apostolic mandate was fulfilled, too, by those apostles and apostolic men who, under the inspiration of the same Holy Spirit, committed the message of salvation to writing" (ibid.).

For more than a century after its foundation, the church was without a canonical list of Holy Scriptures. The Christians did of course read the sacred books of the Jews, but there seems not to have been as yet a "Hebrew canon," still less an "Alexandrian canon" or a "Christian canon," accepted by the church. Instead there was a rather indefinite set of books, including the Pentateuch, the prophets, the psalms, and other "hagiographa." As we can see from the New Testament, the Christians in their citations made no clear distinction between books that were later received as canonical and others that are today regarded by most Christians as apocryphal. For example, the Letter of Jude cites the Assumption of Moses and the Book of Enoch as authoritative.[19] We may therefore agree with Oscar Cullmann that the oral proclamation of the gospel had a clear preeminence over the written during the first few decades of the Christian era.[20] The spoken gospel, even though Paul and others received it through the church, was not seen as a merely human tradition, because the Lord was held to stand behind the apostles as they transmitted his words and deeds. In Cullmann's words, "Transmission by the apostles is not effected by men, but by Christ the Lord himself who thereby imparts this revelation."[21]

Paul can therefore insist that the tradition he proclaims is truly the word of God (1 Thess. 2:13; cf. Gal. 1:8-9; 1 Cor. 7:25; 11:23). He puts his oral doctrine and his letters on the same authoritative level (2 Thess. 2:15). The epistles of

---

19. Jude 6, 9, and 14-15. Allusions to, and echoes from, books that Protestants do not accept as canonical may be found in Rom. 1:19-32 (Wis. 13:1-15), 1 Pet. 1:7 (Wis. 3:5-6), and Heb. 11:35 (2 Mac. 6–7). These books, however, belong to the Catholic Old Testament.

20. See especially the essay "La Tradition," which appears in English translation as chapter 4 of Oscar Cullmann's *The Early Church* (Philadelphia: Westminster, 1956), 55-99.

21. Ibid., 73.

Paul began to be collected at a relatively early period, thus preparing them to be incorporated into what would eventually become the New Testament (cf. 2 Pet. 3:16).

In one concise sentence Vatican II summarizes the stage of oral apostolic preaching: "The apostles, after the Lord's Ascension, passed on to their hearers what he had said and done, together with that fuller understanding which they now possessed, instructed by the glorious life of Christ and taught by the light of the Spirit of Truth" (DV 19, which refers to a number of passages from the Fourth Gospel).

An official footnote at this point in *Dei Verbum* refers to the Instruction of the Pontifical Biblical Commission *Sancta Mater Ecclesia* (1964), which points out that after the resurrection of Jesus the apostles "faithfully explained his life and words." As an example the Biblical Commission mentions the speech of Peter to Cornelius and his household, summarized in Acts 10:34-43. Just as Jesus after his resurrection interpreted to his disciples the words of the Old Testament as well as his own previous teaching (Luke 24:27, 44-45; cf. Acts 1:3), the disciples later interpreted his words and deeds according to the needs of their listeners. "'Devoting themselves to the ministry of the word,' they preached and made use of various modes of speaking that were suited to their own purpose and the mentality of their listeners" (SME 8, with reference to Acts 6:4). For this reason, the Biblical Commission observes, it is necessary to distinguish in the surviving records of the apostolic preaching a variety of literary forms, such as catechesis, story, *testimonium,* hymn, doxology, and prayer.

As this last sentence implies, the apostolic proclamation was much more than a mere relaying of historical information about the words and deeds of Jesus. It was a creative interpretation of the teaching and career of Jesus, accomplished under the revealing light of the Holy Spirit, and designed to arouse and confirm Christian faith. Because the early tradition has the Lord as its true author, it is an intrinsic element of constitutive revelation.

Although the church did not yet have a fixed collection of canonical Scriptures, it was not a totally fluid community. Tradition, without being crystallized in rigid formulas, was a stabilizing force. The apostles exhorted their converts to hold fast to the traditions that had been committed to them (2 Thess. 2:15; 1 Cor. 15:1-11). These traditions, according to Vatican II, were not merely historical and doctrinal; they included "everything that helps the people of God to live a holy life and grow in faith" (DV 8). Vatican II's Constitution on the Liturgy, *Sacrosanctum concilium,* explains in greater detail the mission of the apostles to "carry on the work of salvation that they were announcing, by means of sacrifice and sacraments, around which the whole of liturgical life revolves" (SC 6). The formation of the will, emotions, and imagination of the faithful through prayer and actual practice is an integral part of the tradition.

The community and its tradition were under the authoritative direction of the apostles who, as *Dei Verbum* reminds us, "left as their successors the bishops, 'handing on their own teaching function to them'" (DV 7).[22] The Pastoral Epistles enable us to glimpse the handing over of apostolic authority from the apostles to the heads of local churches through delegates such as Timothy and Titus. The Constitution on the Church, *Lumen gentium*, cites Tertullian and Irenaeus to the effect that the bishops became the guardians of the apostolic tradition (LG 20).[23] For these second-century theologians the teaching of the apostolic churches and their respective bishops was the principal norm of faith.

The Scriptures and Revelation

In the course of time the church did develop its own Bible, formed out of a combination of Jewish Scriptures with newly written Christian Scriptures. The apostolic message was committed to writing by the apostles and their co-workers (DV 7). Recognizing the eminent status of the Bible as a document of revelation, *Dei Verbum* devotes the last four of its six chapters to the Bible. In line with the teaching of earlier popes and councils, it asserts that the biblical books are inspired; that is to say, they were written under the influence of the Holy Spirit (DV 8). The nature of inspiration is explained in ways that bypass the mythological (or at least metaphorical) conceptions that had been current among the rabbis and some early church fathers. Inspiration, as understood by Vatican II, involves neither a "mantic" or "ecstatic" loss of the writer's faculties nor a process of verbal dictation from God to the human scribe. In positive terms, God is said to have brought about the composition of the sacred books by employing human agents, using their own powers and faculties, so that they wrote as authors in a true sense, and yet in such a way that they set down all that God intended, and nothing else (DV 11). The Council does not go into a speculative discussion of how God brings about this result.

In Catholic theology, Scripture is often said to be the inspired word of

---

22. The quotation is from Irenaeus, *Adversus haereses,* III.3.1; PG 7:848; SC 210:31.

23. Reference is here made to several patristic texts, including Tertullian, *De praescriptione haereticorum,* 32; PL 2:52-53; CChr 1:212-13; and Irenaeus, *Adv. haer.,* III.3.1; PG 7:848; *SC* 210:31.

God. This terminology, correct though it be, may give rise to some confusion, since orally delivered prophetic utterance can also be the inspired word of God. What is distinctive to the Bible is that it is the *written* word that comes about through divine inspiration.

Vatican II asserts that the Holy Scriptures contain the word of God and, because inspired, really are the word of God (DV 24). Their special dignity is that, "having been inspired by God and committed to writing once for all, they impart the word of God in unalterable form" (DV 21).

Inspiration is not the same thing as revelation. When he reveals, God communicates new knowledge of himself. When he inspires, God moves a human being to communicate and directs the process so that it achieves the divinely intended end. To say that the Scriptures are inspired is not *eo ipso* to say that they are revealed but only to say that they record what God wanted to be recorded.

Many Catholics make a distinction between the revealed word of God (described in the first chapter of *Dei Verbum*) and the inspired word of Scripture (discussed especially in the third and sixth chapters). While this distinction has merit, it should not be pressed to the point of presenting revelation and inspiration as external to each other. For three reasons a very close connection must be acknowledged.

(1) It is quite possible for God to make a revelation through oral or written inspiration. A prophet or apostle who is moved to proclaim a message may be the organ by which God reveals. In the words of von Balthasar, "Revelation to the prophets and promulgation by the prophets tend to merge together, and form virtually a single act of revelation effected by the Spirit in the service of the coming or past incarnation of the Son. . . . Revelation, then, is effected partly before the writing, partly in the actual writing; in other words, Scripture participates in God's self-revelation in Jesus Christ through the Spirit."[24] Thus the oracles of Isaiah and of the Book of Revelation (to mention only two examples) are simultaneously inspired and revealed.

(2) Even when Scripture is not proposing new and original oracles, its contents coincide in great part with what had previously been revealed. This is evidently the case where the Scripture is laying down articles of faith, as occurs in credal or confessional passages such as Deut. 6:4-5, Rom. 10:8-9, and 1 Cor. 15:1-4. Since the prophetic and apostolic proclamation is by its nature transitory, Scripture is needed to give it a public and perduring existence, so that it becomes available in stable form to future generations.

---

24. Hans Urs von Balthasar, *Word and Revelation: Essays in Theology 1* (New York: Herder & Herder, 1964), 11.

(3) The events and words of revelation, given at particular points of salvation history, take on a new significance when viewed in the light of the whole biblical canon, which surveys the course of God's revelatory work from the dawn of history to the end of the apostolic age. This context is indivisible. One cannot carve the Bible up into revelatory and nonrevelatory passages, as though it were possible to make an anthology of the former, excluding the latter. To excise parts of the Bible would alter the meaning of the whole.

Not long ago a distinguished Catholic exegete asserted that certain passages in the Old Testament, such as the genealogies in the first nine chapters of 1 Chronicles, contain no revelation.[25] My own impression would be that these chapters contribute to our grasp of the self-understanding of the people of God of the Old Testament, and more especially their understanding of the Davidic monarchy, which is a type of the kingship of Christ. It might be difficult to distill propositions of faith from these chapters, but they affect our comprehension of what was fulfilled in Christ and the church, and hence pertain to revelation.

The revelatory character of the Bible as a whole has often been seen as precluding error in any detail. The doctrine of inerrancy was vigorously debated at Vatican II, with some defending and others attacking the prevalent Scholastic formulations. Eventually a compromise was reached. Omitting any sweeping claim of inerrancy in all respects, the Fathers contented themselves with declaring:

> Since everything asserted by the inspired authors or sacred writers must be held to be asserted by the Holy Spirit, it follows that the books of Scripture must be acknowledged as teaching firmly, faithfully, and without error that truth which God wanted put into the sacred writings for the sake of our salvation. (DV 11)

Some interpret this statement as though the Bible could be divided into passages that present divinely given truth and others that present fallible human opinions. But according to the intentions of the Theological Commission there was no question of dividing the Bible into materially distinct

---

25. Raymond E. Brown, in *The Critical Meaning of the Bible* (New York: Paulist, 1981), 7, criticizes the position of Vatican II (and my own) to the effect that the whole Bible not only transmits, but is, the word of God. He objects to this statement on the ground that it seems to make inspiration and revelation coextensive. He goes on to say (p. 8) that for his purposes revelation applies only to "biblical claims to receive or transmit the word of God" and not to the church's understanding of the Bible as the word of God. This seems to me to be an unwarranted narrowing of the concept of revelation.

parts, some of which would be subject to error and others guaranteed against error. The distinction is to be understood in terms of the formal object, that is to say, the aspect under which the Bible is considered. When seen with reference to the communication of salutary truth, the Bible as a whole is free from error. Every passage has its place in this communicative process, since the purpose of the Holy Spirit in inspiring the sacred writers was to point the way to salvation. Certain sentences, if read with a view to scientific or historical information, or without regard to the total biblical context, might seem to be misleading, but within the framework of the entire Bible, viewed as the inspired record of God's gradual self-revelation to his people, these passages can be seen as contributing to the divine message of salvation, and thus as revelatory.[26]

If this be true, it follows that the Bible, inspired in its totality to guide the church in the way of salvation, is a document of revelation. The church does not interpret it from a merely human point of view, as a document of science or secular history. To understand what God wanted to communicate for the sake of our salvation, we must read the Scriptures, as a work composed under the influence of the Holy Spirit, with the help of that same Spirit (DV 12). If the interpreter stops at the merely philological or empirical level, without rising to the perspective of faith, the resulting exegesis will be deficient, with the result that the word of God will not be found in the sacred text. But once the interpreter adopts the perspective of faith, reading the Bible from within the living, worshiping, praying church, the whole Bible can be seen as revelatory and as the word of God. In its total significance it communicates what is salvifically important about God and God's ways.

Some authors have raised the question whether the Bible is itself revelation or simply the record of revelation already given. In the light of the preceding paragraphs we may reply that it both transmits past revelation and completes that revelation. As noted above, the particular revelations that had occurred in the course of salvation history, including the apostolic age, were recorded in the Bible, which consequently serves as a channel of transmis-

---

26. On this point see A. Grillmeier, "Excursus on Article 11," in Vorgrimler, *Commentary on the Documents of Vatican II*, 3:233-37; Johannes Beumer, *Die katholische Inspirationslehre zwischen Vatikanum I und II* (Stuttgart: Katholische Bibelwerk, 1967), 92-95; more briefly, R. A. F. MacKenzie in *The Documents of Vatican II*, ed. Walter A. Abbott (New York: America Press, 1966), 119 n. 31. Grillmeier and Beumer both point out that the Theological Commission, in its responses to proposed changes in the text, insisted that the text implied no restriction of inspiration or inerrancy to certain portions of Scripture. For an argument to the effect that Vatican II disavowed the idea of biblical inerrancy see Oswald Loretz, *The Truth of the Bible* (New York: Herder & Herder, 1968), 92-95 and passim.

sion. But when so recorded, the revelations took on added significance as components of a single process and were made permanently available for the guidance of God's people. Since Christian revelation is by its very nature organic, public, and enduring, the production of the inspired text is integral to the very bestowal of revelation. By God's grace, the church in the formative period was able to express her faith in an original manner that could enlighten all future generations. By producing normative documents of faith the apostolic church was able to make herself, for the sake of posterity, a "historically tangible concretization of God's grace in Christ."[27] The production of Holy Scripture therefore pertains to the process by which the church is constituted as a living community of faith.

Post-Biblical Tradition

The church's acquisition of a full set of canonical Scriptures required a considerable period of time. By the middle or the end of the second century the main questions appear to have been settled. Debates concerning the precise limits of the canon continued, of course, down through the fourth century, and have erupted from time to time since that date. Only with the passage of time did the councils of the church (beginning late in the fourth century) seek to achieve complete uniformity regarding the canon. For present purposes, however, we may regard the canon as substantially settled in the practice of the church some time before the councils issued their decrees.

As Oscar Cullmann and others have pointed out, the church drew up her biblical canon at a time when oral tradition was ceasing to serve as a reliable source of information. This unreliability may be illustrated from the surviving fragments from Papias, who accepted some relatively recent legends as though they were apostolic traditions.[28]

Cullmann combines this assertion with another, more controversial. He regards the adoption of the canon as a great act of humility by which the church submitted all her judgments to the norm of Scripture as the final word.[29] Cullmann's position rests upon a theory of the formal sufficiency and clarity of Scripture that Catholics find unconvincing. The acceptance of the Scriptures as a trustworthy guide does not logically demand the rejection of every other guide, at least where the guides do not disagree. In her proclama-

---

27. Rahner, *Inspiration in the Bible*, 48-49.
28. Cullmann, *Early Church*, 89.
29. Cullmann, *Early Church*, 90.

tion the church has used her authenticated tradition conjointly with Scripture and not in opposition to it.

Cullmann's position, to be sure, contains an element of truth. By the time the canon was drawn up, tradition as a distinct quarry of revealed truth was disappearing from view. In the first few generations the apostolic churches, under the direction of their bishops, were accepted as authoritative witnesses to particular teachings and practices instituted by the apostles. As late as the sixteenth century the Council of Trent rejected the Protestant *sola scriptura* by asserting that the church was perpetually bound to unwritten traditions that had been passed down from the apostles as it were from hand to hand (Session IV, DS 1501).

The Council of Trent in its official acts refrained from giving examples. In the conciliar discussions mention was made of practices such as infant baptism, the sign of the cross, and turning toward the East in prayer, and of beliefs such as the perpetual virginity of Mary, and the identity of Anne as Mary's mother.[30] Some of the Fathers at Trent spoke as though certain revealed truths were contained in tradition alone. But with the introduction of more critical methods in history, increasing numbers of Catholic theologians came to the conclusion that at our present distance from the apostolic age, we have no means of historically verifying the apostolic origin of doctrines and practices in no way attested by the New Testament.

Aware of this difficulty, Vatican II adopted a somewhat different concept of tradition, partly drawn from the Catholic Tübingen theologians of the nineteenth century. Unlike Trent, which had spoken only of traditions (in the plural), *Dei Verbum* spoke of tradition in the singular.[31] Tradition, in this dogmatic constitution, consisted not in particular truths but in a dynamic process of transmission under the guidance of the Holy Spirit. By continuously handing down the faith received from the apostles "the Church, in her teaching, life, and worship, perpetuates and transmits to all generations all that she is and all that she believes" (DV 8). Tradition is seen as progressing in the church, bringing about a growth of understanding that moves forward to the day when the words of God reach their fulfillment in her (ibid.).

This global, dynamic, nonverbal concept of tradition differs markedly from the atomized, static, and oral view usually (but somewhat too simplistically) attributed to the Council of Trent. Far from entering into competition

---

30. Joseph Ratzinger, "On the Interpretation of the Tridentine Decree on Tradition," in Karl Rahner and Joseph Ratzinger, *Revelation and Tradition* (New York: Herder & Herder, 1966), 50-68, 73-78. See esp. 61.

31. The only exception is in a quotation from 2 Thess. 2:15 in DV 8.

with Scripture, tradition disposes the faithful to apprehend more fully and accurately what is implied in Scripture. By dwelling in the faith-community and participating in its living heritage, the Christian believer becomes more responsive to what authors such as Cullmann call the interior witness of the Holy Spirit.[32]

As an example of what is known only with the help of tradition, and not by Scripture alone, *Dei Verbum* mentions "the full canon of the biblical books" (DV 8). This statement need not and should not be understood as though the apostles or their associates had provided a full list of the canonical books, which was then handed down by word of mouth. As Karl Rahner shows, this hypothesis is historically unfounded and is difficult to reconcile with the known facts about the history of the canon. The meaning is rather that the post-apostolic church was in a position to judge which books were pure expressions of the faith because the church already possessed the apostolic faith thanks to the tradition that had been handed on. In Rahner's apt expression, the church had acquired a certain "connaturality" with the authentic revelation through her participation in the living tradition of faith, and was thereby equipped to discern the books of the apostolic age that embodied the true faith.[33] The decision regarding the canon is an early instance of what Catholic theologians call the development of doctrine.

Without seeking to settle the question raised at the beginning of this article, that of the "material sufficiency" of Scripture, Vatican II seemed to favor the view that the totality of revelation is somehow contained both in Scripture and in apostolic tradition. A number of passages from Vatican II suggest that there are no truths contained in Scripture alone or in tradition alone. "Sacred tradition and sacred Scripture are in close connection and communion, for both of them, flowing from the same divine wellspring, merge together in some fashion and tend toward the same end" (DV 9). "Tradition and Scripture together form a single deposit of the word of God, entrusted to the Church" (DV 10). They are so intimately connected with each other, and with the magisterium, that none of the three can stand without the other two, but all together contribute effectively to the salvation of souls (ibid.).

With regard to the revelatory character of tradition, a distinction should be made between tradition in its apostolic and post-apostolic phases. In each case we have to do with apostolic tradition (tradition stemming from the apostles), not with merely ecclesiastical tradition (which originates from the church). In the apostolic period the tradition was still developing under the

32. Cullmann, *Early Church*, 97.
33. Rahner, *Inspiration in the Bible*, 67-72.

active influence of the Lord, who was at work through the Holy Spirit, completing the revelation. In the post-apostolic stage we have to do with tradition as the transmission of a revelation that is already complete.

Even in its post-apostolic phase, tradition is not a merely human process of transmission. In every generation tradition is sustained by the Holy Spirit. The Spirit makes the documents of revelation, so to speak, come alive, so that the church can hear God's revealing voice in the Scripture. Thanks to tradition, says the Council, "the Holy Spirit is active, making the living voice of the gospel resound in the Church, and through it in the world, bringing believers into the fullness of the truth, and making the word of Christ dwell in them in all its richness" (DV 8). Tradition enables the word of Scripture to become effective as revelation for its readers today, rather than being a document of merely historical interest.

Since both tradition and Scripture are divinely given channels of revelation, and since neither is independent of the other, it would be a mistake to subject either to the other as inferior to it. From a Catholic point of view it would be unwarranted to say that the Bible alone is the word of God, or that tradition is totally dependent on Scripture as a prior given. Together, and not separately, both Scripture and tradition embody and transmit the word of God. From its own perspective, therefore, Vatican II was able to reaffirm what Trent had said four centuries earlier: that Scripture and tradition are to be accepted and revered with the same sense of devotion and reverence (Trent, DS 1501; Vatican II, DV 9).

Vatican II and Montreal

The chapter on tradition in *Dei Verbum* was composed almost at the same time that the Fourth World Conference on Faith and Order, meeting at Montreal in 1963, drew up its statement on "Scripture, Tradition and Traditions." The authors of this statement were familiar with the debates at the first session of Vatican II, and the final version of *Dei Verbum* was influenced by the Montreal statement.[34] Convergences between the two documents have often been noted.[35] Montreal, like Vatican II, describes tradition as a "living reality transmitted through the operation of the Holy Spirit" (no. 46). It agrees with

34. Riccardo Burigana, *La Bibbia nel Concilio: La redazione della costituzione 'Dei Verbum' del Vaticano II* (Bologna: Il Mulino, 1998), 224-29.

35. See, for instance, Jean-Louis Leuba, "La tradition à Montréal et à Vatican II: Convergences et Questions," in Bernard-Dominique Dupuy, ed., *La Révélation divine* 2 (Paris: Cerf, 1968), 475-97.

the Council that, "when the canon of the New Testament had been fully defined and recognized by the Church," tradition needed to be understood in relation to Scripture (no. 49). Like Vatican II, again, Montreal looks upon the life of the church as a "continuous recalling, appropriation, and transmission" of the once-for-all event of Jesus Christ (no. 56) and dwells on the "dynamic element in the Tradition, which comes from the action of God within the history of his people and . . . looks to the consummation of the victory of the Lord at the end of time" (no. 64). All churches, according to Montreal, live by their traditions — even churches that claim to attribute no weight to tradition (no. 44).

Notwithstanding the remarkable convergences, there are significant differences between the two documents. While both alike recognize the "prospective" as well as the "retrospective" orientation of tradition, *Dei Verbum* goes beyond Montreal by seeming to acknowledge that tradition undergoes cumulative progress. Although Montreal does not deny such progress, I do not find in its text anything corresponding to Vatican II's statement that "the tradition which comes from the apostles progresses in the Church under the assistance of the Holy Spirit" (DV 8). Vatican II here is speaking not of progress in revelation but of progress in the church's grasp of a revelation already complete.

A second difference between the Montreal statement and *Dei Verbum* is that the former makes considerable use of the term "tradition" in the plural. Montreal goes beyond *Dei Verbum* in raising the question about the legitimacy of different denominational traditions (a question it leaves unresolved in nos. 57-59) and in recognizing that different cultures require different expressions of tradition (nos. 65-66, 69).

From *Dei Verbum,* by contrast, one might get the impression that there is only one tradition — that which stems from the apostles and is sustained in the entire church by the Holy Spirit. Other Vatican II documents, however, use the term "tradition" in the plural. The Decree on the Church's Missionary Activity, *Ad gentes,* directs the young churches to borrow "from the customs and traditions of their people . . . all those things which can contribute to the glory of their Creator, the revelation of the Savior's grace, or the proper ordering of human life" (AG 22). The "particular traditions" developed in this way "can be illuminated by the light of the gospel and then taken up into Catholic unity." The individual young churches "adorned with their own traditions," will have their own place in the ecclesiastical communion (ibid.).

The question regarding denominational traditions is treated in the Decree on Ecumenism, *Unitatis redintegratio,* which speaks at some length of the different "traditions" of the Eastern (Orthodox) and Western churches. It states:

> The heritage handed down from the apostles was received in different forms
> and manners, and from the earliest times of the Church it was explained var-
> iously in different places, owing to diversities of character and conditions of
> life. (UR 14)

The churches of the East have their own liturgical forms, spiritual traditions
(UR 15), disciplines, customs, and observances (UR 16). Still more significantly, the Council adds that in the expressions of doctrine "sometimes one
tradition has come nearer than the other to a full appreciation of some aspects of the revealed mystery, or has expressed it to better advantage" (UR 17).
The "authentic theological traditions" of the Orientals are declared to be "ad-
mirably rooted in holy Scripture," in the living tradition of the apostles, and
in the works of the Eastern fathers and spiritual writers (ibid.). Thus the different theological formulations accepted in the East and the West "are often
to be considered mutually complementary rather than conflicting" (ibid.).

A third difference between the two documents is that Montreal is more
concerned than Vatican II with finding criteria to distinguish genuine tradition from "impoverished tradition or even distortion of tradition" (no. 48).
While recognizing that the letter of "Scripture alone" is not an adequate criterion (no. 49), Montreal does not speak of the magisterium as a criterion except when describing the Roman Catholic position (no. 53). The Faith and
Order Conference recommends that the different churches seek to resolve
their differences by common study of Scripture and of the fathers of the
church (no. 55).

At Vatican II the Council fathers were aware of the problem of deviant or
distorted tradition, but did not expressly address it. The Council documents
provide several criteria for assessing the validity of traditions. *Dei Verbum*
makes it evident that any tradition that conflicts with God's word in Scripture
could not be authentic. It also speaks of the power of discernment of the ecclesiastical magisterium, which has received what Irenaeus called the "sure
charism of truth" (DV 8). The task of authentically interpreting the word of
God, whether in Scripture or in tradition, has been entrusted exclusively to
the living magisterium, which exercises its authority in the name of Christ
(DV 10).

A significant contribution of Montreal was the threefold distinction between Tradition (with a capital T), tradition as a process of transmission, and
traditions as diverse forms of expression of the gospel. Vatican II did not
make this threefold distinction, but it has been taken up by some Catholics
since the Council and seems to be reflected in an address of Paul VI of August
7, 1974:

Here we should explain what we mean by tradition in this religious sphere, both a constituent, together with Sacred Scripture, of revelation [sense #1], and as authentic and compelling transmission, with the assistance of the Holy Spirit through the teaching of the Church, of revelation itself [sense #2]. We consider that these are ideas acquired from our common culture and are held distinct from those commonly called traditions [sense #3] which can rather be said to be usages, customs, styles — transient and changeable forms of human life without the charism of a truth which renders them unchangeable and obligatory. We add, rather, that these purely historical and human traditions not only contain many contingent and perishable elements, towards which criticism is liberal in judgment and reform. They often indeed must be criticised and reformed because of the ease with which human things age, or are distorted, and they need to be purified and even supplanted. Not for nothing do we speak of "modernization" and renewal: and you know with how much energy and breadth of application.[36]

This Tradition/tradition/traditions distinction has proved useful in giving the church continuity and flexibility in dealing with its own heritage in fields such as liturgy, spirituality, theology, and canon law. In opposition to certain rigid "traditionalists," such as Archbishop Marcel Lefebvre, the church has had to justify its updating of this heritage without incurring the charge of being unfaithful to tradition in the strict theological sense. The terminology of the Montreal Faith and Order statement has thus been helpful to the Catholic Church in refining the terminology.

Conclusion

A correct theology of Scripture and tradition requires a sound theology of revelation. The first schema offered at Vatican II was rejected partly because it seemed to give the impression that Scripture and tradition were the basis of revelation, rather than the reverse. The schema represented the "regressive" method, which works from the present to the past. The Council, however, preferred to follow the genetic or causal order, beginning from the origins. The final text therefore began with the concept of revelation and then proceeded via tradition to Scripture. This order is fundamentally correct insofar as Scripture presupposes tradition, while tradition presupposes revelation.

36. Paul VI, "Tradition Explains the Old and the New," General Audience, August 7, 1974; *L'Osservatore Romano* (English weekly edition), 15 August 1974, 1. The words within brackets are my own insertions.

Yet revelation was not complete without its expression in tradition and Scripture. The revelation that lies at the basis of Christian faith was destined to be publicly proclaimed in the apostolic tradition and formulated in the inspired language of Holy Scripture. Even after that, the apostolic tradition and the canonical Scriptures still had to be recognized and interpreted in the tradition of the church in order for the revelation to be effective in later generations. The relationship, therefore, is not linear but rather circular. Revelation gives rise to tradition and Scripture, but Scripture and tradition embody revelation and effectively transmit it to the minds and hearts of believers today.

Tradition, which may be understood as the apostolic heritage living on in the church through the Holy Spirit, is expressed and communicated by means of multiple traditions. These traditions, while they transmit divine tradition, are not identical with it. In order to clarify the distinction, some Catholics have made use of the threefold distinction made by the Montreal conference on Faith and Order.

The Catholic Church has not ignored the problem of unauthentic or distorted tradition, which was examined ecumenically at Montreal. As previously noted, *Dei Verbum* addresses this problem by referring to Scripture as an inviolable norm and to the ecclesiastical magisterium, which Catholics understand as enjoying the prerogative of divine assistance. In a fuller discussion it might be noted that the hierarchical magisterium, before reaching its verdict, normally consults various loci of tradition, such as the church's authorized forms of prayer, the sense of the faithful, and views of trustworthy theologians. The hierarchy also examines whether the teaching in question enhances or weakens the unity and faith of those who hold it.[37] Under certain conditions the magisterium, with the promised help of the Holy Spirit, can make infallible pronouncements, putting an end to further debate within the church.[38]

Today as in the past, the Catholic Church views tradition as an indispensable vehicle for the transmission of revelation. While revering Scripture as containing the word of God in unalterable form, she denies that Scripture is sufficient in the sense that the whole of revelation could be known without tradition. Most Catholic theologians today would hold that every revealed truth is in some way attested by Scripture, but that some revealed truths are not explicitly mentioned by any texts in Scripture. Since the nineteenth cen-

37. Avery Cardinal Dulles, "Tradition: Authentic and Unauthentic," *Communio: International Catholic Review* 28 (Summer 2001): 377-85.

38. The question of magisterial infallibility is too complex to be dealt with in this paper. I have dealt with the subject from an ecumenical point of view in *A Church to Believe In* (New York: Crossroad, 1982), chapter 10 (pp. 133-48).

tury, tradition has been increasingly seen as a process whereby revelation is handed down, but it is not sheer process. The transmission conveys a content, which can to some extent be formulated in propositional truths. Although particular traditions are subject to critical scrutiny, tradition as a Spirit-governed transmission of the gospel in the church, is to be revered, like Holy Scripture, as a form of the word of God. Tradition hands on the word of God in such a way that it can be grasped by the faithful of every time and place.

The Bible in Use: Evangelicals Seeking Truth from Holy Scripture

J. I. PACKER

This presentation is a response to a request that I speak from, and for, the tradition of Protestant evangelicalism. First, therefore, I need to say how I understand the range of my assignment.

Evangelicalism Today

I begin by observing that, whatever else Protestant evangelicalism may be, it is a going concern, a currently expanding global reality that embraces something approaching a quarter of the world's professing Christians. The figures are roughly as follows. Well over a billion professed believers, more than half the total number, are Roman Catholic. Over 200 million are Orthodox, and 400 million, including Anglicans, are mainline Protestants, that is, members of Protestantism's relatively old and large denominational families, which for the most part liberals now lead. But then it is reckoned that 450 million are Pentecostal-charismatic, either in Pentecostal denominations or in independent congregations or in the mainline, and Pentecostal-charismatic Christianity is a mutation of evangelicalism, though it is not always recognized as such. Posit, then, a further 50 million evangelicals in the mainline or in small denominations who would not call themselves charismatic (that is, I think, a reasonable guess), and you reach a total of half a billion, almost a quarter of the whole.

It seems that the rapid spread of Pentecostalism in particular has caused the number of evangelicals to grow in this century in a way that significantly outstrips the proportionate growth of world population, and that growth is apparently continuing. The population explosion in Africa and Asia might account for the increase in Roman Catholic numbers, which also grow impressively, but the evidence suggests that evangelical numbers increase chiefly if not entirely as a result of intentional evangelism, church-planting and church-extending in its thrust, which involves both Pentecostal-charismatic and other evangelicals on equal terms and often collaboratively.

Thus I identify the constituency that I am to scrutinize and characterize, and about which I must in due course try to generalize.

The fundamental claim made for evangelicalism is that it represents the main stream of authentic Christian development over two millennia, even though, like the rest of Protestantism, it has been formally cut off from the Eastern churches for almost half that time and from the Roman Catholic communion for about a fifth of it. Evangelicalism is a convictionally focused point of view that traces its lineage back to the theology and religion of the New Testament via the Fathers, the orthodox scholastics of the West, the medieval teachers of spiritual life, the magisterial Reformers and their Puritan and Pietist successors, and the exponents of theological, spiritual, cultural, and missional renewal of both Reformational and Wesleyan type from the eighteenth century to the present day. The theologians of evangelicalism see it as basic Christianity in all essentials, though they gladly recognize that there has been much mainstream development of Christian specifics outside evangelical circles, and they sadly detect much eccentricity and worse within their own ecclesial backyards as well as in other places. What is urged throughout, however, is that evangelicalism is the true faith of the gospel, and as such yields the true pattern of personal and corporate Christian life. The evangelical understanding of Christianity admits of being amplified but not altered.

Evangelical spokesmen in North America are currently getting over the extreme of cultural and institutional isolation into which, driven by premillennial pessimism and what they saw as deviant denominational leadership, the self-styled fundamentalists retreated earlier in this century. Outside North America, there was less separatist retreating to get over; the self-sufficient ideology of fundamentalism did not take hold elsewhere to any degree, and in, for instance, Britain and Australasia there was never need for the overt reappropriating of wider churchly and cultural involvement that marked the so-called post-fundamentalist neoevangelicals in America in the 1950s. Sub-evangelical leadership in the mainline has for the present, it seems, come to stay; nonetheless, most mainline evangelicals today, like most evangelicals outside North America all along, practice some form of constructive bilateralism, maintaining closest cooperative fellowship with their own kind across denominational boundaries while actively involving themselves in their own historic church family to work for reform and renewal there.

But there is nothing like uniformity at this point. The mainliners' vision is rarely matched by the much larger numbers in independent congregations or distinctively evangelical denominations. Defensive separation as the only way of safeguarding the gospel is still canvassed on the evangelical right wing, while pietistic-charismatic communities tend to display a disturbing lack of knowledge and concern about the full evangelical legacy of faith, thought, rationality, spirituality, liturgy, dignity, and unity. The gulf between the cool cognitive stance of some and the passionate exuberance of others is wide, and the sharpness of the former accusing the latter of incoherent irreverence and of the latter accusing the former of irrelevant intellectualism is sometimes very great. Observing some of the exchanges, you might think evangelicalism is falling apart. I, however, doubt that, for the following reason.

Within the evangelical community three processes counter the disruptive impact of these vocal extremes. The first is a *participative* process whereby opposed and competing positions interact, debate, and assimilate such truth, wisdom, and integrity as they find in each other. Journals, books, college and seminary courses, and now the internet, carry the discussions through which this happens, and since most if not all the protagonists desire evangelical solidarity as the outcome, the initial fury of exchange regularly gives way to tolerance, though agreement may never be reached.

The second is a *political* process of consultation whereby missional strategies are formed through the agency of parachurch institutions and networks which, with their international links, correspond more and more to the multinationals of the business world. Most evangelicals think denominationalism as an ideology is dying and parachurch alliances are on the leading edge, and continual strategizing in terms of this outlook cements their solidarity at all levels. For over two centuries, togetherness in the varied forms of witness and service that the Christian mission requires has been a strong bond of evangelical unity, and it remains so.

It is true that for half a century now evangelical publicists have been taking a leaf out of the Roman Catholic and Orthodox books, speaking of "the evangelical church" as if it is a uniform integrated collective. But the facts make such talk inappropriate. Theologically, evangelicals conceive the church as the one universal community of the regenerate, those who put faith penitently, practically, and so savingly in Jesus Christ the Lord. To this one church belong all the groups that regularly gather to do all the things the church does (that is, to praise and pray, with biblical preaching and teaching; to celebrate sacraments and practice pastoral care; to uphold pure faith and life, and to reach out to a needy world). These groups are outcrops, microcosms, and samples of the one great body of Christ. Parachurch bodies are then seen as expressions of Christ's kingdom that are more or less churchly according as they augment the ministry of the congregations more or less directly. Organizationally, however, there is no collective "evangelical church," nor in any case is churchliness the primary focus of the unity with each other that evangelicals feel. ("What is, then?" we ask. My next paragraph shows.)

The third process keeping evangelicals together is *procedural,* namely the practice of seeking biblical warrant and control for all aspects of personal and corporate Christian living. This is the central, heart-of-the-matter focus both of evangelical identity and of evangelical unity. Evangelicals maintain that as God has enthroned his Son, the living Word, as Lord of the universe, so he has enthroned the Bible, his written word, as the means of Christ's rule over the consciences of his disciples. The 66-book Protestant canon is held to be divinely inspired and authoritative, true and trustworthy, informative and imperative, life-imparting and strength-supplying to the human heart, and to be given to the church to be preached, taught, expounded, applied, absorbed, digested and appealed to as arbiter whenever questions of faith and life, belief and behavior, spiritual wisdom and spiritual welfare, break surface among the saints. Of the unifying bonds of evangelicalism, this view and use of Scripture is the strongest of all.

An explicit spelling-out of the nature of evangelicalism's internal unity will clarify the thrust of what has been said. This is most simply done in Chinese-box terms. Evangelical unity, as a particular mode of generic Christian unity, begins with belief in the trinitarian fundamentals of the ecumenical creeds, which biblical teaching establishes. Says Anglican Article 8: "The Three Creeds, *Nicene* Creed, *Athanasius's* Creed, and that which is commonly called the *Apostles'* Creed, ought thoroughly to be received and believed: for they may be proved by most certain warrants of Holy Scripture." Evangelicals do not see themselves as in unity with biblicist sects (Mormons, Jehovah's Witnesses, Moonies, or other such) that use the Bible to undermine the trinitarianism of the creeds, the soteriology that rests on it, and the authenticity of the universal church.

Then, within this doctrinal frame, the second element in evangelical unity is a shared experience of fellowship with God in peace through the living Christ of the Bible, the crucified and risen Jesus of the Gospels who is the divine and divinely enthroned Son of God in the epistles. Evangelicals do not see themselves as one with any who still lack a life-giving disciple relationship of trust and obedience to Jesus Christ as their Savior, Lord, and Friend.

Finally, within the double frame of credal orthodoxy and regenerate experience, the third element in evangelical unity is the above-described faithful use of the Scriptures as the ongoing source of vision, direction, wisdom, encouragement, and hope from God for all facets of personal and communal Christian life. Evangelicals do not see themselves as in full unity with any who do not live in this overtly Bible-based way.

It is safe to say that as long as the processes discussed — intramural interacting, transdenominational strategizing, and biblically-informed living — are maintained, evangelicalism will remain a distinct and stable reality on the world Christian stage.

Exploring the Evangelical Heritage

Against this background I shall now take some soundings in the great ocean of British and American evangelical use of the Bible, not now to reshape faith and order in the churches, but to deepen and enrich personal spiritual life through response to the realities that the Bible reveals. I shall look seriatim at evangelical expectations from the Bible; evangelical elucidations of the Bible; immersion in the Bible as an evangelical discipline; and (a bleak theme) isolation of the Bible as an evangelical failing.

In doing this I shall treat the convictional piety of the magisterial Reformation and the Puritanism that sought to complete it as evangelicalism in its original Western form, the spiritual seedbed of the revival conversionism that came after. The eighteenth-century movement on both sides of the Atlantic is sometimes seen as the birth of evangelicalism, but nobody who lived then would have agreed with that, and nobody who has looked into sixteenth and seventeenth century church history could agree with it either. There was, indeed, a big difference between the Christian-nation mindset within which the Reformers and Puritans practiced their Augustinian devotion and the pietistic society-structure within which the Methodists taught faith and holiness, just as there was a big difference between the didactic elitism of evangelical preachers before the revivals and the sanctified populism of the pulpit barnstormers who followed them. But the personal religion of salvation from sin through the death and mediation of Jesus Christ and the regenerating power of the Holy Spirit — in other words, evangelical godliness itself — has been essentially unchanged from the sixteenth century to the present day.

My exploration of the evangelical heritage is itself, of course, a study of tradition. Tradition, as Jaroslav Pelikan said somewhere, is the living faith of the dead, as opposed to traditionalism, which is the dead faith of the living. I shall present the tradition much as our Orthodox brothers present the conciliar and Cappadocian heritage, as in substance the teaching of the Holy Spirit — in this instance, on the life of God in the soul of man (to borrow the title of Henry Scougal's little book that so helped Charles Wesley and George Whitefield). I do so because I think Scripture itself justifies this estimate.

Evangelical Expectations from the Bible

The Reformation movement, with all the intellectual brilliance and personal magnetism of its leaders, rode into Western Europe on the back of the Renaissance renewal of literary learning, which itself rode on the back of the newly-born printing industry. The battle-cry, *Ad fontes!* (To the sources!) referred to sources that were in print; it served both to focus and to heighten the excitement of discovery through reading that was permeating Northern European culture. It is no surprise, then, to find that the Reformers wanted everyone to be literate and to have the Bible in their own language, and that the sixteenth century was a great era of Bible translation and elementary education conjoined. Of the translations made, two were particularly outstanding and influential, Luther's in German and Tyndale's in English. The Reformers wanted their translations diligently and reverently read, as being the word of God delivered in and through the words of men, and their confident hope was that the Holy Spirit who gave the Scriptures would use them, thus translated, to lead readers into a transforming knowledge of Jesus Christ. Said Luther: "Scripture is God's writing and God's word." "Whoever would know God and have eternal life should read this book with diligence and search for its testimony of Christ, God's Son."[1] In his preface to England's Geneva Bible, Calvin wrote, coolly and analytically:

> The Bible was not given to us to satisfy our foolish curiosity and pride. Yet Paul says it is useful. For what? To instruct us in sound doctrine, to comfort us, to inspire us, and to make us able to perform every good work . . . through it we learn to place our trust in God and to walk in fear of him.[2]

And in his preface to the French translation of the New Testament by his cousin Olivetan, more warmly and pointedly:

> This is what we should in short seek in the whole of Scripture: to know Jesus Christ, and the infinite riches that are comprised in him and are offered to us

---

1. Luther, WA 50:282; 48:146; cited from Ewald M. Plass, *What Luther Says* (St. Louis: Concordia, 1959), 65, 80. Pages 61-109, extracts 166-331, elaborate these sentiments from many standpoints.

2. Cited from H-J Kraus, "Calvin's Exegetical Principles," *Interpretation* 31 (1977): 11.

by him from God the Father. If one were to sift thoroughly the Law and the Prophets, he would not find a single word that would not draw and bring us to him. . . . Our minds ought to come to a halt at the point where we learn in Scripture to know Jesus Christ and him alone, so that we may be directly led by him to the Father who contains in himself all perfection.[3]

England's archbishop of Canterbury, Thomas Cranmer, writing while Henry VIII, whom the pope had dubbed *Fidei Defensor* for writing against Luther, was still his royal master, had to be careful what he said. Nonetheless, his preface to the Great Bible, written in 1540, is really very forthright:

> In the Scriptures be the fat pastures of the soul; therein is no venomous meat, no unwholesome thing; they be the very dainty and pure feeding. He that is ignorant shall find there what he should learn. He that is a perverse sinner shall there find his damnation, to make him tremble for fear. He that laboureth to serve God shall find there his glory, and the promissions [promises] of eternal life, exhorting him more diligently to labour. Herein may princes learn how to govern their subjects: subjects, obedient love and dread to their princes. Husbands how they should behave them unto their wives, how to educate their children and servants; and contrary, the wives, children, and servants may know their duty to their husbands, parents, and masters. Here may all manner of persons, men, women, young, old, learned, unlearned, rich, poor, priests, laymen, lords, ladies, officers, tenants, and mean men, virgins, wives, widows, lawyers, merchants, artificers, husbandmen, and all manner of persons of what estate or condition soever they be, may in this book learn all things what they ought to believe, what they ought to do, and what they should not do, as well concerning Almighty God, as also concerning themselves and all other . . . it is convenient and good (for) the Scripture to be read of all sorts and kinds of people, and in the vulgar tongue. . . .[4]

Every man that cometh to the reading of this holy book ought to bring with him first and foremost this fear of Almighty God; and then next, a firm and stable purpose to reform his own self according thereunto.[5]

---

3. Calvin, *Commentaries*, ed. J. R. Haroutunian (Philadelphia: Westminster, 1958), 70.

4. *Thomas Cranmer*, ed. G. E. Duffield (Appleford: Sutton Courtenay Press, 1964), 37.

5. Ibid., 41. The first sermon of the 1547 book of Homilies, written by Cranmer, is titled "A Fruitful Exhortation to the Reading and Knowledge of Holy Scripture," and makes the same points in a more emphatic way. "As drink is pleasant to them that be dry, and meat to them that be hungry, so is the reading, hearing, searching, and studying of Holy Scripture to them that be desirous to know God or themselves, and to do his will." "These books therefore ought to be much in our hands, in our eyes, in our ears, in our mouths, but most of all in our hearts. For the Scripture of God is the heavenly meat of our souls;

The need to read Holy Scripture, and the benefit of doing so, have been constantly affirmed by evangelicals ever since, with stress on the importance of reading the whole Bible regularly and not limiting oneself to a few favorite passages. Here is John Owen, the Puritan, making that point.

> *Frequent reading of the word* more generally and cursorily, whereunto all Christians ought to be trained from their youth, 2 Tim iii.15, and which all closets and families should be acquainted with, Deut. vi.6-9, is of great use and advantage; and I shall, therefore, name some particular benefits which may be received thereby: —
>
> 1. Hereby the minds of men are brought into a *general acquaintance* with the nature and design of the *book of God;* which some, to their present shame and future ruin, are prodigiously ignorant of.
>
> 2. They who are exercised herein come to know *distinctly* what things are treated of in the particular books. . . .
>
> 3. Hereby they exercise themselves unto *thoughts of heavenly things* and a holy converse with God; if they bring along with them, as they ought, hearts *humble* and sensible of his authority in the word.
>
> 4. Their minds are insensibly furnished with *due conceptions about God, spiritual things, themselves,* and *their conditions;* and their memories with expressions proper and meet to be used about them in prayer or otherwise.
>
> 5. God oftentimes takes occasion herein to *influence their souls* with the efficacy of divine truth in particular, in the way of *exhortation, reproof, instruction,* or *consolation;* whereof all who attend diligently unto this duty have experience.[6]

---

the hearing and keeping of it maketh us *blessed, sanctifieth* us, and maketh us holy: *it turneth our souls: it is a light lantern to our feet: it is* a sure, *steadfast, and everlasting* instrument of salvation." "Chrysostom saith, that 'man's human and worldly wisdom or science needeth not to the understanding of Scripture, but the revelation of the Holy Ghost, who inspireth the true meaning unto them that with humility and diligence do seek therefore.' . . . If we read once, twice, or thrice, and understand not, let us not cease so, but still continue reading, praying, asking of other; and so, by still knocking, at the last the door shall be opened as St. Augustine saith." "Let us thank God heartily for this his great and special gift. . . . Let us hear, read, and know these holy rules. . . . Let us ruminate and as it were chew the cud, that we may have the sweet juice, spiritual effect, marrow, honey, kernel, taste, comfort, and consolation of them. . . . Which he grant us all that died for us all, Jesus Christ" (Cranmer, *Homilies* [London: SPCK, 1938], 1, 3, 8, 9f.).

6. John Owen, *Works* (London: Banner of Truth, 1967), IV.200; from *The Causes, Ways, and Means of Understanding the Mind of God as revealed in his Word, with Assurance therein: and A Declaration of the Perspicuity of the Scriptures, with the External Means of the Interpretation of them* (1678). Richard Rogers, the first Puritan to write a full treatise on the Christian life, had made the same point long before: "And first this is to be observed, that in reading the Scriptures, they (Christians) reade not heere and there a Chapter . . . but the

Luther read his Bible from cover to cover twice a year. Daily use of Cranmer's 1549 lectionary (unchanged in 1552 and 1662) will take you through the Old Testament once and the New Testament three times annually, and the psalter twelve times. In the 1830s Robert Murray McCheyne drafted his plan for reading the whole Bible once a year, and many still use it. Several such schemes have appeared since, and the flow of printed helps for Bible reading (devotional notes and expositions, questions for group work with leaders' notes, Bibles with annotations, guides for personal, "inductive," applicatory Bible study, and so on) is at least a century old. You could not stress the importance of daily Bible reading for spiritual health more than evangelicals actually have done during the past 250 years. With the Reformers and Puritans, evangelicals since the eighteenth century have expected that reflective Bible reading will energize the soul, guide the conscience on matters of duty, discipline, and vocation, excite faith and hope, and sharpen the sense of God's constant presence and care. Evangelicals I knew when I was young sought to distill from each day's reading a "best thought," just as Francis de Sales taught his readers to "pick a nosegay" from their rather more formalized daily meditations on gospel stories. In this century, "Bible teachers" have been a recognized category of evangelical ministers; weekly "Bible schools" have adorned many churches; small group Bible studies have become legion; and in many quarters expository preaching, understood as preaching that opens up whole passages of Scripture in an applicatory way, is viewed as the supreme homiletical craft.

Writes Thomas Howard, now a Roman Catholic, of the evangelicalism in which he was reared:

> Evangelical spirituality stands or falls with private Bible reading. . . . In the household where I grew up, family prayers occurred twice a day. . . . my father read the Bible to us . . . and . . . led us in prayer. . . . Sunday school took us to the Bible as well. Its agenda concentrated almost exclusively on familiarizing us with the text of Scripture. . . . The actual frame of mind of an evangelical as he comes to the Bible in his daily devotions is a matter of some importance. His whole ambition is to "get a blessing." This can take on a somewhat magical aspect at times. I remember struggling to wring spiritual counsel from the lists of names in 1 Chronicles or from the hair-raising tales of

---

Bible in order throughout, and as oft as they can, that so by little and little they may bee acquainted with the Histories, and the whole course of the Scriptures, (having before the grounds of Christian religion laid)" (*Se(a)ven Treatises Containing Such Direction as is Gathered out of the Holy Scriptures, leading and guiding to true Happiness both in this life and in the life to come: and may be called the practise of Christianity*, 3rd ed. 1610, 314).

butchery in Judges. Generally speaking, however, the attempt turns out to yield fruit if it is pursued consistently. There is an agile immediacy about an evangelical's attitude towards Scripture.[7]

This evangelical discipline of Bible reading assumes three things. The first is the essential clarity of Scripture: the thoughtful reader will be able to see what the texts are saying about what matters. The second is the ministry of the Holy Spirit, who gave the Scripture, in illuminating our hearts to understand how it touches us. John Paul II well articulates the evangelical mind about this when he says: "to arrive at a completely valid interpretation of words inspired by the Holy Spirit, one must first be guided by the Holy Spirit and it is necessary to pray for that, to pray much, to ask in prayer for the interior light of the Spirit and docilely accept that light, to ask for the love that alone enables one to understand the language of God, who 'is love' (1 Jn. 1:8, 16). While engaged in the very work of interpretation, one must remain in the presence of God as much as possible."[8] The third thing assumed is that the thoughts and words of the biblical writers, their indicatives and imperatives, which the Holy Spirit brings home to our hearts, are demonstrably in line with the credal, confessional, and catechetical dogmas of the evangelical communions to which the Bible students belong. The characteristic evangelical mentality is churchly, not sectarian; the attitude of those who manipulate Bible texts to overthrow established Christian beliefs and institutions is not evangelical, and evangelicals ordinarily oppose such endeavors more vigorously than anyone else.

Evangelical Elucidations of the Bible

Evangelicalism began with learned men opening up the Bible in pulpits and classrooms according to the Renaissance rule of seeking the meaning that was expressed, and therefore presumably intended, by the human writer. This was what they called the *literal* sense, as distinct from various time-honored ways of allegorizing the text. They quoted texts as proofs, but were not proof-texting in the modern meaning of that term; the biblical book from which they took the texts was in each case their unit for study, commentary, and use as a source for pastoral and theological instruction. The flow of thought running through

7. Thomas Howard, *Evangelical Is Not Enough* (Nashville: Thomas Nelson, 1984), 15-17.

8. John Paul II and the Pontifical Biblical Commission, *The Interpretation of the Bible in the Church* (Boston: St. Paul Books and Media, 1993), 19f.

the book was what they were after, as Calvin's classic commentaries and recorded sermons working through whole books in the pulpit, as was his habit, clearly show. Censuring the medievals for quoting texts out of context and hence misunderstanding and misapplying them, the Reformers were careful not to fall into the same trap themselves. Responsible evangelical expositors from the sixteenth century to the present day have followed the Reformers in all of this; compare, for instance, with Calvin's commentaries the scholarly popular expositions of Matthew Henry in the early eighteenth century[9] and John Stott in the second half of the twentieth.[10] The more technical commentary series currently produced by evangelical teams for evangelical publishers tell the same story.[11] Reformational exegetes believe that the way into the mind of God is through the mind of the human writer, and hence labor to draw out the didactic content of each biblical book with pastoral and apologetic application, rating the end-product in each case as a message from God himself.

Formally, reflective evangelical interpretation of Scripture assumes the inspiration and inerrancy of the text as originally given, and its organic revelational link and substantive divine-human parallelism with Jesus Christ our Lord. Again I quote John Paul II as saying in his own way what evangelicals characteristically affirm on these matters.

> The strict relationship uniting the inspired biblical texts with the mystery of the incarnation was expressed by the encyclical *Divino Afflante Spiritu* [1943] in the following terms: "Just as the substantial Word of God became like men in every respect except sin, so too the words of God, expressed in human languages, became like human languages in every respect except error." Repeated almost literally by the conciliar Constitution *Dei Verbum,* this statement sheds light on a parallelism rich in meaning.

9. Matthew Henry, *Exposition of the Old and New Testaments* (6 vols., 1704-20, with the final volume finished by his friends from his notes after his death). Henry's work, which is still in print, has been uniformly praised from its first appearance to our own day. It is scholarly, drawing on the best exegetical helps available (such as Matthew Poole's exhaustive five-folio *Synopsis Criticorum* [Utrecht, 1684], the ICC of its day, plus his *Annotations* [London, 1685] in three folios), and is full of pastoral applications distilled from a century of Puritan practical writing.

10. John Stott has authored expositions of the Sermon on the Mount, Acts, Romans, Galatians, Ephesians, the Thessalonian letters, and 2 Timothy: all published by InterVarsity Press (Leicester, UK, and Downers Grove, IL).

11. On page 133 of *Between Faith and Criticism* (San Francisco: Harper & Row, 1986), Mark Noll lists no less than ten evangelical commentary series that were in process of production at that time. The New American Commentary (1991-) can now be added to that number.

It is true that putting God's words into writing, through the charism of scriptural inspiration, was the first step toward the incarnation of the Word of God. These written words, in fact, were an abiding means of communication and communion between the chosen people and their one Lord. On the other hand, it is because of the prophetic aspect of these words that it was possible to recognize the fulfillment of God's plan when "the Word became flesh and made his dwelling among us" (Jn. 1:14). After the heavenly glorification of the humanity of the Word made flesh, it is again due to written words that his stay among us is attested to in an abiding way. Joined to the inspired writings of the first covenant, the inspired writings of the new covenant are a verifiable means of communication and communion between the believing people and God, the Father, Son and Holy Spirit.[12]

In line with this approach, evangelical exegesis assumes throughout the internal coherence of biblical teaching (the principle that Calvin called *the analogy of faith*), and the significance of the closed canon as constituting the ultimate context within which each text, and each book of which it is a part, must be set for full understanding.

Three fundamental convictions control mainstream evangelical exegesis of Scripture. Each is drawn directly from the dominical and apostolic handling of the Old Testament, as the New Testament documents display and attest that. Because they are presuppositional they are not often made explicit, but no evangelical will have doubts about them when they are laid on the table. They are as follows.

First, the Lord Jesus Christ, who is the Son of God and cocreator and is now incarnate for saving mediation and royal rule as prophet, priest and king, has been the focus and, if one may so speak, subtext of all God's revelatory words and deeds, just as God's plan for him has been the rationale of God's shaping of world history, from Eden on; and Christ's honor and glory will continue to be the divine goal to all eternity.

Second, God has always willed that the relationship between himself and his human creatures should take the form of a covenantal bond of mutual self-giving, calling for faith, hope, love, adoration, loyalty, and righteousness on man's part; and all God's gracious dealings with mankind have been, are, and always will be intended to instill and deepen this relationship.

Third, human nature, like God's character, remains unchanged at heart, so that though many politico-socio-economic factors changed for God's people during the period of the Bible story, and have changed again many times since, and though the externals of the various cultures in the world today are

12. John Paul II, *The Interpretation of the Bible*, 16.

significantly different at many points, the basic perceptions of God and responses to God that the Bible calls godliness — awe and reverence before the divine Creator and Disposer who is holy, just, and good, and humble "fear" of him; faith, fidelity, repentance, love, peace, assurance and gratitude; praise, prayer, and patient perseverance in well-doing — are essentially the same from Genesis to Revelation.

Thus the biblical interpreting that mainstream evangelicals do has a characteristically christocentric, covenantal, doxological, and devotional cast. Its purpose is the upbuilding of Christians and so of the church, and its usual point of reference is the many-sided reality of Christian discipleship. In this it is following in the footsteps not only of the magisterial Reformers and their Puritan successors, but also of such as Augustine and Chrysostom. Its solidarity with patristic exposition is currently coming to light through the *Ancient Christian Commentary* series that Professor Oden is masterminding,[13] and its solidarity with itself is shown by, among other things, the ready market that reprints of older commentaries from the evangelical stable regularly find.[14] A potent tradition, not definitive yet stabilizing and orienting, operates in the world of evangelical exegesis; its reality must not be overlooked.

So far I have sought to profile almost a half-millennium of Bible work that would, I think, be generally recognized as responsible, learned, pastorally sensitive, and, within the limits of pre-Hegelian historical theory, historically aware. It operated within a credal and confessional heritage that the interpreters thought the Bible supported and beyond which they saw no reason to go. It must be said, however, that, outside this mainstream, Bible searching by imaginative individuals has sometimes produced erratic results. It did so spectacularly among the Anabaptists of the Reformation era and during the Commonwealth years in England, and has continued to do so down to the present day, as evangelical Bible searchers have explored themes on which the confessional heritage did not pronounce. Eschatological expectation is one area where Bible-based fantasy (I choose my words with care) has had a field day, as various forms of premillennialism were embraced, the return of Jesus Christ was confidently proclaimed as imminent, and some, not grasping the genre and idiom of biblical apocalyptic, thought they could forefancy and even date in advance the momentous event of the Savior's reappearance, partly by chronological computation from figures in the books of Daniel and Revelation, partly

---

13. *Ancient Christian Commentary on Scripture,* ed. Thomas C. Oden et al. (Downers Grove, IL: InterVarsity Press, 1998-). Volumes on Romans and Mark have appeared so far.

14. Banner of Truth led the way here. The Crossway Classic Commentary series (Wheaton: Crossway, 1993-) has completed its coverage of the New Testament.

from supposed correspondences between world events and biblical visions and predictions.

This frame of popular evangelical interest in "prophetic study" (a code-phrase, as used) goes back without a break to the opening of the nineteenth century, when the French ran the pope out of Rome in 1798, thus (it was said) fulfilling the prediction that after 1260 "days" the rule of Antichrist would end,[15] and Napoleon himself was being widely identified with the Beast of Revelation 13. From "prophetic study" there emerged in the 1830s premillennial dispensationalism, the brainchild of J. N. Darby, positing that God has two distinct peoples, the Jewish nation and the Christian church, and that he plans separate and contrasting destinies for each.[16] Dispensational teachers, with their notions of a raptured church, a Jewish millennium, and Christ reigning from Jerusalem over a basically unchanged planet Earth, all set forth with enormous confidence, were amazingly influential in the English-speaking world until about 1950, and in the USA, where dispensationalism has been heavily institutionalized and passionately embraced by fundamentalists to counter their despair at mainline churches' apostasy, dispensational ideas command a large following still.[17]

Then, among Pentecostals and charismatics, who also think the end is near, recent decades have seen the spread of theologies of restoration or "latter rain," which hold, as did Edward Irving in the 1820s, that in this final run-up to Christ's return God is giving back to the church all the distinctive gifts and phenomena of apostolic days (tongues, visions, dreams, gifts of prophecy

15. This kind of prophetic interpretation assumed that a day in predictive passages meant a year, justifying the assumption from Num. 14:33-34 and Ezek. 4:4-6, "each day for a year."

16. See on this Timothy P. Weber, *Living in the Shadow of the Second Coming: American Premillennialism 1875-1982* (Grand Rapids: Zondervan, 1983). Several theological teaching institutions have premillennialism in their doctrinal statement, some in an explicitly dispensational form. The continuing popularity of this view can be gauged from the fact that the "Left Behind" series of novels by Tim La Haye and Jerry B. Jenkins on what happens after the rapture of the church sells literally millions.

17. On dispensationalism, which has proved unstable under modern scrutiny, see among other discussions, O. T. Allis, *Prophecy and the Church* (Philadelphia: Presbyterian and Reformed, 1945); Clarence B. Bass, *Backgrounds to Dispensationalism* (Grand Rapids: Eerdmans, 1959); Curtis I. Crenshaw and Grover E. Gunn III, *Dispensationalism Today, Yesterday, and Tomorrow* (Memphis: Footstool, 1985); John H. Gerstner, *Wrongly Dividing the Word of Truth* (Brentwood, TN: Wolgemuth and Hyett, 1991); *Continuity and Discontinuity: Perspectives on the Relationship between the Old and New Testaments,* ed. John S. Feinberg (Westchester, IL: Crossway, 1998); *Dispensationalism, Israel and the Church,* ed. Craig A. Blaising (Grand Rapids: Zondervan, 1992).

and healing, and so on). A range of lurid ideas about demons and spiritual warfare has appeared too.[18]

The romantic era in Western culture has produced among its other fruits a strong fascination with secrets, as the plots of novels over two centuries abundantly show, and one assumption behind exegesis of this sort is that there are secrets in the Bible that had to wait many centuries before anyone detected them. With this has often gone the further assumption that there are sentences in the Bible which through the Holy Spirit's ministry will convey to latter-day believers messages from God that could not have been in the minds of the original human writers — messages, in other words, that are read into the texts rather than read out of them. Prayerful, devoted, unself-critical Bible reading informed by the expectations that such ideas create can have odd results. A lady I knew in my boyhood was sure that the power of the air, of which the KJV of Ephesians 2:2 says that Satan is the prince, was the radio, so she would not have one in her home. An Irish preacher told how a man testified to him that he was growing a third set of teeth according to Scripture: when asked what Scripture, he quoted Isaiah 41:15 (KJV once again), "I will make thee a new sharp threshing instrument having teeth." A theological student committed to ordination in an English north country parish but attracted by a counter-invitation to South Wales was sure that the first words of Isaiah 43:6 (KJV), "I will say to the north, Give up," were God telling him that his commitment would be cancelled. (It wasn't, and he later realized that he had deluded himself. He told the story often as a cautionary tale.) All evangelicals seek personal guidance from the Bible, and surely they are right to do so, but God guides by rational discernment of how principles apply, not by giving biblical sentences senses that their biblical context will not support. The Bible should not be handled as if it were written in code, and nowadays, happily, not many evangelicals do.

Dispensational premillennialism and Pentecostal restorationism are perhaps the most striking products of popular evangelical romanticism in the West in recent years. My impression is that with the current global burgeoning of evangelical scholarship they are on the wane, and my opinion is that all will benefit if in fact they are.

Evangelical Immersion in the Bible

Evangelicals see their Bible as the primary means of God's grace to their minds and hearts, and have therefore labored to immerse themselves in it by

18. See the series of novels by Frank Peretti, which also sell by the million.

constantly reading it, memorizing it, meditating on its promises and encouragements, displaying texts in their homes, and generally doing all they can to ensure that Bible truths will always be before their minds. This concern has in the past produced, at least in the Caucasian West, a recognizable mindset and lifestyle. I spoke above of romanticism: it seems to me that *romanticism,* with its focus on emotions and reactions, drama and conflict, agonies and ecstasies in personal life; and *pietism,* with its quest to experience what, on biblical grounds, we believe, and its insistence that true Christian experience is something of which the world has no knowledge and the church, by and large, has very little; are the two words that best describe the distinctive blend of elitism, ardor, humility, swagger, and domesticity that has long been a mark of the evangelical world. Out of the cultural matrix, between the mid-nineteenth and mid-twentieth centuries, there grew a home-, church-, and parachurch-based family-style spirituality — intimate, cozy, gossipy, Sabbatarian, conscientiously cheerful, somewhat simplistic, somewhat exhibitionist — which Thomas Howard, who was brought up in it, is able to describe to us vividly. Here are some of the things he tells us about it.

> Evangelicals have made a major specialty out of fellowship. They talk to each other about the Lord. They meet in groups whose sole purpose is to bring Christians together for informal Bible study, often without any teacher, and for prayer and "sharing." They speak openly about their inner burdens and about what God is teaching them. . . .
>
> Testimonies play a major role in evangelical spirituality. In a testimony someone . . . says something about his present experience of the Lord. He might recount some victory in his personal life, such as the overcoming of some temptation, or perhaps tell of a decision God has helped him make. . . .
>
> It is difficult for nonevangelical Christians to appreciate the place occupied by hymn-singing among evangelicals. We sang and sang. Isaac Watts, William Cowper, John Newton, Charles Wesley — these were the big names. My father would sit down as he came through the living room at odd moments and play "When All Thy Mercies, O My God," or "There is a Fountain Filled with Blood," or "Praise Him, Praise Him, Jesus Our Blessed Redeemer." . . . Nineteenth- and twentieth-century revivalist hymns and gospel songs form a major part of the literature. . . . There is also an enormous number of "choruses." . . . [19]

(Since the charismatic mutation of evangelicalism spread, far more choruses have been added to that already large number, many of them simply setting to

19. Howard, *Evangelical Is Not Enough,* 17-18.

music Bible words, or a direct echo of them.) Sociologists might see this life-style as one brand of Victorianism or Edwardianism, but the claim made for it was, and is, that Bible teaching shapes it — in other words, that it is a direct product of immersion in the Scriptures. And that is undoubtedly true.

This corporate spirituality still exists, but it has to struggle, and mean-time new modes of immersion in the depths of Bible truth are appearing. With the weakening of family life and the increasing pressures of loneliness and rootlessness in the secular city, the quest for a personal spirituality — that is, as generally understood, an inner ascesis that satisfies, pacifies, unifies, and energizes the frazzled heart — has become a major cultural concern among us, and it is not surprising that in this milieu evangelicals should be found going on retreats, consulting spiritual directors (often Roman Catho-lic), experimenting with fasts, and trying out modes of meditation and con-templation that they never knew before, in order to center their souls more directly on God and his word. In particular, some evangelicals are laboring to regain a skill in which their forebears excelled, but which had largely withered on the vine, to wit, the art of meditation on biblical truths as described by its classic evangelical exponents — namely, the seventeenth-century Puritans. Foremost among them, at this point as at so many others, were John Owen and Richard Baxter, and it is worth noting how they conceived the nature and benefit of the discursive meditation that they taught.

Owen describes the meditative immersion in biblical truth that he rec-ommends in the following way:

> By solemn or stated meditation, I intend the thoughts of some subject spiri-tual and divine, with the fixing, forcing, and ordering of our thoughts about it, with a design to affect our own hearts and souls with the matter of it. . . . By this design it is distinguished from the study of the word, wherein our principal aim is to learn the truth, or to declare it unto others; and also from prayer, whereof God himself is the immediate object. But in meditation it is the affecting of our own hearts and minds with love, delight, and humilia-tion.[20]

Owen does not restrict the doctrinal themes on which it is good to medi-tate, though his own preferred topic, as it seems, was the glory of Christ (his own last work was a set of meditative broodings on this). Baxter, however, wants everyone to meditate regularly on the hope of heaven, the saints' ever-lasting rest (that is the title of his best-selling treatise on "heavenly medita-tion," as he called it). Here is how he describes the "consideration" (reflective

---

20. John Owen, *Works* VII.384 (*The Grace and Duty, of Being Spiritually Minded*).

brainwork) with which the meditative exercise of mind and heart on this promised blessedness must begin.

> It is by consideration that we first have recourse to the memory and from thence take those heavenly doctrines that we intend to make the subject of our meditation — such as promises of eternal life, descriptions of the saints' glory, the resurrection, etc. We then present them to our judgment that it may deliberately view them over and take an exact survey . . . so as to magnify the Lord in our hearts till we are filled with a holy admiration. . . . But the principal thing is to exercise, not merely our judgment, but our faith in the truth of the everlasting rest; by which I mean both the truth of the promises and our own personal interest in them. . . . Never expect to have love and joy move, when faith stands still, which must lead the way. . . . Thus when the judgment hath determined, and faith hath apprehended the truth of our happiness, then may our meditation proceed to raise our affections and, particularly, love, desire, hope, courage or boldness and joy.[21]

The strategy of meditation, as thus conceived, is that verbal and vocal reflection on biblical teaching about God and godliness should stir up and lead what seventeenth-century psychology referred to as our affections (that is, dispositional attitudes of reaction and response, with their own emotional overtones and motivating force). Such meditation, modeled as it is on a great deal of the Psalms, is essentially talking to oneself about God and oneself in the realized presence of God himself; and as it naturally leads into prayer, so it should produce a degree of inner integration, stability, and devotional delight that would not otherwise be known. It is apparent that this form of focused immersion in Bible truths can be, among other things, an effective counter to anti-intellectual shallowness and laziness and sentimental religious emotionalism, also a habit that prevents yielding blindly to feelings and moods, and a step, or series of steps, towards spiritual wisdom and maturity. It will be interesting to see how far the attempt to recover this element in the evangelical heritage will get.

Evangelical Isolation of the Bible

On a sadder note, evangelical emphasis on the Bible has often led to the neglect of other important elements of Christian thought. It has meant evangelical

---

21. Richard Baxter, *The Saints' Everlasting Rest.* Quoted from Peter Toon, *The Art of Meditating on Scripture* (Grand Rapids: Zondervan, 1993), 126-27.

isolation from the mainstream Christian heritage of Bible-based theology and wisdom over two millennia, which evangelicals should claim but which few seem to know or care about; from evangelicalism's own heritage of theology and exposition, which most simply ignore; and from the searchings and findings of the physical, historical, and human sciences, with their never-ending quests to push out further the walls of human knowledge. It seems as if some have drawn out of the Reformation slogan, *sola scriptura,* a meaning that it was never intended to bear. *Sola scriptura,* a.k.a. the sufficiency of Scripture, is a phrase standing for several salutary things. As a critical principle (which is how it first emerged) it means that all projected doctrines must pass the biblical test. As a principle of doctrinal construction, it affirms that all the raw material is embodied in the Bible, and nothing substantive going beyond this may be brought in from outside. As a principle of nurture, it declares that the only truths that God blesses to our upbuilding in Christ are truths revealed somewhere in Scripture. So far, so good, and there should be nothing controversial in any of that at the present time. But *sola scriptura* was never meant to imply that what is not mentioned in the Bible is not real, or is unimportant and not worth our attention, or that the history of biblical exegesis and exposition, and of theological construction and confession, over two millennia, need not concern us today, or that we should restrict our interest in God's world and in the arts, sciences, products, and dreams of our fellow-human beings to matters which at least one Bible writer directly discusses.

The common idea that evangelicalism is intrinsically obscurantist comes from observing actual obscurantism of this kind; in the earlier years of the twentieth century there was, unhappily, a good deal of it to observe. Some evangelicals have had such a fixation about separating from error and sin that they have fallen into cultish sectarianism in relation to the Christian world and into what Chesterton saw as Protestant Manichaeism in relation to the real though marred goodness of the created order. Also, some have looked to the Bible, in its character as divine instruction, to give information that resolves scientific questions about the beginning and age of the earth, the origin of human life, the antiquity of the human race, the factors that operate in physical and mental illness, and so on. Fundamentalism, which is evangelicalism rationalistically on the defensive against theological liberalism, has in its defensive zeal and its wish to exalt the Bible often made this mistake. Scientific accounts of realities are based on analytical observation and experiment, and declare what things are there and how they work. Biblical accounts of realities declare why those things exist at all, and what their significance is for the God-mankind relationship. The two sorts of account cannot be contradictory, for they are answering different questions; they are, rather, complementary, and are to be integrated in a way that preserves and indeed highlights the integrity of both, without either seeking to rubbish the other. Our task is to bring them together, not keep them apart. *Sola scriptura* does not mean Bible-without-science. The Bible has been given us, not to define for us the realities of the created order, nor to restrain our interest in them, but to enable us to diagnose, understand, appreciate, and handle them as we meet them, so that we may use and enjoy them to the Creator's praise. The mistake here, however, does not seem to be entrenched, and the lesson here is, if I am any judge, progressively being learned by the younger evangelical generation.

Catholic Reflections on Discerning
the Truth of Sacred Scripture

THOMAS G. GUARINO

I. Introduction

Pope John Paul II, in his encyclical *Ut Unum Sint,* noted that "Dialogue is not simply an exchange of ideas. In some ways, it is always an exchange of gifts" (*Ut Unum Sint* #28, citing *Lumen Gentium* #13). The gifts which Evangelicals and Catholics share are well-known, but are deserving of emphasis nonetheless. Together, we acknowledge that there is one God, three-personed, the creator of heaven and earth. We acknowledge as well that God the Father sent his only-begotten Son, Jesus Christ, as Savior and Redeemer to bestow salvation on a fallen world. There are many other elements of the Christian faith that we hold in common. These should not be forgotten; they should, indeed, constitute the wider context for the discussions taking place between us.

In this paper, I hope to outline several points fundamental to the Catholic position on discerning the truth of sacred Scripture. While both Evangelicals and Catholics firmly believe in the inspired truth of the Bible, there is some difference in how this truth is precisely determined. Certainly, if there is one affirmation of the ancient church that is repeated with unremitting conviction it is this: *Deus auctor sacrae scripturae.* The subtle hermeneutical question remains: how is God's Word to be understood by us? This question will necessarily require a discussion of tradition, how it is viewed by Catholics and how it is understood by contemporary theologians.

Evangelicals, of course, have generally followed the Reformation dictum of *sola scriptura.* The essence of this phrase has a long and interesting theological history and is, with nuances, accepted by many, if not most, contemporary Catholic theologians. The slogan received a burst of energy during the Reformation with its attempt to cut through what was perceived as the overgrown thicket of human traditions surrounding and clouding the foursquare gospel. Among the alleged brambles were indulgences, prayers for the dead, overwrought Marian devotion, and a host of other practices. A stark formulation of the *sola scriptura* position may be found in Martin Luther's claim in *The Babylonian Captivity of the Church*, "We ought to see that every article of faith of which we boast is certain, pure and based on clear passages of Scripture."[1]

II. The *Loci Theologici*

In Luther's wake, the issue of properly interpreting Scripture, never before fully examined, came to the fore of Catholic thought. Pressed by the challenge of the Reformers, several Catholic theologians began to study the way in which Scripture's truth was determined by the Catholic Church. They came to see that such discernment was not the result of any algorithmic formula or inchoate development, but occurred through a variety of ecclesial and theological "places" or sources. The best known of these tracts is certainly that of the Spanish theologian, Melchior Cano, whose *De locis theologicis* was published in 1563. Cano listed several authorities undergirding theological teaching. Among those registered are Scripture, oral tradition, the general councils, the fathers of the church, the scholastic thinkers, and philosophy and history. All of these are theological authorities except the final two, which are extrinsic to the theological disciplines.

Contemporary Catholic theologians would find Cano's list useful if not exhaustive. They would no doubt agree that both the church fathers, the first witnesses to Christ after the apostles, and the ecumenical councils, the collective representation of the apostles' successors, are important for a normative reading of Scripture. They would likely add to these criteria factors such as the liturgical worship of the church. Indeed, it was the belief that the church's prayer was a legitimate source for interpreting Scripture which gave rise to the dictum rooted in the fifth-century Christian writer, Prosper of Aquitaine: *lex orandi, lex credendi*, the law of praying is the law of believing. In explaining this axiom, the theologian C. Vagaggini notes: "The prayer of the liturgy indicates what must be believed and that which must be believed influences our prayer."[2] An even more forceful witness was made by Pope

1. Martin Luther, *The Babylonian Captivity of the Church*, in *Three Treatises*, trans. A. T. W. Steinhaeuser (Philadelphia: Muhlenberg Press, 1943), 225.

2. Cipriano Vagaggini, *Theological Dimensions of the Liturgy*, trans. L. Doyle and W. Jurgens (Collegeville, MN: Liturgical Press, 1976), 509.

Pius XI to Dom B. Capelle: "The liturgy . . . is the most important organ of the ordinary magisterium [teaching authority] of the Church. . . . The liturgy is not the didascalia of this or that individual but the didascalia of the Church."[3] An example of this from Christian tradition may be found in the Creed of Constantinople of 381, dedicated primarily to defending the divinity of the Holy Spirit. The council, in defining the consubstantiality of the Spirit, does so not in an ontological but in a liturgical key: "*. . . cum Patre et Filio simul adoratur et conglorificatur. . . .*" In recent Catholic theology, one may note the statement of the Vatican's Congregation for the Doctrine of the Faith regarding purgatory: "The Church excludes every way of thinking or speaking that would render meaningless or unintelligible her prayers, funeral rites and religious acts offered for the dead. All these are, in their substance, *loci theologici.*"[4]

Also on the contemporary list of theological places would be the *sensus fidelium* or sense of the faithful insofar as the faithful have been reflective of proper Catholic teaching through their own faith, prayer, and devotion. Other additions to the Catholic list of sources would be the witness to the truth evidenced by the lives of the saints as well as the teaching of Catholic theologians.

All of the above criteria, ecumenical councils, church fathers, teaching of bishops, work of theologians, liturgy of the church, *sensus fidelium,* and lives of the saints, are, taken together, properly grouped under the word "tradition." Together, they form the composite life of the church; they are a witness to the Catholic belief that the Holy Spirit is actively working through the church in her attempt to praise God properly and understand his Word correctly. All of these theological "places" have but one goal: to ensure that the apostolic witness to Christ is preserved in its entirety. As Newman states: "I think I am right in saying that the tradition of the apostles, committed to the whole Church . . . manifests itself variously at various times: sometimes by the mouth of the episcopacy, sometimes by the doctors, sometimes by the people, sometimes by liturgies, rites, ceremonies and customs, by events, dis-

---

3. For the text of the private audience in which this remark was made, please consult A. Bugnini, *Documenta pontificia ad instaurationem spectantia* (Rome, 1953), 70-71. The remark may also be found in the work authored by Dom Capelle himself, *Le Saint-Siége et le mouvement liturgique* (Louvain, 1936).

4. Congregation for the Doctrine of the Faith, "On Certain Questions Concerning Eschatology" (May 17, 1979), Denzinger-Hünermann (Freiburg: Herder, 1991), no. 4654. An English translation may be found in *The Christian Faith,* ed. by J. Neuner and J. Dupuis (New York: Alba House, 1990), 775. All further citations will be from Denzinger-Hünermann (DH).

putes, movements and all those other phenomena which are comprised under the name of history."[5]

Newman's formulation of the *loci*, accepted as it is by many Catholic theologians, is at some remove from the notion that a separate but equal "oral tradition" is passed down to bishops, from age to age, containing aspects of revelation complementary to those found in Scripture itself. It is true, of course, that some theologians, especially after the Council of Trent, assumed that there was a tradition mediating a definitive content of faith which had been passed down from apostolic times and which is not found in Scripture. But as Karl Rahner says, this theory was always a theological construct and was certainly never a binding doctrine of the Catholic faith.[6]

From the above discussion, one sees a fundamental principle emerge, viz., that the Catholic Church believes it has a constant help and guide in its listening to, praying with, and discerning the truth of sacred Scripture. This guide and help is the Holy Spirit who, Catholics believe, unfailingly leads the church to understand more completely the fullness of revealed truth. This is how Catholics interpret and understand the scriptural passages of Matt. 28:20 and John 14:25.

Of course, the Catholic Church had not precisely formulated its view on the proper discernment of Scripture until the challenge of the Reformation forced it to examine the issue more intensely. Given that the Council of Trent's statements on Scripture and tradition are important to Catholics and something of an anomaly to Evangelicals, it will be worthwhile to examine the teachings of this council a bit more closely.

III. The Council of Trent

Many are familiar with the famous passages from the Council of Trent which have long been sticking points between Catholics and Protestants. The two neuralgic extracts are (1) that the saving truth and rule of conduct promulgated by Christ ". . . are contained in the written books and unwritten traditions which have come down to us, having been received by the apostles from the mouth of Christ himself . . ."; and (2) the council ". . . receives and venerates with the same sense of loyalty and reverence all the books of the Old and

5. John Henry Newman, "On Consulting the Faithful in Matters of Doctrine," in *Conscience, Consensus and the Development of Doctrine*, ed. James Gaffney (New York: Doubleday, 1992), 398.

6. Karl Rahner, *Foundations of Christian Faith*, trans. William Dych (New York: Seabury, 1978), 364.

New Testament — for God alone is the author of both — together with all the traditions concerning faith and morals, as coming from the mouth of Christ or being inspired by the Holy Spirit and preserved in continuous succession in the Catholic Church."[7]

A. *"Written Books and Unwritten Traditions"*

The Council of Trent, before it could properly respond to the theological challenges of the Reformation, had first to be clear on the source of revealed truth. To this end, the council started with a list of the sacred books of the Bible, ultimately repeating, not without prior debate, the list drawn up by the Council of Florence in 1442. From there the council, pricked by Luther's cry of *sola scriptura,* moved to the relationship between Scripture and tradition. To forestall the possibility of dismissing Trent as merely a reactionary conclave, it is worthwhile to listen carefully to its measured words and evangelical spirit.

"The Council of Trent has always this purpose in mind that in the Church errors be removed and the purity of the Gospel be preserved." The motives of the council are unimpeachable, preserving the church from error and preaching the gospel in its totality and purity. The council goes on to say: "Our Lord Jesus Christ, Son of God, first promulgated [the gospel] from his own lips. He in turn ordered that it be preached through the apostles to all creatures as the source of all saving truth and rule of conduct." One should notice the use of the singular, *fons* or source, rather than the plural, *fontes,* which became so popular in later Catholic post-Reformation writers. The one source of divine truth is neither Scripture nor tradition but the gospel preached by Jesus Christ, the Son of God. And this one gospel is the source of saving truth for all men and women.

It is only after these important considerations that the council logically asks: Where is this saving gospel, which Jesus bestowed on us and we are now to preach, to be found? Trent responds: "The council clearly perceives that this truth and rule are contained in the written books and unwritten traditions which have come down to us. . . ." Where did the council find this language? Certainly earlier ecumenical councils had spoken this way. One sees this language adumbrated at the Second Council of Constantinople in 553. One sees it even more clearly at the Second Council of Nicea, the assembly upholding the legitimacy of icons, in 787. This latter council notes: "Anyone

7. DH, no. 1501; *The Christian Faith,* 77.

who does not accept the whole of the Church's tradition, both written and unwritten, anathema sit."

But most prominent in the Tridentine discussion of "written books and unwritten traditions" is the work of the fourth-century father of the church, Basil of Caesarea. An example of Basil's influence can be found in the *Acta* of the council. In preparation for the conciliar discussions, Cardinal Sirleto, a noted humanist, had done extensive research in the writings of the church fathers. On January 3, 1545, he wrote a letter from Rome to one of the council presidents, Cardinal Cervini, indicating that he was passing on some sentences of Basil pertinent to the authority of ecclesiastical traditions. He notes, in particular, chapters twenty-seven and twenty-nine of the treatise, *De spiritu sancto*. "*Plurima ex iis,*" he writes confidently. He also mentions that certain texts of sacred Scripture, 1 Cor. 11:23 and 2 Thess. 2:15, are supportive of the Catholic position.[8]

What was the original context of the passages borrowed by the Council of Trent? The intention of Basil's treatise, of course, is to demonstrate, against various opponents, that the Spirit is, like the Son, one and the same nature as the Father and deserving of the same honor and worship as the Father and the Son. But the immediate point of chapter twenty-seven is more focused, requiring a bit of explanation. Basil begins his argument in chapter twenty-four by noting that many created things, even men, are glorified (as is clear from the Psalms). Why, he asks, would this honor be denied the Spirit? Basil notes that some do give the Spirit honor and glory, but not equally with the Father and the Son. By citing various New Testament passages, he attempts to show the uniqueness of the Spirit. Nonetheless, his opponents remain unconvinced. In chapter twenty-five, Basil recounts their charge: "How is it that Scripture nowhere describes the Spirit to be glorified together with the Father and the Son?"[9] The New Testament speaks of "in the Spirit" rather than "with the Spirit." For his opponents, the Spirit is not quite equal to the other two divine persons. As Basil says, "They insist we must give glory to God *in* the Spirit, but never *and to* the Holy Spirit, passionately clutching this one word as if it contained power to lower the Spirit." Basil devotes the remainder of the chapter to discussing the use of different words in various scriptural passages and their relative interchangeability. In chapter twenty-six, Basil shows that there are many ways "in" may

8. *Concilium Tridentinum,* vol. X, ed. *Societas Goerresiana* (Freiburg in Breisgau: Herder, 1965), 932.

9. Basil the Great, *On the Holy Spirit,* trans. David Anderson (New York: St. Vladimir's Seminary Press, 1980). Most of the following translations are from this edition.

be used in proper reference to the Spirit. For example, one says "we worship in the Spirit." But, he claims, this is not to deny the coordinating preposition "with." In chapter twenty-seven, Basil says that even though some argue that honoring the Spirit "with" the Father and the Son is innovative, "it remains for me to describe the origin and force of the word 'with' and to show that its usage is in accord with Scripture."

In what will be the key passage for Trent, Basil then describes one reason why "with" may be used. The text in Latin translation (which was ultimately used at Trent) reads: "*Ex asservatis in Ecclesia dogmatibus (dogmaton) et praedicationibus (kerugmaton), alia quidem habemus* e doctrina scripto *prodita; alia vero nobis in mysterio tradita recepimus* ex traditione aposto-lorum. . . ." A serviceable translation of this text might read: "Among the doc-trines and proclamations preserved in the Church, some we have derived from *written teaching;* others we have received delivered to us in mystery from the *tradition of the Apostles. . . .*"[10] It was this text that served as the immediate source of Trent's formulation.

Trent used Basil's particular point, that some traditions, such as the phrase "with the Holy Spirit," have been handed down to us, in order to es-tablish a more general point: that tradition has an important, indeed essen-tial, role in the life of the church. This is hardly to claim the thought of Basil for Trent. It does illustrate that Trent's theological rationale, as well as that of subsequent councils, is not misplaced when exalting the central role of tradi-tion in the church's teaching.

Several historians have noted that the change in the decree from "this truth and rule are contained partly in written books and partly in unwritten traditions" *(partim . . . partim)* to "this truth and rule are contained in writ-ten books and unwritten traditions" *(et),* was, most likely, nothing more than a stylistic alteration on the part of the authors. If this were true, then the textual change hardly reflected a new acceptance of the material suffi-ciency of Scripture. Yves Congar notes, however, that although the change was probably not made to favor explicitly the material sufficiency of Scrip-ture, the fact remains that, theologically speaking, room was now made for this thesis. The conciliar decree is open to this interpretation inasmuch as Catholics believe that statements of ecumenical councils are providentially guided by the Holy Spirit. Congar closes by noting that the proper way of summing up the relationship between Scripture and tradition as found in both the Fathers and the pre-Tridentine period is in the formula used by

10. Basil the Great, in Migne, *PG* no. 32, col. 187A (emphasis added). Also, *Sources Chrétiennes, Traité du Saint-Esprit,* trans. B. Pruche (Paris: Cerf, 1946), 232-233.

Newman and the nineteenth-century theologian, J. E. Kuhn: *Totum in scriptura, totum in traditione.*[11]

While Congar and J. Geiselmann believe that Trent left the door open for the thesis of the material sufficiency of Scripture, Joseph Ratzinger stakes the same claim for the Dogmatic Constitution of Vatican II, *Dei Verbum* #9. This text is ". . . the product of the attempt to take into account, to the widest possible extent, the points made by the Reformed churches and [was] intended to keep the field open for a Catholic idea of sola scriptura. . . ."[12] If these theologians are correct, and the majority of contemporary Catholic theologians surely agree with them, then Catholics, in their own way, could agree with the position that the entire truth of salvation is found in Scripture.

B. Pari Pietatis Affectu

Let us now turn to the other disputed passage of Trent, that part of the decree reading: "Following, then, the example of the orthodox Fathers, [the council] receives and venerates with the same sense of loyalty and reverence all the books of the Old and New Testaments — for God alone is the author of both — together with all the traditions concerning faith and morals as coming from the mouth of Christ or being inspired by the Holy Spirit and preserved in continuous succession in the Catholic Church."

As Professor George pointed out, this sentence (and particularly the word *pari*) was not only the subject of heated debate at Trent, but remains a stumbling block for many Evangelicals.[13] Of course, the sweeping statement of the council that it venerates with the same loyalty and reverence both Scripture and *all the traditions* coming from Christ or inspired by the Spirit

---

11. Yves Congar, *Tradition and Traditions,* trans. M. Naseby and T. Rainborough (New York: The Macmillan Company, 1967), 412-13. Avery Dulles makes a similar point when he notes, "It would be an exaggeration to say that Catholics and Protestants have switched positions, as though Catholics were, today, the spokesmen of *sola Scriptura* and Protestants [referring to the Faith and Order Conference in July, 1963] were championing *sola traditione.* But . . . it is no longer accurate to say that the basic difference consists in the fact that Protestantism advocates Scripture as the one source of revelation whereas Catholicism looks to Scripture plus tradition." *Revelation and the Quest for Unity* (Washington: Corpus Books, 1968), 68-69.

12. Joseph Ratzinger, "Commentary on *Dei Verbum,*" in *Documents of Vatican II,* vol. 3, ed. H. Vorgrimler, several translators (New York: Herder & Herder, 1969), 192. Ratzinger also notes here both his reservations and those of various Protestant commentators.

13. See above, Timothy George, "An Evangelical Reflection on Scripture and Tradition," 23.

should alert us to the difficulties Trent faced regarding the enumeration of properly venerated traditions. More than one bishop at the council noted that several traditions had changed over the centuries. As Nacchianti said: "How can I accept the practice of praying eastward with the same reverence as St. John's gospel?"[14] And Bertano, who was also against the word *pari,* argued that even traditions that were of great age, such as Communion under both kinds, had fallen into desuetude. Of course, the Jesuit Lejay had earlier offered a useful distinction: there were traditions *quae ad fidem pertinent* as well as others which were not foundational to the Christian faith. But the bishops at the council had no desire to enter into a detailed debate concerning particular traditions. And we can perhaps imagine that the council presidents, realizing the mountain of theological and disciplinary work still before them, discouraged an elongated discussion of particular traditions. On April 5, 1546, a vote on the question of parity was taken. While thirty-three bishops thought the original wording preserved the mind of the church, another eleven wished *pari pietatis affectu* to be replaced by *simili pietatis affectu.* The debate continued for another two days with little change in the argument. Finally, on April 8, 1546, the decree was once again examined and the word *pari* finally approved.

The language of tradition in the decree remains general and vague. We can assume that this represents both a desire to avoid protracted discussions separating dogmatic from non-essential traditions as well as a desire to conform to the fundamental hermeneutical principle of the council, viz., to resolve only those doctrines on which there was general agreement and to eschew those points on which there was serious divergence.[15] Of course, it was adherence to this principle that led Trent to refrain from any statement concerning the disputed issue of the Immaculate Conception of the Blessed Virgin Mary.

Of great importance to this section of the decree is the provenance of the phrase *pari pietatis affectu.* What is its lineage? How did the fathers at Trent arrive at it? Again, we turn to chapter twenty-seven of *On the Holy Spirit* of St. Basil. As we noted above, Basil claimed that some doctrines we have from written teaching while we have received others, as in a mystery, from the tradition of the apostles. After this statement Basil says (in Latin translation): ". . . *quorum utraque vim eamdem habent ad pietatem; nec iis quisquam contradicet; nullus certe, qui vel tenui experientia noverit quae sint Ecclesiae*

---

14. Hubert Jedin, *A History of the Council of Trent* v. 2, trans. Dom Ernest Graf (St. Louis: Herder, 1957), 87.

15. Congar, *Tradition and Traditions,* 412.

instituta. Nam si consuetudines quae scripto proditae non sunt, tanquam haud multum habentes momenti aggrediamus rejicere, imprudentes Evangelium in ipsis rebus praecipuis laedemu, imo potius praedicationem ad nudum nomen contrahemus." This may be translated as follows: ". . . Both sources have equal force in true religion. No one would deny either source — no one, at any rate, who is even slightly familiar with the ordinances of the Church. If we attacked unwritten customs, claiming them to be of little importance, we would fatally mutilate the Gospel, no matter what our intentions — or rather, we would re-duce the Gospel teachings to bare words."

After this Basil mentions a long list of unwritten traditions, most of which the Catholic Church would classify as non-doctrinal. To give just a sampling I cite a brief passage: "Which book teaches us to pray facing the East? Have any saints left for us in writing the words to be used in the invoca-tion over the Eucharistic bread and the cup of blessing? . . . We bless baptis-mal water and the oil for chrismation as well as the candidate approaching the font. By what written authority do we do this, if not from secret and mys-tical tradition? What about . . . other baptismal rites, such as the renunciation of Satan and his angels? Are not all these things found in unpublished and unwritten teachings, which our fathers guarded in silence, safe from med-dling and petty curiosity?"[16] All of Basil's examples are intended to lead to his central point, viz., adoration should be extended to the Spirit as well as the Father and the Son. In the end, one wonders if the Council of Trent, with the *pari pietatis affectu,* did not have in mind something similar to J. E. Kuhn's *Totum in scriptura, totum in traditione.*

Perhaps useful in its analysis of the Tridentine decree on Scripture and tradition is the work of G. C. Berkouwer, *The Second Vatican Council and the New Catholicism.* Berkouwer, who died in 1996, was a Reformed theologian and committed Calvinist who spent his teaching career at the Free Univer-sity of Amsterdam. According to several observers, he stands in the same line of theologians as H. Bavinck and A. Kuyper. He was also an officially ap-pointed observer at Vatican II. Berkouwer notes that while Trent was content to "contradict the Reformation with an expression of great respect for tradi-tion, the relationship between Scripture and Tradition is a completely open matter." Further, "What is important is that Trent said nothing that would put tradition on a par with Scripture in the sense that it complements Scrip-

---

16. Basil, *On the Holy Spirit,* chapter 27. Luther, apparently, did not have much use for Basil. As he says in the *Tischreden,* "Basil doesn't amount to a thing; he was a monk after all, and I wouldn't give a penny for him." *Werke* vol. 40, no. 252, p. 33. Cited by Edward Oakes in *Pattern of Redemption* (New York: Continuum, 1994), 107 n. 10.

ture."[17] Berkouwer points out that nothing in the council itself supports the Counter-Reformation's claim that tradition adds to the revelation given with Scripture. And he notes that while the word "tradition" evoked "negative emotional accompaniments" in large segments of Protestant theology, the phrase *sola scriptura* meant ". . . to bind the Church with its confessions and its preaching to the apostolic witness. Clearly, therefore, the phrase *sola scriptura* was not meant to suggest an opposition between Scripture and tradition; it was meant to be a sign pointing to the danger zones where the sound of the gospel might not be heard."[18] Already in 1965, Berkouwer was perceptive enough to note that, according to much Catholic theology, "Scripture is sufficient for *all* truth and tradition only interprets the truth of Scripture."[19]

Let us now turn to a wider examination of how tradition functions in the Catholic Church.

Excursus on Tradition

Trent spoke of receiving and venerating ". . . all the traditions concerning faith and morals as coming from the mouth of Christ or being inspired by the Holy Spirit. . . ." Newman outlined the variety of places where the proper tradition could be found. Vatican II, as *Dei Verbum* #8 witnesses, holds that tradition, properly understood, is neither a dead hand nor a hanging millstone stifling the Holy Spirit. For the council, tradition is dynamic and alive; it is, in fact, the work of the Holy Spirit himself, guiding the people of God into the fullness of revealed truth. Describing this idea of tradition, the French theologian, Henri de Lubac, says: "Tradition, according to the fathers of the church, is in fact just the opposite of a burden of the past; it is a vital energy, a propulsive . . . force, acting within an entire community as at the heart of each of the faithful because it is none other than the very Word of God both perpetuating and renewing itself under the action of the Holy Spirit."[20]

It is true, as has been noted, that some Counter-Reformation theologians held to the position that tradition constituted a "separate" source for revelation. But this understanding was never seen as a basis for *expanding or creat-*

17. G. C. Berkouwer, *The Second Vatican Council and the New Catholicism* (Grand Rapids: Eerdmans, 1965), 96-97.

18. Berkouwer, *Second Vatican Council,* 107.

19. Berkouwer, *Second Vatican Council,* 108.

20. Henri de Lubac, *The Motherhood of the Church,* trans. Sr. Sergia Englund (San Francisco: Ignatius Press, 1982), 91.

THOMAS G. GUARINO

ing some new revelation of God. In fact, the Catholic Church has never allowed a *productive* notion of revelation, whereby tradition would actually add something to the deposit of faith. Vatican II was careful to repeat what the church had already said in response to some Catholic modernists of the late nineteenth century: the church awaits no new public revelation. The Father has revealed himself finally and definitively in the life, death, and resurrection of his Son, Jesus Christ. Revelation continues in the church only in the limited sense that God continues to touch the hearts of his people and to pour the new life of the Spirit into their souls. Of course, there is a sense of "passing on" tradition, but this is not a determined process, nor even simply an oral one. Vatican II rightly speaks of tradition developing in the church, under the Holy Spirit, through a growth in the understanding of the words and realities [of salvation history] which have been handed down (*Dei Verbum* #8). This growth and development of tradition happens, the council continues, through the prayer, contemplation, and study made by believers, through their experience of spiritual realities, through the wealth of sacred writings, especially the fathers of the church, and through the preaching of bishops. In passages like these, one sees the church's sense of the coinherence or circumincession existing among the Scriptures, the Fathers, the liturgy, theologians, and the spiritual lives of believers.

In the nineteenth century, men like Newman and J. A. Möhler sought to revive patristic images comparing the development of tradition with organic growth. One finds such images of harmonious development as far back as the fifth-century father of the church, Vincent of Lerins. The image of a boy growing to full stature or of a seed maturing to a blooming tree had the significant advantage of preserving fundamental and essential elements of identity while still allowing for growth, development, and architectonic progress in the understanding of revelation. In his famous book, the *Commonitorium*, Vincent traced the dialectic whereby the church teaches both that public revelation is closed and the church is always led to a fuller understanding of revealed truth. Inasmuch as Vincent's thought typifies aspects of a Catholic notion of tradition, I will summarize his work briefly. The *Commonitorium* was written about 430 A.D., only about one hundred years after the Council of Nicea and fifty years after the divinity of the Holy Spirit was indisputably established at the Council of Constantinople. Vincent tells us that he wrote it because his memory was becoming weak and reviewing the notes he set down helped him to see important matters more clearly. Of particular concern to Vincent are various heresies that have sprung up under the name of development or progress of the faith. His work is a plea for the genuine development of the faith, but with the caution that such development must be architec-

90

tonic in kind, tightly linked to what has been handed on rather than a fundamental change or distortion of content.

In chapter twenty-three, he tackles the question in a classic passage:

> But perhaps someone will say: Is there no progress of religion in the Church of Christ? There is progress, even great progress. . . . But it must be progress in the proper sense and not a change in faith *(profectus non permutatio)*. Progress means that each thing grows within itself, whereas change implies the one thing changes into another *(aliquid ex alio in aliud)*. Hence, it must be that understanding, knowledge and wisdom grow and advance strongly in individuals as well as in the community, in a single person as well as in the Church as a whole and this gradually according to age and history. But they must progress within their own limits, that is in accordance with the same teaching, the same meaning and the same judgment.[21]

In Vincent of Lerin, we have a good example of how the Catholic Church understands both development of doctrine and the role of tradition in the life of the church. Both tradition and development must be in fundamental accord with Scripture and keep to "the same teaching, meaning and judgment." Other phrases, sprinkled throughout the *Commonitorium,* sound the same theme. Of the deposit of faith, Vincent notes that the task of the church is neither to add nor to subtract, *nihil addit, nihil minuit.* The church's preaching and teaching is always to say things newly, but never to say innovative things, *dicit nove non dicit nova.* It should come as no surprise that the Catholic Church cited passages from Vincent at critical moments of the church's life, e.g., during the definition of the Immaculate Conception in 1854, when cautioning against fideism and rationalism at Vatican I (1870), and in statements issued during the modernist crisis at the turn of the century.

For Catholics, the Marian dogmas serve as examples of Scripture and tradition working in concert, of organic growth and harmonious development, of the *profectus non permutatio* counseled by Vincent. In the constitution defining the Assumption, for example, the pope is sensitive to the task of justifying this development in the Christian tradition. Of the Assumption, he says: "This truth is based on Sacred Scripture and deeply embedded in the minds of the faithful; it has received the approval of liturgical worship from the earliest times; it is perfectly in keeping with the rest of revealed truth, and has

---

21. Vincent of Lerins, *Commonitorium,* in *Corpus Christianorum* LXIV, ed. R. Demeulenaere (Turnholti: Brepols Editores, 1985). English translation by Rudolph Morris, *Fathers of the Church,* vol. 7 (New York: Fathers of the Church, Inc., 1949). I have slightly modified the translation.

been lucidly developed and explained by the studies, the knowledge and the wisdom of theologians. Considering all these reasons, we deem that the moment . . . has now arrived for us to proclaim solemnly this extraordinary privilege of the Virgin Mary. . . ."

Several of the criteria important to the Catholic Church are invoked by the constitution. Not only does the pope cite Scripture, but he notes as well the tradition of ancient liturgical feasts in East and West, the *sensus fidelium*, the work of theologians, and the relationship among the mysteries (or what Vatican I called the *nexus mysteriorum inter se*). As regards the biblical citations, early in the decree the Protoevangelium (Gen. 3:15) is invoked while, somewhat later, Pauline passages regarding Christ's victory over sin and death (Romans 5 and 6) as well as our final passage to imperishability and immortality (1 Cor. 15:54) are cited. Of course, the ultimate basis for the privilege of the Assumption is Mary's unique status in the economy of salvation as the Mother of God. Evangelicals will find the biblical evidence for this dogma to be tenuous at best. The differing Catholic and Evangelical views regarding scriptural justification and proper development will be discussed in the next section.

IV. Disputed Questions

A. Sola Scriptura

At one point in his work, Calvin notes, "Here then is the difference between us; they attribute authority to the Church without the Word: we, on the contrary, inseparably unite the one with the other."[22] Prescinding from the charges and countercharges of the sixteenth-century debates, there is no doubt that Catholic theologians would plead innocent to Calvin's charge. Catholics argue, on the contrary, that the church may never proceed without the Word; to do so would be fatal to the church's own life and work. The issue, then, crystallizes around the question of precisely how the Catholic Church proceeds with the Word. A further question asks how this Catholic proceeding with the Word differs from an Evangelical proceeding, or Protestant proceeding generally.

One difference between the two approaches to the *sola scriptura* issue can be seen in the maxim "justification by faith alone." On one reading of Scrip-

---

22. Calvin, *CR, Opera Calvini* IV, col. 736. Cited by Congar, *Tradition and Traditions*, 141 n. 5.

ture, Protestants of many stripes, following Luther, have reached the conclusion that justification by faith alone is the *articulus stantis et cadentis Ecclesiae*. Catholics, while recently admitting that justification by faith alone is an important, indeed a foundational teaching of the Christian church, have stayed away from language implying that it is the fundamental teaching of the New Testament. As Cardinal Ratzinger noted in his comments on the original document between Catholics and Lutherans, all Catholic teachings must by synthetic with the *regula fidei* of the church. This patristic phrase indicates a concern both with the tradition of the church and with the *nexus mysteriorum* suggesting, perhaps, a set of criteria more relevant to Catholicism than to Evangelical churches.

This concern with tradition is evident even in the ecumenically motivated Catholic theologian Karl Rahner. He thinks that while the questions of *fides sola et gratia sola* may be solved without difficulty, the issue of Scripture alone is more complicated.[23] He argues that for the earliest church, a legitimate succession of both witnesses and of what is being witnessed to, is clearly evident. At the same time, Rahner says: "It is taken for granted by the Catholic understanding of the faith and of the church . . . that Scripture as such and as written is a real norm for the post-apostolic church. The church does not receive any new revelation over and beyond the scripture, nor over and beyond the apostolic preaching of the original church. Rather, the church's understanding of the faith and its teaching office have no other tasks except to remain with the ultimate and eschatological revelation which has been handed down."[24]

As has already been noted, one possible and legitimate way of interpreting significant passages of both Trent and Vatican II is by the phrase *sola scriptura*. Congar, in particular, has shown that the *sola scriptura* position is entirely congruent with the Council of Trent. And Joseph Ratzinger has successfully argued that Vatican II is clearly open to this interpretation. Karl Barth himself noted that while there is one chapter on tradition in *Dei Verbum*, and this always in relationship to Scripture, there are four chapters on Scripture exclusively.[25]

Many Evangelicals pause, however, when Catholics proceed to explain how *sola scriptura* is understood in the Catholic Church. Fair to say, it is not the way in which Luther expressed in it *The Babylonian Captivity of the*

---

23. Karl Rahner, *Foundations*, 361.

24. Rahner, *Foundations*, 363.

25. Karl Barth, *Ad limina apostolorum*, 51 n. 4. Cited by J. Ratzinger in *Documents of Vatican II*, ed. Vorgrimler, 192.

Church (cf. note #1). Nonetheless, most Catholic theologians agree that all saving truth is contained in the written Word of God. By this they mean that the Scriptures contain, either explicitly or implicitly, all of the dogmatic teachings of the Catholic Church. Ecumenically and historically motivated Catholic theology, by and large, holds that Scripture is sufficient for all the revealed truths of salvation while tradition, the life of the church under the Holy Spirit, enables the church to penetrate the truth and meaning of Scripture more fully.

B. Critical Principle

During Vatican II, prominent Protestant theologians such as Oscar Cullmann and J. K. S. Reid were disappointed that the council did not go on to develop Trent in such a way that possible distortions within the tradition would be mentioned. Their comments crystallized one of the main problems that many Protestant theologians have with the Catholic discernment of Scripture: the lack of a critical scriptural principle to separate, as Harnack once claimed, the gospel from the rank growth of tradition.

Catholic theologians argue that there is, indeed, a critical principle of tradition, a divine one no less: the Holy Spirit himself guides the church into the fullness of truth and directs her in avoiding error. No other critical principle need exist. One reason for this is that Catholicism thinks of Scripture, tradition, and the church as intrinsically interrelated. A kind of coinherence exists among the three. Sacred Scripture is inspired by the Holy Spirit, the church is guided by the Holy Spirit, allowing the church to interpret Scripture properly, and tradition (with varying levels of authority, of course) is the history of the church reading Scripture with the divine assistance of the Spirit. The three terms are not thought of dialectically, as if in opposition to one another, but analogically, as interrelated and interwoven. J. Ratzinger expressed something like this years ago when he noted that the New Testament issues forth from the church's reading of the Old Testament in light of Christ, while tradition issues forth from the church's reading of the New Testament in the light of the Holy Spirit.[26] Sacred Scripture, then, is a gift given to the church by the Lord, and the church is commissioned by Christ to safeguard Scripture's truth with the unfailing aid of the Holy Spirit. Scripture is God's Eternal Word to the church and the church is charged with the continuing task of guarding it, lis-

---

26. Joseph Ratzinger, "On the Interpretation of the Tridentine Decree on Tradition," in *Revelation and Tradition* (New York: Herder & Herder, 1966), 50-72.

tening to it, living it, and interpreting it properly. This is the meaning of the passage in *Dei Verbum* no. 10, which reads, "The task of authoritatively interpreting the word of God, whether written or handed down, has been entrusted exclusively to the living teaching authority of the Church, whose authority is exercised in the name of Jesus Christ. This teaching office is not above the word of God, but serves it, teaching only what has been handed on, listening to it devoutly, guarding it scrupulously and explaining it faithfully by divine commission and with the help of the Holy Spirit. . . ."

Of course, when speaking of the tradition and teaching of the Catholic Church, a caveat must be issued, viz., there are different levels of authority connected with church teaching. Some teachings are fundamental and irreformable; many others do not have that status. Catholic theology readily admits that inasmuch as church teachings are issued with varying levels of authority, certain teachings may be subject to reform. Not every teaching is endowed with the charism of infallibility nor is every teaching to be equated with the divine law. It is no secret, for example, that Vatican II reversed several teachings of the prior ordinary papal magisterium, e.g., the previous teaching on religious freedom. One must not think, then, of every individual ecclesial tradition as monolithically taught by the church with the same weight or authority. We should remember the statement of Vatican II's *Unitatis Redintegratio* #6: "Christ summons the Church . . . to that continual reformation of which she always has need, insofar as she is an institution of men here on earth. Therefore, if the influence of events or of the times, has led to deficiencies in conduct, in Church discipline, or even in the formulation of doctrine (which must be carefully distinguished from the deposit of faith itself), these should be rectified at the proper moment." There is an understanding, without question, that at a certain level, ecclesial teaching may become distorted and ultimately abandoned. This issue, traditionally related to "theological notes," cannot be fully broached here. But perhaps it is just at this point that we may see some rapprochement with our Evangelical brethren on the issue of human fallibility, weakness, and sin.

Ultimately, for Catholicism, no radical chasm can develop between Christ and the church, even with the sinfulness that is characteristic of all members of the church, including those who have occupied and continue to occupy important and honored offices. Christ, the guarantor of truth, has promised that he abides with the church to the end of days. The Catholic Church takes this to mean that Christ will not allow the church to deviate from his truth or to lead his flock into serious error.

This latter point, I suspect, indicates the problem most Evangelicals have with Catholicism, a sense that it fails to recognize fully that human sinfulness and pride has deeply attenuated the ability of the church to follow Christ in all things. By ignoring or downplaying the depth of anthropological corruption, Catholicism tends to stray from the pure truth of the Bible in favor of human ingenuity, invention, and even idolatry. The result is dogmatic "truth" based not on the inspired Word of God, but on the fallible word of men. Evangelicals hold that the Bible alone must judge and norm the church's action and curb the desire of sinful men to exercise authority over God's Word or use it to their own advantage. Of course, as should become clear below, Catholics would agree with this statement as well, claiming that the church is the servant of God's Word, seeking only to follow it and propose it anew.

C. Development of Doctrine or Extra-Biblical Teaching?

Professor George, while defending the *sola scriptura* principle, notes that because of changed linguistic and cultural horizons through the centuries, some kind of theological development is always necessary. Along similar lines, J. Daryl Charles raises questions about an uncritical use of the phrase, *sola scriptura.* "Scripture never exists *sola;* rather it is understood and interpreted via the collective wisdom of the Christian church in all ages and communions. For this reason, it is more appropriate to speak of *prima scriptura* — which more adequately represents historic Christian orthodoxy while preserving Scripture's normative place in doing . . . theology."[27] This same position is taken by Berkouwer who notes, "An abstract view of *sola Scriptura,* in which the Bible is kept as a set of propositions to be consulted for proof of one's position, results from insisting on a single source of revelation, exclusive of all other considerations."[28] The ideas of George, Charles, and Berkouwer suggest an important place for tradition in the life of the church — but in such a way as this legitimate emphasis on tradition does not jeopardize the truth of, or primacy of, the written Word of God. For all of these theologians, Scripture must be the unique and final touchstone for all church teaching, including every conciliar or papal decision.[29]

Perhaps these men would be surprised to learn that Catholicism has little problem with this formulation as it stands. Most Catholic theologians accept the phrase *sola scriptura;* they accept as well the claim that the Bible is the *norma normans non normata,* the ultimate touchstone for Christian faith.

---

27. J. Daryl Charles, "Losing Our Moral Theology," *First Things* 89 (Jan. 1999): 52.
28. Berkouwer, *Second Vatican Council,* 101-2.
29. George, "An Evangelical Reflection on Scripture and Tradition," 33 above.

Further, as noted above, Catholic theologians have reconciled "Scripture alone" with the ecumenical councils of Catholicism; the phrase need not stand in tension with either Trent or Vatican II. The difficult issues come to the fore, however, when trying to "unpack" precisely what the phrases *sola scriptura* and *norma normans* mean to Catholics and Evangelicals.

What likely separates Catholics and Evangelicals on this point is their respective view of the church. In matters of doctrine and teaching, Catholics have a difficult time understanding the notion of Scripture as over and against the church. Catholics find the biblical imagery depicting the church as the "pillar of truth" and as the "body of Christ" foremost in their minds. They are at home with the image of "mother church" developed by the North African Fathers Cyprian, Tertullian, and Augustine in the third and fourth centuries. Cyprian's famous sentence, "One cannot have God for a Father who does not have the church for a Mother" [*De unitate ecclesiae,* 6], is an image indicating, for Catholics, the profound link between God, the church, and, a fortiori, Scripture itself. Consequently, Catholics see the Holy Spirit as guiding the church, day by day, into the fullness and complexity of the mystery of salvation revealed in Scripture. This is hardly a license for innovation; rather, it is God's work in the church's daily task of bringing men and women to salvation. The notion of *sola scriptura,* then, would be one in which the immutable deposit of faith, given to us by Christ, develops under the light of the Holy Spirit from age to age.

Of course, many Evangelicals agree that the development of doctrine is possible and even necessary. They add, as Professor George does, that any development must have Scripture as its foundation and base itself upon "the inner logic and inexorable implications of Jesus' words and deeds." Given these criteria, Evangelicals find certain developments in Catholic doctrine, e.g., the Marian dogmas and the teaching on Purgatory, to be illegitimate developments or, in the words of Vincent of Lerins, a collective *permutatio* rather than a *profectus* of the faith.

Evangelicals, however, may be surprised to know that Catholics find nothing objectionable in the criteria suggested by Professor George. For Catholics, too, all development must be based on Scripture and must represent the "inner logic and inexorable implications" of Jesus' life and teaching. The difference between Catholics and Evangelicals might be found in how these "inexorable implications" are discerned by the individual church. For Catholics, this discernment is mediated by all of the formal and informal acts of the church, the *loci theologici* of which we have spoken. Through all of these, the truth of Jesus' words and deeds, as well as the truth of Scripture itself, comes to its full meaning. Catholicism thinks it does nothing more than re-present the essential meaning of the New Testament now more clearly understood in light of the church's tradition of life in the Holy Spirit. All of the councils of the church and all of the church's doctrinal statements, are, for Catholicism, re-presentations of the same gospel of Jesus Christ. The Catholic Church sees its task, then, not as innovating with regard to the deposit of faith, but preserving and conserving the message of the Christ.

Catholics claim that scriptural attestation is important, indeed essential, but they interpret such witness in a global rather than an explicit sense. Evangelicals, on the other hand, think that certain and even explicit attestation of Scripture is necessary in order for the church to teach that any development is, indeed, a result of the inner logic of Scripture itself. Our question, then, remains the one an early ecumenist, John Courtney Murray, asked over thirty years ago: ". . . What is warranted extension of the primitive discipline of the Church and what, on the other hand is accretion, additive increment, adulteration of the deposit, distortion of true Christian discipline?" In short, what is the difference between "true growth" and "rank excrescence"?[30]

In any case, it is important to note that Evangelicals and Catholics do not appear to disagree on the fundamental principle allowing some development in church teaching; they likely disagree on the means of implementing this principle in the life of the church. Congar points out that one statement by Luther could be helpful in moving the question of development along: "Quod non est contra Scripturam pro Scriptura est et Scriptura pro eo."[31]

D. Some Brief Examples of Development

The following examples of development are far too brief to be of great use. I include these, then, not to offer instruction in the controversies themselves, but rather to illustrate certain aspects of development important to Catholic theology.

1. The Divinity of the Holy Spirit

As is well known, even in the year 380, the divinity of the Holy Spirit was still widely debated in Constantinople and its environs. Gregory of Nazianzus

---

30. John Courtney Murray, *The Problem of God* (New Haven: Yale University Press, 1965), 53.

31. Martin Luther, *Briefwechsel* II, pp. 426-27; Congar, *Tradition and Traditions*, 143 n. 3.

tells us, during his funeral oration for Basil the Great, that even Basil could not refer openly to the Holy Spirit as God for fear he would be ejected from the capital city. In Gregory's words, "The enemies were on watch for the unqualified statement 'the Spirit is God' which, although it is true, they . . . in their impiety thought to be impious, so that they might banish him and his power of theological instruction from the city and themselves be able to seize upon the Church and make it the starting point and citadel from which they could overrun with their evil doctrine the rest of the world" *(Epistle 58)*.

And Gregory Nazianzen himself said, "The Old Testament preached the Father openly and the Son more obscurely, while the New revealed the Son and hinted at the deity of the Spirit. Now the Spirit dwells in us and reveals himself more clearly to us. For it was not right, while the deity of the Father had still not been confessed, to preach the Son openly and, before the Son had been acknowledged, to force us to accept the Holy Spirit — and I speak too boldly here — into the bargain. . . . (It was much more suitable that) by gradual advances and, as David said, by partial ascents, moving forward and increasing in clarity, the light of the Trinity should shine on those who had already been given lights" *(Oratio 31.26)*. In the same essay, Gregory tells us that the opponents of the Spirit claimed that some ". . . speak of an alien God [the Spirit] of whom Scripture is silent."

Are we to think that the opponents of Basil and Gregory were simply malicious or malevolent? To the argument that the Spirit was virtually everywhere in Scripture, their opponents claimed that Scripture spoke of the Holy Spirit more as a "force" than as a distinct "person." Basil, in his treatise on the Holy Spirit, appealed, as we have seen, both to Scripture and the tradition of the church. Gregory, in his remarks, suggests that only gradually was it clearly understood that the Holy Spirit was to be honored and glorified with the Father and the Son.

Here, too, of course, both Catholics and Evangelicals will say that the "inner logic and inexorable implications" of Jesus' words and deeds were developed. Catholics will add, however, that while the divinity of the Holy Spirit is part of the logic of the New Testament, the totality of the implications arising from the New Testament have not always been easily discerned or readily apparent in the history of the church. It is precisely here that tradition serves as an important aid to the church in understanding the meaning of Scripture.

2. The Immaculate Conception

A second example illustrating the Catholic understanding of development of doctrine is the Immaculate Conception of the Blessed Virgin Mary. Evangelicals, along with other Protestants, would surely claim that this teaching goes beyond biblical attestation. Catholics, however, would say that while this doctrine is not explicitly attested in Scripture, the unique place of Mary in the life and work of Jesus is indisputable. Without adducing the entire tradition leading to the definition of 1854, one can nonetheless outline the fundamental pillars of the Catholic argument: Mary was chosen by God to give birth to the Savior, inaugurating our redemption. Certain biblical passages were interpreted as applicable, at least symbolically, to Mary, e.g., the Protoevangelium of Gen. 3:15 and the woman clothed with the sun in the book of Revelation (Rev. 12). The New Testament relates the story of her unique vocation, with Luke calling her "favored one" or "full of grace," moving Augustine to remark: Concerning the holy Virgin Mary I wish to raise no question when it touches the subject of sins, out of honor to the Lord. . . ." (*De natura et gratia*, 42.36). Such was the place of Mary in the New Testament and in salvation history that since the time of Justin and Irenaeus she has been thought of as the New Eve. The extraordinary title, Mother of God, was bestowed on Mary by the council of Ephesus in 431, even while some Christians wished to deny Mary this honor. All further Marian titles and privileges ultimately flow from her unique vocation as the Theotokos.

For many Scholastics, the primary difficulty with the Immaculate Conception amounted to reconciling this claim with the universal redemptive work of Christ. The seeming inability to do this was the objection of Albert the Great, Bonaventure, and Thomas Aquinas in the period of the great Schoolmen. This was the case even though Aquinas, seeking to offer an argument for the special station of the Mother of God, noted that the closer anything is to its cause, the greater its share in the effects. Now Christ is the first principle of grace; all grace and truth have come through him. The Blessed Virgin Mary was closest to Christ's human nature, which he received from her. Therefore, fair it was that she should receive a greater measure of God's grace, above others (*ST* III, q.27, a.5).

Duns Scotus reconciled the Immaculate Conception with Christ's universal salvific work by arguing for the prevenient redemption of Mary. Since bodily animation need not precede sanctification, was it not fitting that the Son of God should redeem his mother in this way? With the problem seemingly settled, Mary's Immaculate Conception was endorsed by the theological faculties of Paris in 1496 and Cologne in 1499. At Trent in 1546, the doctrine was still regarded as a somewhat unsettled question and therefore not to be finally resolved. At the same time, the council carefully excluded the Blessed Mother from its decree on the universality of original sin and similarly excluded her, in its decree on justification, from the statement that all men are subject to sin in their daily lives. Ultimately, of course, the Immaculate Conception was defined in 1854 by Pius IX after consultation with various bishops and theologians.

It should be said clearly, however, that for Catholics, the Immaculate Conception does not constitute an addition to the deposit of faith or new revelation. Catholics see this teaching as the work of the Holy Spirit guiding the church to a fuller understanding of revealed truth. Catholics claim that the definition of the Immaculate Conception of Mary, as regards process if not centrality, is entirely similar to the definition of the divinity of Christ by Nicea and the divinity of the Holy Spirit by the Council of Constantinople.

Catholicism regards the Marian doctrines, as much as the christological and pneumatological ones, as presenting the "same" truth as the New Testament, now viewed in a "different" way.

V. Conclusion

Catholics and Evangelicals can, seemingly, agree about much concerning Scripture, tradition, and revelation. In particular, we can agree on a role for the principle of *sola scriptura*, on a role for the principle of tradition, and on some place for a legitimate understanding of development.

At the same time, the major area of disagreement remains precisely how development is guided by the Holy Spirit. To phrase it another way, how does development remain faithful to the teaching of Scripture?

Both our agreements and disagreements we faithfully entrust to the Holy Spirit, asking him to enlighten us and to guide our deliberations.

The Role of "Tradition" in the Life and Thought of Twentieth-Century Evangelicals

JOHN WOODBRIDGE

Introduction

The fingers of the pianist flew back and forth over the keys of the piano, creating swelling crescendos of notes. With a little careful reflection, listeners could discern from the cascade of music pouring forth from the piano the simple melody of a Christian hymn, now greatly embellished by run after run up and down the keyboard. The pianist, Rudy Atwood, thrilled his generation of radio listeners with his musical virtuosity. Atwood was a member of the gospel team that participated in Charles Fuller's "Old Fashioned Revival Hour" — a program that became the staple of Sunday radio listening for millions of Americans in the 1930s, 1940s, and 1950s.

To go to the Municipal Auditorium in Long Beach, California, and sit in on a live broadcast of the "Old Fashioned Revival Hour" constituted the equivalent of a minor Evangelical pilgrimage. Your sense of anticipation would build as you watched the stage where preparations were being made for the coast-to-coast broadcast. You could see members of the "Old Fashioned Revival Hour Choir" taking their places while greeting each other. Charles Fuller (1887-1968) and Mrs. Grace Fuller were talking about last minute details right in front of you. Then, on cue, the "Old Fashioned Revival Hour Choir" opened the broadcast with a rousing, full-throated rendition of "Jesus Saves." As he did every week, Charles Fuller turned to Mrs. Fuller, whom he affectionately called "Honey," and asked her about the contents of the letters they had received from listeners during the week. Then Mrs. Fuller read inspiring selections from five or six letters on the air. Rudy Atwood played one of his popular piano arrangements. A quartet and the "Old Fashioned Revival Hour" choir interjected old favorite songs like "There's Power in the Blood" into the broadcast at carefully chosen moments. Charles Fuller delivered an evangelistic message or sermon. Now the familiar voices and music you heard when you had gathered around the radio with your family week after week were attached to real live persons up on the stage.

In 1943, the *Coronet Magazine* observed: "If you're inclined to wager that America's largest radio audiences tune in on Charlie McCarthy or Bob Hope, ignore your hunch and save your money. For while these comedians are indeed aces of the air, a couple of preachers operating on shoestring budgets are giving them a run for their money. . . . Fuller is the founding father of the 'Old Fashioned Revival Hour,' which has so many outlets there probably isn't a radio set anywhere in the United States which can't pick up his hymn singing and sermons on Sunday Nights."[1] Indeed, the program reached more than ten million people by the early 1940s, the most widely listened to radio program in the United States. By 1944, the audience had climbed to an astonishing twenty million.

If Charles Fuller were asked what was "old fashioned" or traditional about his program, he would have probably replied that he and his colleagues preached the gospel of Jesus Christ as great revivalists and faithful pastors had proclaimed it before his day. Fuller would have had a point. A century earlier, in his book, *Religion in America* (1843) Robert Baird had attempted to explain to Europeans what Americans believed. He claimed that nearly all American Protestants were *Evangelicals* and looked favorably on revivalism.[2]

Charles Fuller was convinced that his was the true "old fashioned" gospel as opposed to the siren messages of "modernists" — those powerful Protestant Liberals (1910s-1930s) who attacked the Evangelical gospel most American Protestants had believed in the nineteenth century. From their point of view, "modernists" like Shailer Matthews and Harry Emerson Fosdick felt that Christianity needed to accommodate to the advances of "modern" knowledge, especially "modern" science, with the goal of commending the faith to thoughtful church people.

More importantly, Charles Fuller believed that the gospel he preached was quite simply what the Bible taught. Brimming with confidence in the power of the gospel of Jesus Christ to transform lives, Fuller would tell his vast radio audience that Christ had died on the cross for their sins and that by

---

1. Cited in Bruce Shelley, "Charles E. Fuller: Old Fashioned Revivalist," in *More Than Conquerors*, ed. John D. Woodbridge (Chicago: Moody Press, 1992), 162-63.

2. Baird was aware of the fact that some Old School Presbyterians, Lutherans, and other Protestants did have serious reservations about the value of "revivalism."

simple faith in Christ they might be forgiven, that they could be "born again" (John 3:3-7) and have eternal life. On Sunday after Sunday, Fuller would say words like these to the five thousand people crowded into the Long Beach Municipal Auditorium: "If you want the joy of being a child of God simply by exercising your faith in Jesus Christ, raise your hand. God bless you down there. I see you, and God bless you. . . . How about those in the first balcony? I see you. . . . Raise your hands way up high. Show the Lord you mean business. . . . Yes, I see. . . . God bless you."[3]

Fuller seemed to have incontrovertible evidence that the gospel he preached was what the Bible taught. The gospel's power was amply displayed in the response to his preaching. At each service many people in the Municipal Auditorium in Long Beach responded to the evangelist's invitation by accepting Christ as their Lord and Savior. Over the years thousands more persons testified in letters to the Fullers or told pastors directly that the gospel message they had heard the evangelist preach had given them Christian hope to face trying circumstances or that they had been "born again" and now experienced a peace "that the world cannot give."

Charles Fuller's evangelistic ministry provides us with an entry door or portal into the Evangelical/Fundamentalist movement of the mid-twentieth century. This was a world of Christian believers who accepted the final authority and inerrancy of the Bible, God's Word, and cherished the powerful and sometimes flamboyant gospel preaching of evangelists like Fuller, Jack Wyrtzen, Percy Crawford, Torrey Johnson, Dawson Trotman, and a young Billy Graham.

In our own day, some fifty years later, agreement still generally exists in various streams of Evangelicalism that the Bible alone is the "final authority" for faith and practice. But during the second half of the twentieth century, "Battles for the Bible" broke out in certain quarters regarding how Scripture's final authority should be described. Not all those who call themselves "Evangelicals" today affirm the doctrine of biblical inerrancy. As for the gospel, the widespread support garnered by the statement, *The Gospel of Jesus Christ: An Evangelical Celebration* (1999), seems to indicate that Evangelicals continue to uphold its central elements (including justification by faith alone).[4]

Critics, both Evangelical and non-Evangelical, have not been stingy in proposing harsh criticisms of the Evangelical movement. They have charged

---

3. Cited in Shelley, "Charles E. Fuller," 164.

4. See *Christianity Today* (June 1999). The document, along with articles amplifying its contents, appears in the forthcoming book, *This We Believe: The Good News of Jesus Christ for the World*, ed. John N. Akers, John H. Armstrong, and John D. Woodbridge (Grand Rapids: Zondervan, 2000), 239-48.

that some Evangelical academics no longer believe in "truth," that the thinking of some Evangelicals is heavily imbued with "secularism," that church ministries are often market-driven, and that the political agendas of the "Religious Right" have diverted the energies of many Evangelicals from Christian witness, acts of love and compassion.

But in a recent book, *Evangelicalism: Embattled but Thriving,* sociologist Christian Smith deflects several of these negative judgments. He reports data from his sociological research suggesting that the Evangelical laity — the particular subject of his study — do believe the conservative Protestant doctrine they profess and that they "walk their talk" in terms of giving and caring. Regarding the Bible, 52% of Evangelicals believe that it is "literally true," 45% think it "true, not always literally," while 3% consider it "true but with errors."[5] Regarding "hope for salvation," 96% of Evangelicals believe that it is through "faith in Christ only," while only 4% believe that there are "other ways to salvation." Regarding the social implications of the gospel, Smith writes that Evangelicalism is the "strongest of all American Christian traditions, especially when it comes to explicitly religious expressions of activism."[6] Smith goes so far as to defend the controversial thesis that the Evangelical movement is the most vital Christian movement in the United States today: "Contemporary American evangelicalism is thriving. It is more than alive and well. Indeed, . . . it appears to be the strongest of the major Christian traditions in the United States today."[7]

In this discussion, we would like to analyze a topic not frequently broached in studies of twentieth-century Evangelicalism and Fundamentalism. Our central question is this: In what ways did Evangelicals of the twentieth century interact with "tradition" as they reflected upon their beliefs and perceptions of the culture in which they lived? As we shall see, potential responses to our question almost inevitably angle back towards the definition one assigns to the word *tradition.* The present study will be admittedly tentative and certainly not exhaustive in scope.

Evangelicals, "Modernity," and Roman Catholic Tradition

Upon first reflection our central question may appear singularly unpromising. For one thing, a number of scholars have portrayed "Fundamentalists,"

5. Christian Smith, *Evangelicalism: Embattled but Thriving* (Chicago: University of Chicago Press, 1998), 23.

6. Smith, *Evangelicalism,* 36.

7. Smith, *Evangelicalism,* 20.

an Evangelical subgroup, as "non-traditionalist" partisans of "modernity" (not to be viewed as synonymous with theological "modernism"). Bassam Tibi, a participant in the University of Chicago Fundamentalism Project, reiterates a premise of that project: "Fundamentalists, again, are modernists, not traditionalists, because they evaluate tradition in the light of modernity."[8] Indeed, several commentators have proposed that American Fundamentalists were as equally committed to "modernity" in epistemology (reason as a final criterion for establishing truth) as any of their foes, the "modernists" of the Twenties and Thirties. Whatever the strengths and weaknesses of this interpretation, the fact remains that notable scholars view "Fundamentalists" as essentially "non-traditionalists." Despite their rhetoric urging the return to another era that was more "Christian," the actual interest of "Fundamentalists" in listening to and being guided by "tradition" are allegedly not very great.

Then again, a number of academics who see themselves as Evangelicals, having rejected "modernity" (its underlying philosophical "Foundationalism" assumed to have been vanquished), find themselves confronted with a vexing problem: How can the meaning of the text of Scripture (if there is such a thing as meaning) be appropriated? Is its meaning ultimately dependent on the meanings brought to the text by the interpreter herself? If this is so, would not the meaning of the text change dramatically dependent upon the "traditions" of the various communities from which interpreters come? A skeptical entailment would follow to the effect that no community of interpreters could persuade another community that their interpretation is the "right one" except through the use of "political" power. Whereas certain Fundamentalists have been charged as "anti-traditionalists" due to their alleged "modernism," some of these "postmodern" Evangelicals could be viewed as "anti-traditionalists" of another kind despite their frequent allusions to "community traditions" and claim that "God's action in Jesus of Nazareth" is the ultimate criterion for truth.[9]

---

8. Bassam Tibi, *The Challenge of Fundamentalism: Political Islam and the New World Disorder* (Berkeley: The University of California Press, 1998), 14. Tibi is the coauthor of *Fundamentalisms and Society* (1993), volume 2 of the Fundamentalism Project of the American Academy of Arts and Sciences. This assessment of Fundamentalism differs widely from J. Gresham Machen's perception that conservative Christians of the 1920s actually believed a gospel that was based on Scripture and found in the creeds of the early Christian church. Daryl Hart, Machen's most recent biographer, portrays the Princetonian as a "traditionalist."

9. In *A Primer on Postmodernism* (Grand Rapids: Eerdmans, 1996), Stanley Grenz writes: "But we add although all interpretations are in some sense invalid, they cannot all

In the main, however, the more powerful impetus for "anti-traditional-ism" for many "Bible-believing" Evangelicals and Fundamentalists has come from another quarter. Often, they have not been favorably disposed to "Tradition" owing to long-standing polemical conflicts with Roman Catholicism. This negative assessment apparently stems from their conviction that "Tradition" serves as the warrant for a number of Roman Catholic doctrines they deem "unbiblical." As defenders of *sola scriptura* (Scripture alone is the sufficient and infallible rule for faith and practice), they have judged the Council of Trent's definition of "Tradition" as unacceptable. According to their reading of Trent, the Council stipulated that "Tradition" is a form of unwritten divine revelation, equal in authority with Scripture, God's written revelation; further, "Tradition" is a potential source of doctrine (faith and morals) not found in Scripture.

It is easy to understand why these Protestants read Trent this way. The fathers at Trent did declare that the saving truth and rule of conduct taught by Christ "are contained in the written books and unwritten traditions which have come down to us, having been received by the apostles from the mouth of Christ himself . . ."; moreover, they received and venerated with "the same sense of loyalty and reverence all the books of the Old and New Testament — for God alone is the author of both — together with all the traditions concerning faith and morals, as coming from the mouth of Christ or being inspired by the Holy Spirit and preserved in continuous succession in the Catholic Church."

In his essay, "Catholic Reflections on Discerning the Truth of Sacred Scripture," Professor Thomas Guarino helps Evangelicals to understand that this reading of the Council of Trent does not reflect what many contemporary Catholics think Trent actually taught. According to Guarino, contemporary Catholic theologians believe that room exists in Roman Catholic teaching for the doctrine of *sola scriptura*. He contends that Yves Congar, in particular, has "shown that the *sola scriptura* position is entirely congruent with the Council of Trent."[10]

Not only has Congar claimed that the *sola scriptura* position was congru-

---

be *equally* invalid. We believe that conflicting interpretations can be evaluated according to a criterion that in some sense transcends them all. Because we believe that 'the Word became flesh' in Jesus Christ, we are convinced that this criterion is the story of God's action in Jesus of Nazareth" (165). How the use of this criterion avoids Grenz's criticisms of Foundationalism is difficult to surmise. Moreover, are there any grounds for accepting the criterion other than dependence on a form of very strong fideism?

10. See above, Thomas Guarino, "Catholic Reflections on Discerning the Truth of Sacred Scripture," 93.

ent with the Council of Trent, he has also argued that a position similar to it finds a home in the Middle Ages: "It was generally held that Scripture contained all the truths of faith necessary for salvation. If a question was put concerning a non-scriptural doctrinal formulation, attempts were made to provide some scriptural reference which was at least equivalent or indirect."[11] As for the origins of the two-source theory in which Tradition was deemed to carry doctrine not explicitly found in Scripture, that position appears to have been a doctrinal innovation of canon lawyers in the late Middle Ages. Richard Muller, a distinguished historian in his own right, cites the work of Heiko Oberman regarding its origins: "Oberman argues that this two-source theory is evident as early as Ivo of Chartres (d. 1116) and Gratian of Bologna (d. 1158) and that they rested their view on an argument made by Basil in his treatise *On the Holy Spirit* that 'equal respect and obedience' be given 'to the written and the unwritten ecclesiastical traditions.'"[12]

With this historical background in mind, Professor Guarino's complementary claim becomes more understandable in terms of historical precedents: "Nonetheless, most Catholic theologians agree that all saving truth is contained in the written Word of God. By this they mean that the Scriptures contain, either explicitly or implicitly, all of the dogmatic teachings of the Catholic Church."[13] He does acknowledge, however, that a number of Roman Catholic Counter-Reformation apologists did read Trent as proposing a two-source theory of revelation with unwritten traditions passing on "a definite content of faith": "It is true, of course, that some theologians, especially after the Council of Trent, assumed that there was a tradition mediating a definitive content of faith which had been passed down from apostolic times and which is not found in Scripture. But as Karl Rahner says, this theory was al-

---

11. Yves M.-J. Congar, *Tradition and Traditions: An Historical and a Theological Essay,* trans. M. Naseby and T. Rainborough (New York: Macmillan, 1967), 87.

12. Richard A. Muller, *Post-Reformation Reformed Dogmatics, Volume 2: Holy Scripture: The Cognitive Foundation of Theology* (Grand Rapids: Baker Books, 1993), 40. Consult Heiko Oberman, *The Harvest of Medieval Theology: Gabriel Biel and Late Medieval Nominalism* (Grand Rapids: Eerdmans, 1967), 361-411; Oberman writes regarding Basil's *On the Holy Spirit:* "We find here for the first time explicitly the idea that the Christian owes equal respect and obedience to written and to unwritten ecclesiastical traditions whether contained in canonical writings or in a secret oral tradition handed down by the Apostles through their successors" (369). He observes: "If for clarity's sake we call the single-source or exegetical tradition of Scripture held together with its interpretation 'Tradition I' and the two sources theory which allows for an extra-biblical oral tradition 'Tradition II,' we may say that both Tradition I and Tradition II had their medieval partisans" (471).

13. Guarino, "Catholic Reflections," 94.

ways a theological construct and was certainly never a binding doctrine of the Catholic faith."[14]

Protestants will hopefully be excused if they have thought for centuries that the Council of Trent taught a two-source theory of revelation similar to the one well-schooled, Counter-Reformation Catholic apologists propounded — not as a theory but as orthodox Catholic doctrine. The Jesuit Robert Bellarmine (1542-1621), a very eminent Roman Catholic theologian of the late sixteenth century and early seventeenth, wrote: "The controversy between the heretics [Protestants] and ourselves focuses here on two points: first, when we affirm that the Scriptures do not contain the totality of necessary doctrine, for faith as well as for morals; then when we say that apart from the Word of God written, it is necessary to have his non-written Word, that is to say, divine and apostolic traditions."[15] In a catechism of 1609, the Roman Catholic Guillaume Baile, echoing Ballarmine and ostensibly Trent, provided this question and answer: "Are all things necessary for our salvation found expressly in Scripture? No. It is for this reason that Scripture sends us back to Tradition some of which being divine have as much authority as if they were written."[16] Protestant apologists of the sixteenth and seventeenth century also thought that Trent taught the view their Counter-Reformation Roman Catholic opponents defended.

And it is hostility towards this perception of the Roman Catholic teaching about "Tradition" that courses through many writings of Evangelicals and Fundamentalists during the twentieth century. An early example of this hostility appears in *The Fundamentals: A Testimony to the Truth,* a series of pamphlets distributed widely (2-3 million copies) throughout the English-speaking world. English and American theologians and pastors from various Protestant church backgrounds wrote these influential pamphlets.

14. Guarino, "Catholic Reflections," 82.

15. Often the infallibility of the Scriptures was related to the original autographs. The Roman Catholic biblical critic, Richard Simon (1638-1712), wrote: "But in that men were given the Sacred Books, as well as all other books, and in that the first Originals *(Originaux)* had been lost, it was not surprising that several changes occurred, through the passage of time as well as through the negligence of the Copyists. It is for this reason St. Augustine recommends to those who wish to study the Scripture, that above all, they apply themselves to the criticism of the Bible, and to correct the mistakes in their copies" (*Histoire critique du Vieux Testament* [Rotterdam: Reinier Leers, 1685], 1). See the studies of Randall Balmer on the widespread advocacy of the original autographs proposal among American Protestants *before* A. A. Hodge and B. B. Warfield published their study on the inspiration of the Bible.

16. Bibliotheque Nationale D 2204: Baile, *Catechisme et abbrege des controverses de nostre temps* (Paris: Pierre Chevalier, 1607), 12-20.

Historians have often compared the "irenic" discourse of these pamphlets with the harsh rhetoric of certain Fundamentalist spokespersons in the 1920s and 1930s. But an irenic tone does not characterize articles devoted to Roman Catholicism. For example, in the article, "Is Romanism Christianity?", T. W. Medhurst of Glasgow, Scotland, did little to soften his criticisms of a Tridentine definition of "Tradition": "What, then, according to it [the Council of Trent], is *the standard of truth?* It tells us that Rome receives *The Sacred Scriptures* and *'The unwritten Traditions* . . . preserved in continuous succession in the Catholic Church, with *equal affection of piety and reverence'* (Session 4): also that 'no one may dare *to interpret* the Sacred Scriptures' in a manner contrary to that 'Church *whose it is to judge respecting the true sense and interpretation* of the Sacred Scriptures'; nor may anyone interpret them 'in any manner contrary to the unanimous consent of *the fathers'* (Session 4)."[17] Medhurst believed that the Roman Catholic Church's reliance upon "unwritten Traditions" as a source for doctrine constituted a primordial reason it had departed from Christian orthodoxy. Perhaps in reference to the "anti-modernist" oaths contemporary Roman Catholic priests were obliged to sign, Medhurst minced few words in describing their alleged mindset: "The Romanist must not dare to have an opinion of his own; his mind must exist in the state of utter prostration and bondage; he must not attempt to understand the Scripture himself."

By contrast, Medhurst extolled Protestants who by yielding to the Bible's authority and it alone thereby embraced true Christianity: "*The Bible, the whole Bible, nothing but the Bible,* is the standard and the rule of Christianity. To know its meaning for ourselves, to receive its teaching, to rely on its promises, to trust in its Redeemer, to obey Him from delight of love, and to refuse to follow other teaching, is Christianity itself. But Romanism denies all this; and therefore, Romanism is not Christianity."

In "Holy Scripture and Modern Negations," James Orr, the well-known Scottish theologian, paradoxically enough, tried to overthrow the Roman Catholic doctrine of "Tradition" by appealing to "tradition." He stated that "the idea of the authority of Scripture is not younger, but older than Romanism."[18] He claimed that in writings of the church fathers the Scriptures were "treated in precisely the same way as they are used in the Biblical literature of today; namely, as the ultimate authority on the matters of which they speak."

17. T. W. Medhurst, "Is Romanism Christianity?" in *The Fundamentals: A Testimony to the Truth* (Chicago: Testimony Publishing Company, 1910-1915), vol. XI, 102-4.

18. James Orr, "Holy Scripture and Modern Negations," in *The Fundamentals,* vol. XI, 32-33.

Anti-Catholicism remained prevalent among Protestants in general during the Twenties and especially the Thirties as they became increasingly alarmed by the growing power of the Roman Catholic Church in the United States. In fact, anti-Catholicism hovered behind the creation of the National Association of Evangelicals (1942). Harold Ockenga, a key founder of the organization, cited the Roman Catholic menace along with the powerful influence of Protestant Liberalism and Secularism as principal reasons Evangelicals needed to unite together in an organization.[19] Don Sweeting's recent doctoral dissertation devoted to Evangelical-Roman Catholic relations (1960 to 1997) reiterates the supposition that not until President Kennedy's election in 1960 did noticeably better relationships begin to emerge between some Evangelical Protestants and Roman Catholics.

Nonetheless, the authoritative documents of Vatican II and the *Catechism of the Catholic Church,* appearing in the second half of the century, did little to palliate Evangelicals' basic unease regarding Roman Catholic teaching about "Tradition." Evangelicals were generally unfamiliar with the perspectives on Tradition that Professor Guarino has described with such care. Few Evangelical scholars were experts in twentieth-century Roman Catholic theology. Moreover, on the face of it the *Catechism of the Catholic Church* does seem to reiterate the two-source theory: "Sacred Tradition and Sacred Scripture make up a single sacred deposit of the Word of God. . . ."[20] In addition, the catechism continues to join the magisterium to both Scripture and Tradition in a way not acceptable to most Evangelicals: "It is clear therefore that, in the supremely wise arrangement of God, Sacred Tradition, Sacred Scripture, and the Magisterium of the Church are so connected and associated that one of them cannot stand without the others."[21]

Sensing that support for the value of tradition was absent in corners of the Evangelical world, Christopher Hall, in his *Reading Scripture with the Church Fathers,* sought to explain its usefulness within parameters laid down by the Evangelicals Thomas Oden, H. O. J. Brown, and others. Hall summarized what he thought was a common view of many Evangelical Protestants in the late 1990s: "Many view the church's history from the second to the six-

---

19. Consult Ockenga's speech, "The Unvoiced Multitudes," in *Evangelical Action! A Report of the Organization of the National Association of Evangelicals for United Action* (Boston: United Action Press, 1942). For a review of Evangelical and Roman Catholic relations, consult Don Sweeting, "From Conflict to Cooperation? Changing American Evangelical Attitudes Towards Roman Catholics: 1960-1997" (Ph.D. dissertation, Trinity Evangelical Divinity School, 1998).

20. *Catechism of the Catholic Church* (1995), 97.

21. *Catechism of the Catholic Church* (1995), 95.

teenth century as a succession of mistakes upon mistakes. For many Protestants much of church history remains a barren wasteland, a desert of error strikingly characterized by the absence of the Holy Spirit's guidance and discernment. . . . Does not the Reformers' insistence upon *sola scriptura* cast grave doubt on the church fathers' marked tendency to read Scripture in the light of the church's tradition?" For Hall, Evangelicals had deprived themselves of a major source of instruction and guidance in reading Scripture by their disdain for church history and tradition.[22]

We have seen, then, that whether at the century's beginning or at its end, many Evangelical Christians have expressed resolute opposition to the concept of Tradition as defined by their reading of the Council of Trent. Why have they been so intransigent? Protestant Christians in general have maintained the conviction that the Roman Catholic view of Tradition as defined by Trent represents a prime illustration of a doctrinal innovation by the Roman Catholic Church. As noted, this innovation consisted of the creation of a two-source theory of revelation in which "Tradition and Scripture" are deemed to have equal authority. From an Evangelical perspective *(sola scriptura)*, the two-source theory constitutes a doctrinal innovation of enormous import. Not only does it depart from the Bible's view of its own authority, but the theory abandons the stance of many of the church fathers and theologians of the Middle Ages. As James Orr pointed out, the church fathers generally accorded to Holy Scripture an "ultimate" authority superior to Tradition. Apostolic tradition had to conform to Holy Scripture.

Obviously, throughout the centuries some Roman Catholic theologians have seen things otherwise. Scripture and Tradition have equal authority. Moreover, these theologians have made the pragmatic argument that Christians will falter in their understanding of Scripture if they do not rely upon "Tradition" and the guidance of the magisterium to help them interpret Scripture. Did not Protestants twist Scripture like a wax nose in any direction to make it say whatever suited their fancy or whim? Was not this Protestant travesty a necessary entailment of "the priesthood of all believers" and "the right of private judgment"? Did not François de Sales rightfully complain long ago that the Protestants' vaunted principles for arriving at a proper in-

---

22. Christopher Hall, *Reading Scripture with the Church Fathers* (Downers Grove: InterVarsity, 1998), 13. Hall writes: "The slogan *sola Scriptura*, then, is the frank assertion and admission, as Anthony Lane puts it, 'that the church can err.' The fathers themselves insisted that the church be held accountable to Scripture. At the same time *sola Scriptura* has never meant that the only resources the Christian needs to understand God's Word well are the Bible and the Holy Spirit" (p. 13). One useful patristics resource is the Ancient Christian Commentary on Scripture edited by Thomas Oden.

terpretation of Scripture (Scripture interpreting Scripture, reliance upon the illuminating work of the Holy Spirit, the use of regenerated reason . . .) had not protected them from arriving at different interpretations of the same text?[23] Had not Protestants created new churches, further splitting the unity of Christendom? Did they not sow seeds of skepticism because no Protestant church could persuade other ones that it was the "true church," the sole possessor of true doctrine?[24] Had not Protestants fallen into these deep pits due to their neglect of Tradition and the infallible guidance of the magisterium?

Responsible Protestant scholars could not brush aside these Roman Catholic criticisms with a mere wave of the hand. These were serious charges. In response Protestant theologians often argued that the Scripture's clarity regarding matters of faith and practice did not preclude the fact that portions of Scripture remain difficult to interpret. But owing to God's gracious accommodation of Scripture to the frailty of our human understanding, we can understand sufficiently well what it says about matters of salvation and how we should live.[25] The Bible is an infallible rule of faith and practice and tells us all we need to know about salvation. Article 6 of the Thirty-Nine Articles of the Church of England reads: "Holy Scripture containeth all things necessary to salvation: so that whatsoever is not read therein, nor may be proved thereby, is not to be required of any man, that it should be believed as an article of the Faith, or be thought requisite *or* necessary to salvation."

Given the sufficiency of Scripture, Christians do not need to repair to Roman Catholic traditions or to the magisterium to find an infallible interpretation of Scripture or to be instructed about doctrines of soteriological import, ostensibly absent in Holy Scripture itself. For that matter, the magisterium is

23. Regarding the canon of the Bible, François de Sales wrote: "Now let us see what rule they have for discerning the canonical books from all of the other ecclesiastical ones. 'The witness,' they say, 'and inner persuasion of the Holy Spirit.' Oh God, what a hiding place, what a fog, what a night! We are not in this way very enlightened in so important and grave a matter." Cited in Richard Popkin, *The History of Skepticism: From Erasmus to Descartes* (New York: Harper & Row, 1968), 710.

24. On the use of arguments drawn from new pyrrhonism in Roman Catholic apologetics, see Popkin, *The History of Skepticism;* Bibliotheque Nationale D54285: François Veron, *Briefve methode pour reduire les devoyez et convaincre les ministres de la parole de Dieu reformee* (Lyon: Jean Lautret, 1618).

25. It is very important to distinguish between Socinian and Augustinian forms of accommodation. The first assumes that there will be material errors in the text due to the impress of the cultural values of the human authors upon the Bible. The second assumes that God accommodates his Word to us in ways that allow us to understand it despite our human frailties. For Augustine this form of accommodation did not necessitate that there would be errors in the text. Copiest errors existed in the text, however.

not infallible and the "Traditions" of the Roman Catholic Church are sometimes indubitably contradictory. Whereas Luther and Erasmus struggled mightily with each other over issues of free will, they did agree that church councils and popes had erred in the past and that church traditions had contradicted each other. Regarding the church fathers, Luther wrote: "But everyone, indeed, knows that at times they [the fathers] have erred as men will; therefore, I am ready to trust them only when they prove their opinions from Scripture, which has never erred."[26] Robert Coogan, an Erasmus expert, summarizes Erasmus's position as follows: "Erasmus offers dogmas decreed by councils which the Church now condemns as heretical. For Erasmus, the testimony of Scripture provides the last word; and lacking that, one relies then on the authority of the Church."[27]

In his *Disputation on Holy Scripture* (1588), William Whitaker, a Cambridge professor admired by Bellarmine, put the Protestant position this way: "We say that the Scriptures are a rule, because they contain all things necessary to faith and salvation, and more things may be found in them than absolute necessity requires. . . . But, say they [Roman Catholics], the church never errs, the pope never errs. We shall shew both assertions to be false in the proper place. We say that Scripture never errs, and therefore judge that interpretation to be the truest which agrees with Scripture."[28] Nonetheless, many Protestants did argue that the creeds of church councils were authoritative and helpful to the extent that they reflected biblical teaching.

J. I. Packer has summarized well three assumptions of Bible reading that various Evangelical communions have accepted for centuries: "The first is the essential clarity of Scripture: the thoughtful reader will be able to see what the texts are saying about what matters. The second is the ministry of the Holy Spirit, who gave the Scripture, in illuminating our hearts to understand how it touches us. . . . The third thing assumed is that the thoughts and words of the biblical writers, their indicatives and imperatives, which the Holy Spirit

26. Cited in Paul Althaus, *The Theology of Martin Luther,* trans. Robert C. Schultz (Philadelphia: Fortress Press, 1966), 6 n. 12.

27. Robert Coogan, *Erasmus, Lee and the Correction of the Vulgate: The Shaking of the Foundations* (Geneva: Droz, 1992), 47.

28. William Whitaker, *A Disputation on Holy Scripture . . . ,* ed. William Fitzgerald (Cambridge: Cambridge University Press, 1849), 476. The Roman Catholic Richard Simon (1638-1712) viewed the debate between Bellarmine and Whitaker as a very significant polemical contest: "In addition, I have gone into more detail about the sentiments which Whitaker had of Bellarmine and other Jesuits, because that ought to serve as a key for understanding countless books which have been written thereafter by Protestants of France, England, and Germany against the books of Bellarmine" (*Histoire critique du Vieux Testament,* 472).

brings home to our hearts, are demonstrably in line with the credal, confessional, and catechetical dogmas of the evangelical communions to which the Bible students belong."[29]

While attempting to answer Roman Catholic criticisms, Protestant polemicists were not reluctant to launch their own attacks on their perception of Trent's teaching about "Tradition." Protestant theologians argued that Roman Catholics used "Tradition" as an invalid authority to justify innovative doctrinal beliefs that have no warrant in Holy Scripture. In his remarkably thorough critique, *Examination of the Council of Trent* (1565-1573), Martin Chemnitz (1522-1586) analyzed eight different kinds of "tradition."[30] A learned Patristics scholar, Chemnitz reserved special criticism for those traditions (the eighth kind) "which pertain both to faith and morals and which cannot be proved with any testimony of Scripture but which the Synod of Trent nevertheless commanded to be received and venerated with the same reverence and devotion as the Scripture itself." Chemnitz claimed that Roman Catholics overthrew clear scriptural teaching by appealing to tradition's authority: "For what more comprehensive license could be thought out, to invent whatever you please freely and with impunity in the church, than if against all the very firmest and clearest arguments from Scripture the mere title of traditions may be turned like the head of the Gorgon, so that it is not right to search further if a thing is said to be tradition?" Chemnitz went further and labeled the "papalists'" arguments about traditions "a complete repertory of errors and superstition."[31]

According to Protestant apologists, Roman Catholics invented a whole series of doctrines claiming unwritten tradition as the warrant; these doctrinal innovations included the infallibility of the popes, the invocation of saints, the immaculate conception of Mary, and so on. Protestant apologists questioned further if these doctrines met the Roman Catholics' own standards for establishing authenticity. Following the teachings of Vincent of

---

29. See above, J. I. Packer, "The Bible in Use: Evangelicals Seeking Truth from Holy Scripture," 68.

30. Martin Chemnitz, *Examination of the Council of Trent Part I,* trans. Fred Kramer (St. Louis: Concordia Publishing House, 1971), 217-307. Lutherans sometimes say of Martin Chemnitz: "If the second Martin (Chemnitz) had not come, the first Martin (Luther) would scarcely have endured" (24). For Lutheran views on Scripture in the seventeenth century, see Robert Preus, *The Inspiration of Scripture: A Study of the Theology of the 17th Century Lutheran Dogmaticians* (London: Oliver & Boyd, 1957). For Roman Catholic views on tradition, see George Tavard, *La tradition au xviie siècle en France et en Angleterre* (Paris: Les Editions du Cerf, 1969).

31. Chemnitz, *Examination,* 272-73.

Lerins, Roman Catholics had accepted the principle that an authentic tradition was "that which has been believed everywhere, always, and by all."[32]

Retaining these criteria in mind, what warrant did "Tradition" actually afford for the doctrine of the immaculate conception of Mary when Aquinas, by all accounts an authoritative teacher of the church, apparently opposed the doctrine? Jaroslav Pelikan observes: "The most formidable argument that Bernard of Clairvaux and then Thomas Aquinas, as well as their later followers, had directed against the immaculate conception of Mary was the charge that if she had been conceived without original sin, she did not need redemption — which would detract from 'the dignity of Christ as the Universal Savior of all.'"[33] If Aquinas and other leading Roman Catholic teachers opposed the belief, the doctrine does not appear to have passed the bar of the Vincentian criterion, "believed . . . by all." As Professor Guarino observes, Protestants also think "the teaching goes beyond biblical attestation." Obviously, Roman Catholic scholars have thoughtful responses to these kinds of charges — responses that from their point of view are cogent and persuasive. Professor Guarino himself sets forth a Roman Catholic case for the immaculate conception of Mary, taking into account Aquinas's objection and reflections on that doctrine.[34]

Our purpose in sampling these debates is to underscore the high stakes Roman Catholics and Protestants have invested in their opposing assessments of tradition as an infallible warrant and source of doctrine. For Protestants, Roman Catholics' reliance on tradition provided a justification to add elements to their doctrine of salvation — elements quite foreign if not inimical to the Bible's actual teachings. For Roman Catholics, what Protestants condemned as theological innovations do have biblical warrant and must be considered in any responsible Roman Catholic soteriology. According to contemporary Roman Catholics, these doctrines are often based on theological trajectories issuing from the Bible, even if their textual foundation appears scant. Moreover, they claim that without tradition and the magisterium, Protestants do not have the means with which to interpret

32. *Commonitorium*, II, 3. Vincent of Lerins wanted to identify authentic tradition so that it might be used to help in interpreting Holy Scripture: "Here, it may be, some one will ask, Since the canon of Scripture is complete, and is in itself abundantly sufficient, what need is there to join to it the interpretation of the Church? The answer is that because of the very depth of Scripture all men do not place one identical interpretation upon it" (II, 2).

33. Jaroslav Pelikan, *Mary Through the Centuries: Her Place in the History of Culture* (New Haven: Yale University Press, 1996), 195.

34. Guarino, "Catholic Reflections," 100-101.

Scripture in a way that is faithful to the doctrine of the Roman Catholic Church.

We have reached the point in our discussion where a first response to our central question is possible. And the response looks very much like a platitude — something we might have anticipated. For centuries, long-standing differences of perspective regarding the relationship between Scripture and tradition have divided Roman Catholics and Evangelicals. During the twentieth century, these divisions continued to influence the thinking of American Evangelicals and Fundamentalists towards tradition. In our own day the vast majority of Evangelical Protestants object to the concept of tradition if it is explained to them in the terms of the Council of Trent.

Professor Guarino's perspectives regarding how certain post–Vatican II Roman Catholic scholars view Trent and *sola scriptura* are not apparently widely known in the Evangelical community. He proposes that both Roman Catholics and Evangelicals believe in *sola scriptura* and both look to the Holy Spirit for guidance in biblical interpretation. At the same time, he understands that official Roman Catholic doctrine and the doctrine of Evangelicals are not in agreement on significant teachings. Perhaps for this reason, Professor Guarino asks, ". . . how does development remain faithful to Scripture?"[35] His question forces us to ask if the interdependent relation of the authority of Holy Scripture, Tradition, and of the magisterium in Roman Catholicism's theology so influences their understanding of *sola scriptura* for the Roman Catholic Church that its dogmatic definition is really quite removed from what Evangelical Christians have meant by *sola scriptura*. Evangelicals believe that the Bible alone is their final authority. Their definition excludes tradition and the magisterium as interdependent authorities with Holy Scripture.

Evangelical Identity and Tradition

Whatever the level of accuracy of our first response regarding Evangelicals' attitudes towards tradition as defined by Trent, the answer leaves much unsaid. It does not advance our understanding in any substantial fashion regarding the ways tradition has sometimes shaped the identity of Evangelicals and acted as an authority for them.

If we define the word *tradition* in a more flexible fashion, not isolating its definition to a Tridentine formulation, we discover that Evangelicals have had

35. Guarino, "Catholic Reflections," 101.

beliefs, customs, and practices that have functioned as their own "traditions" even if they are sometimes not acknowledged as such.[36] Do not many Evangelicals today speak of their beliefs as faithfully representing "The Reformed Tradition," or "The Lutheran Tradition," or the "Pentecostal Tradition"?[37] Is it not the case that in certain Evangelical churches fierce battles have erupted between those who favor "traditional worship styles" and those who champion "contemporary worship styles"?[38] Do not Evangelical church members sometimes resort to the expression, "This is not the way we have traditionally done this in our church," to trump an appeal for reform in the life of the church — a reform that appears well-grounded in Holy Scripture?

The point does not need belaboring. Some "traditions" with a small "t" have informed the thought and practice of Evangelicals. And it must be confessed that Evangelicals can become so attached to past practices, customs, and beliefs that they sometimes resist needed reform even when these "traditions" manifestly are inimical to biblical teaching. During a recent interview on the "Larry King Show" (May 18, 2000), Anne Graham Lotz, Billy Graham's daughter, pointed out how certain unfortunate "traditions" had long staying power within the life of certain Evangelical churches. She urged that these negative traditions (abuses) be reformed in the light of the teachings of Holy Scripture.

---

36. H. O. J. Brown writes: "If we look at the free churches in the Protestant communions, even those which claim to have 'no creed but the Bible' show that they have plenty of tradition, though they may formally disdain the concept" ("Proclamation and Preservation: The Necessity and Temptations of Church Tradition," in *Reclaiming the Great Tradition*, ed. James S. Cutsinger [Downers Grove: InterVarsity Press, 1997], 83). Our discussion will be based in part on the following definitions of Tradition: 1. ". . . an inherited, established, or customary pattern of thought, action, or behavior (as a religious practice or a social custom)"; ". . . the handing down of information, beliefs, and customs by word of mouth or by example from one generation to another without written instruction"; ". . . cultural continuity in social attitudes, customs, and institutions" *(Merriam Webster Collegiate Dictionary);* or, ". . . the transmission of customs or beliefs from generation to generation" *(New Oxford Dictionary of English).*

37. George Marsden writes about the power of religious traditions to shape (Evangelical and Fundamentalist) institutions and the lives of individuals: "So the heritages themselves exercise implied authority by providing accepted traditions of interpreting experience and recognizing authorities. Thus the history of institutions and of the people in them must always be considered in the context of the movements and traditions to which they are remarkably bound" *(Reforming Fundamentalism: Fuller Seminary and the New Evangelicalism* [Grand Rapids: Eerdmans, 1987], 3).

38. Donald E. Miller, *Reinventing American Protestantism: Christianity in the New Millennium Inside Calvary, Vineyard, & Hope Chapel* (Berkeley: University of California Press, 1997), 90-91.

More than they sometimes care to acknowledge, then, the identity of "Bible-believing" Evangelicals sometimes has been fashioned in considerable measure by powerful cultural forces and by powerful "traditions." Some of the "traditions" have been very supportive of biblically-derived Evangelical beliefs whereas others have exerted a destructive influence.

Indeed, to talk about "Evangelical" identity takes us into the multi-faceted world of conservative Protestantism with its denominational coalitions like the National Association of Evangelicals; independent churches and mega-churches; thousands of para-church groups; theological societies, publishing houses, and journals; Bible colleges, liberal arts colleges, and universities; and television and radio networks. It draws us into a world where we find Evangelical Methodists and Episcopalians who highly esteem "church tradition" as a legitimate authority in shaping their theology and Independent Baptists who often have little good to say about "Tradition," liturgies, and the like. The centuries' old debates regarding what is legitimate in worship lingered into the twentieth century: Should worship patterns only follow the explicit teachings of Scripture or can they include practices and "traditions" of long standing, neither explicitly taught nor forbidden by Holy Scripture?

It has been proposed that nothing seriously theological holds the Evangelical movement together, its various subgroups and "traditions" being so disparate, its teachings so drained of actual biblical content by cultural influences. Some commentators have proposed that Evangelicals, if they are unified at all, are brought together by appreciation for certain worship styles, warm feelings of spirituality, commitment to voluntary societies, desires "to save America" through national revivals and the like — but certainly not by doctrine. But these kinds of critical assessments are not persuasive. They overlook the fact that many Evangelicals and Fundamentalists of the twentieth century did share a good number of common "fundamental" theological beliefs and do so today as Christian Smith's analysis demonstrates. Among these are the full deity and full humanity of Christ, the Virgin Birth, justification by faith alone, the substitutionary Atonement of Christ, the bodily resurrection of Christ, the Second Coming of Christ, and for much of the century, the inerrancy of Holy Scripture.[39] In distinction from Evangelicals, many Fundamentalists expanded the core of indispensable beliefs beyond these to include "ecclesiastical separation" — a doctrine they thought would preserve doctrinal purity. Moreover, for George Dollar, an "insider" historian of Fundamentalism, it was indispensable for true Fundamentalist identity that a

39. Marsden, *Reforming Fundamentalism*, 4.

person be "dispensational" in theology.[40] The Fundamentalist should also be "militant" in the defense of the faith. In an oft-cited description (1920), Curtis Lee Laws defined a Fundamentalist as one who would do "battle royal" for the "fundamentals." Indeed, Fundamentalists did take very firm stands against "modernism" and the "Social Gospel." They were often suspicious of "Evangelicals" like Carl F. H. Henry, who in writing *The Uneasy Conscience of Modern Fundamentalism* (1947) called conservative Protestant Christians to greater social and political engagement.

Despite shared doctrinal commitments, Fundamentalists and Evangelicals of the twentieth century displayed such a range of disparate traits that historian Timothy Smith described Evangelicalism as a mosaic or kaleidoscope. Not only did differences in theology, worship styles, and church governance exist between Episcopalian Evangelicals and Independent Baptists, but issues of racial prejudice and patterns of economic and social stratification also contributed to the separation of members of Afro-American, Hispanic, Asian, and white Evangelical churches from each other. Then again, a baffling number of "Fundamentalisms" existed in the twentieth century. Members of one Fundamentalist group often looked to a powerful leader (a magisterium of sorts) to give guidance on what to think about the Christian faith, the larger world beyond the group, as well as other Fundamentalist leaders. William Bell Riley, an early Fundamentalist leader, had a fairly ecumenical attitude towards Christians remaining in the mainline denominations, whereas Carl McIntire, likewise a Fundamentalist, championed a more radical form of biblical "separatism." In disputes between Fundamentalists, the opposing parties often accused each other of "compromise" with worldliness, with "Liberalism," or of consorting with Evangelicals or with "Neo-Evangelicals." Especially after 1957, Fundamentalists practiced "second degree separatism" in an attempt to maintain purity of doctrine. Some of them feared that Evangelicals were intent upon wooing the Fundamentalist faithful to the "compromised" banner of Evangelicalism. The Evangelicals were thought to be "taking over" the reins in traditionally Fundamentalist Bible schools, colleges, denominations, and presses. Divisions ensued between Fundamentalists and the "New Evangelicals" — divisions made all the more painful because many of those in the parties had been such close personal friends. Edward J. Carnell's statement of 1959 that "Fundamentalism was orthodoxy gone cultic" did not ease tensions. As Fundamentalists rigorously pursued the

---

40. For a discussion of Dispensationalism, see Timothy Weber, *Living in the Shadow of the Second Coming: American Premillennialism 1875-1982* (Grand Rapids: Zondervan, 1983), 16-24, 45-51, 242-44.

principle of "second degree separation" — a premise not much in evidence in the Fundamentalism of the 1920s — their own movement fractured time and time again, Fundamentalist separating from Fundamentalist.[41]

As for Evangelicals, Bruce Shelley has listed seven "traditions" in the movement: "1. Evangelicals in the Reformation tradition, primarily Lutheran and Reformed Christians 2. Wesleyan evangelicals, such as the Church of the Nazarene 3. Pentecostal and charismatic evangelicals such as the Assemblies of God 4. Black evangelicals, with their own distinctive witness to the gospel 5. The counterculture churches (sometimes called peace Churches), such as the evangelical Quakers and Mennonites 6. Several traditionally white Southern denominations, led by the Southern Baptists 7. The spiritual heirs of Fundamentalism found in independent church and many para-church agencies."[42] In this world of conservative Protestantism, the task of defining and identifying who was a "true" Fundamentalist, Evangelical, Wesleyan, Calvinist, Lutheran, Pentecostal, or Mennonite periodically provoked passionate verbal interchanges. To demonstrate that one was a "true believer," a person whose "faithfulness" was being questioned often attempted to use "tradition" to prove that his or her beliefs were in line with those of an earlier well-known stalwart of a particular movement.

Little wonder that the historiography of Evangelicalism and Fundamentalism is complex and the object of rather heated debate.[43] Little wonder that

---

41. In his autobiography William Bell Riley, a founder of the World's Christian Fundamentals Association (1919), spoke of his friendship with a number of modernists. According to Douglas Huffman, "By differentiating between the man and his views, Dr. Riley retained the friendship, and, at times, the ardent admiration of not a few of the modernistic leaders. . . . On more than one occasion Dr. Riley has in the same breath expressed his contempt for the *theology* but ardent admiration for the *personalities* of such men as Professor Shailer Matthews and Dr. Harry Emerson Fosdick." Douglas S. Huffman, "Reformulating Fundamentalism: The Fundamentalism of William Bell Riley (1861-1947)," Doctoral Seminar Paper, Trinity Evangelical Divinity School (December 5, 1990), 27.

42. Bruce Shelley, "Evangelicalism," *Dictionary of Christianity in America* (Downers Grove: InterVarsity Press, 1990), 416.

43. For "insider" books on Fundamentalism, consult George Dollar, *A History of Fundamentalism in America* (Greenville, SC: Bob Jones University Press/Unusual Publications, 1973); David O. Beale, *In Pursuit of Purity: American Fundamentalism Since 1850* (Greenville, SC: Unusual Publications, 1986). For Evangelicalism, see John Fea, "American Fundamentalism and Neo-Evangelicalism: A Bibliographic Survey," *Evangelical Journal* 11 (Spring 1993): 21-30; Douglas Sweeney, "The Strange Schizophrenia of Neo-Evangelicalism: A Bibliography," *Evangelical Studies Bulletin* 8 (Spring 1991): 6-8; Norris A. Magnuson and William G. Travis, *American Evangelicalism: An Annotated Bibliography* (West Cornwall, CT: Locust Hill Press, 1997). For Pentecostalism, see Cecil M. Robeck, "The Pentecostal Movements in the U.S.: Recent Bibliography," *Evangelical Studies Bulletin* 3 (1986); Charles Edwin

members of the media and secular academics often found it a confusing and perplexing task to make sense of the thought and life of variegated "Evangelical" and Fundamentalist groups. Perhaps for this reason, outside commentators often employed words like *Fundamentalist* and *Evangelical* and *Pentecostal* and *Religious Right* in stereotypical fashions — ways that did not actually capture the self-perceptions of the persons allegedly described. Even in the 1920s William Bell Riley complained that "modernists" and members of the press described Fundamentalists in terms that did not correspond to what they actually believed or how they read the Bible.[44] He was particularly disappointed that critics frequently misrepresented what it meant for Fundamentalists to read the Bible "literally." The scholarly world awaits a fresh reception history of twentieth-century Fundamentalism and Evangelicalism that takes seriously the participants' own self-perceptions of who they were, what they believed, and what they experienced, rather than depending so significantly on the perceptions of their critics.

The general historiography of Evangelicalism and Fundamentalism is linked to the specific historiographies of conservative Lutherans, Pentecostals, Southern Baptists, black Bible believers, and others — some of whom, as Bruce Shelley noted, claimed by the end of the century that they were "Evangelicals" or, on the contrary, protested that they should not be viewed as "Evangelicals." For example, until recent decades, Southern Baptists on occasion dismissed the word *Evangelical,* as a "Yankee" expression. But today, some Southern Baptists will describe themselves as "Evangelical Christians" as well as Southern Baptists. In the 1970s, during debates related to biblical authority and the rights of conscience, "Moderates" and "Conservatives" in Southern Baptist circles employed the expression *Fundamentalist,* loading it with favorable or unfavorable connotations depending on their theological and personal loyalties.[45] Elsewhere, many black conservative Protestants became increasingly wary of the name "Evangelical" or "Fundamentalist,"

Jones, *A Guide to the Study of the Pentecostal Movement* (2 vols.) (Metuchen, NJ: Scarecrow Press, 1983); Edith L. Blumhofer, *Restoring the Faith: The Assemblies of God, Pentecostalism and American Culture* (Champaign, IL: University of Illinois Press, 1993); Donald Dayton, *The Theological Roots of Pentecostalism* (Metuchen, NJ: Scarecrow Press, 1987). For comparative studies of Evangelical movements in different lands, consult George A. Rawlyk and Mark A. Noll, eds., *Amazing Grace: Evangelicalism in Australia, Britain, Canada, and the United States* (Grand Rapids: Baker, 1993), 401-9.

44. For Riley's understanding of what Fundamentalism actually was, see especially William Bell Riley, *What is Fundamentalism?* (Minneapolis: n.p., 1927).

45. See studies by David Dockery and Michael Nolan on the use of terms such as these and others.

thinking these terms denoted forms of "white" Christianity. As William Bentley suggested in 1975, some black Christians preferred to be called "Bible believers."[46] Pentecostal and charismatic Christians, though frequently designated as "Fundamentalists" in the press, historically had uncomfortable relations with Fundamentalism. Dispensational Fundamentalists were often very critical of Pentecostal and charismatic Christians for their beliefs in the gifts of divine healing and speaking in tongues. Some Pentecostals claimed that they read Scripture with a "Spirit"-oriented hermeneutic that differed from more "rationalistic," propositional approaches used by Fundamentalists or Evangelicals.

It would take us too far afield to review the vast historiographical literatures devoted to Evangelicalism, Fundamentalism, Pentecostalism, and the various churches. But a few points should be mentioned because they help explain why it was that some Evangelicals who had not been prone to study their own histories or traditions began to sense the compelling need to do so.

Professor George Marsden has provided what many scholars accept as a standard definition of *Fundamentalism:* a "militantly anti-modernist Protestant evangelicalism."[47] This definition appears quite salient for the period up to approximately 1960. Many "Fundamentalists" used categories of thought formed in the heated controversies of the Twenties and Thirties with modernists in assessing theological controversies of the Forties and Fifties.

Note that Professor Marsden described *Fundamentalism* as a form of *Evangelicalism.* Until the late 1950s many conservative Protestants used the two words interchangeably, believing that while their differences were about strategies for interacting with the "world" (Fundamentalists: separate from the world and thereby retain doctrinal and moral purity; Evangelicals: penetrate the world by preaching the gospel and engaging the "world" intellectually), they at least shared a common commitment to "fundamentals" of the faith and a belief in the inerrancy of Holy Scripture.

As late as 1975, Professor Martin Marty argued that the belief in biblical inerrancy was one common doctrine that Evangelicals and Fundamentalists shared together.[48] But the impact of the historiography of Ernest Sandeen

---

46. William Bentley, "Bible Believers in the Black Community," *The Evangelicals: What They Believe, Who They Are, Where They Are Changing,* ed. David F. Wells and John D. Woodbridge (Nashville: Abingdon, 1975), 108-21. Bentley was President of the National Black Evangelical Association.

47. This is Joel Carpenter's assessment of Marsden's definition (Carpenter, *Revive Us Again: The Reawakening of American Fundamentalism* [New York: Oxford University Press, 1997], 5).

48. Martin Marty wrote: "Even in the midst of heated polemics, evangelicals and fun-

and George Marsden apparently convinced Professor Marty and others to reconsider this point. A powerful new historiography emerged in which it was affirmed that a belief in biblical inerrancy constituted the doctrine *par excellence* of Fundamentalism; it was not a cardinal belief of Evangelicalism. This historiography proposed that in 1881 the Princeton Seminary professors, A. A. Hodge and B. B. Warfield, allegedly created the innovative doctrine of inerrancy in the original autographs as a means to avoid the impact of Higher Criticism.[49] Recent research by Clinton Ohlers, however, has revealed that contemporary theologians of the 1880s and 1890s who criticized the doctrine of biblical inerrancy believed they were overthrowing the traditional Protestant doctrine of Scripture, not a new doctrine whose provenance was recent (1881). Mark Noll has pointed out that "for the first two-thirds of the century . . . it is hard to distinguish the Princeton views on the Bible [infallibility in the original autographs] from those of the American evangelical world at large."[50] For that matter, as Timothy George has reminded us, contemporary Roman Catholics of the late nineteenth century also held the doctrine of biblical inerrancy. Both Protestants and Roman Catholics generally assumed that biblical inerrancy had been a central teaching of the Christian churches. For example, in 1518 Johannes Eck chided Erasmus for proposing that Matthew made a mistake (changing one word for another) due to a lapse of memory. Eck indicated that no Christian would accept Erasmus's contention: "Listen, dear Erasmus: do you suppose any Christian will patiently endure to be told that the evangelists in their Gospels made mistakes? If the authority of Holy Scripture at this point is shaky, can any other passage be free

---

damentalists then tried to remind themselves that they agreed on 'the fundamentals.' More often than not they have boiled down to five 'doctrines that were declared to be essential' by several conservative gatherings: 'the inerrancy of Scripture, the virgin birth of Christ, the atonement of Christ, the resurrection of Christ, and the miracle-working power of Christ'" ("Tensions Within Contemporary Evangelicalism," in *The Evangelicals: What They Believe, Who They Are, Where They Are Changing,* 173).

49. See Ernest Sandeen, *The Roots of Fundamentalism: British and American Millenarianism, 1800-1930* (1970; Grand Rapids: Baker, 1978), 126-31; George Marsden, *Fundamentalism and American Culture: The Shaping of Twentieth-Century Evangelicalism: 1870-1925* (New York: Oxford University Press, 1980), 109-88; Martin Marty, *Modern American Religion, Volume 1: The Irony of It All, 1893-1919* (Chicago: The University of Chicago Press, 1986), 232-37; Carpenter, *Revive Us Again,* 5 ("Fundamentalism was a historically new religious movement with distinctive beliefs, notably premillennialism and the verbal inerrancy of the Bible"); Nathan Hatch and Mark Noll, eds., *The Bible in America: Essays in Cultural History* (New York: Oxford University Press, 1982).

50. Mark Noll, "The Princeton Theology," in *Reformed Theology in America: A History of Its Modern Development,* ed. David F. Wells (Grand Rapids: Baker, 1997), 27.

from the suspicion of error? A conclusion drawn by St. Augustine from an elegant chain of reasoning."[51]

In any case, as the new historiography on the matter took hold in scholarly circles in the 1980s and 1990s, persons who upheld the doctrine of inerrancy could find themselves labeled as a Fundamentalist, even if they personally described themselves as Evangelicals. The aforementioned Fundamentalism Project of the University of Chicago, directed by Professors Martin Marty and Scott Appleby, added its substantial authority to this new historiography by identifying the doctrine of biblical inerrancy as a doctrinal innovation of the 1880s and an indubitable marker of Fundamentalism. An historiographical struggle of sorts that had already broken out earlier in the 1970s over the definition of Evangelicalism and Fundamentalism now continued to expand into new theatres. Historians of various backgrounds began to proffer competing story-lines regarding the histories ("traditions?") of Fundamentalism, Evangelicalism, the Wesleyan movement, the Pentecostal movement, the Southern Baptists, the Missouri Synod Lutherans, and other groups.[52]

Debates over the nature of biblical authority, then, helped provoke this new interest in discovering what particular forces, social, philosophical, or otherwise, had been at work in shaping the thinking of particular groups. Some scholars attempted to demonstrate that their own churches (the Church of the Nazarene, for example) had been negatively affected by Fundamentalism's "leavening" influence and therefore had adopted the doctrine of inerrancy — a doctrine not really reflective of the beliefs of the earliest founders of the movement. These debates also prompted Evangelical Christians to consider in a more sustained fashion what the witness of earlier Christians upholding the "the central tradition" of the Christian churches had been regard-

---

51. Erasmus, *The Correspondence of Erasmus,* ed. Peter Bietenholz (Toronto: University of Toronto Press, 1979), vol. 5, 289-90. The inerrancy position was a common one in the Middle Ages as well. Benedicta Ward and G. R. Evans write: "The general presumption was that even if a writer was capable of error God would not allow mistakes to creep into the text. So that did not diminish the Bible's high authority. Another kind of mistake did arise and had to be allowed for. This was the error not of authorship but of copying" ("The Bible in the Middle Ages," *The World History of Christianity,* ed. Adrian Hastings [Grand Rapids: Eerdmans, 1999], 119).

52. When David Wells and the present author decided to edit a volume on Evangelicalism in the early 1970s, we believed that we knew what Evangelicalism was. Thus we gave our book a title that today appears overstated: *The Evangelicals: What They Believe, Who They Are, Where They Are Changing* (1975). Carl F. H. Henry came out with a book the next year that captured far better the emerging historiographical struggle beginning to wash over the Evangelical movement. Henry's book was entitled: *Evangelicals in Search of Identity* (Waco, TX: Word, 1976).

ing the Bible's authority. In 1979, for example, Jack Rogers and Donald McKim published *The Authority and Interpretation of the Bible: An Historical Approach* in which they argued that the doctrine of biblical inerrancy is not a belief found in the central tradition of the Christian churches.[53] Various rejoinders were written challenging their reading of church history.[54]

Often absent in these controversies was an explicit analysis of what authority the authors gave to the witness or testimonies of the church fathers, medieval theologians, or the Reformers in confirming their historical analysis. Without providing a detailed rationale, Evangelical historians generally assumed that if it could be proven that their beliefs about the Bible were in line with those of certain Reformers or certain church fathers, they had demonstrated the "orthodoxy" of the beliefs. Their underlying assumption was apparently this: God, the Holy Spirit, superintended the development of doctrine within Christ's church. Thus the creeds and beliefs of earlier Christians can serve as "witnesses" *(Formula of Concord)* to right doctrine. But these witnesses are fallible. Consequently the ultimate witness to the authority of the Scripture is the witness of the Holy Spirit within the believing Christian.

Besides the impact of these controversies, the alleged collapse of Foundationalism, the ensuing disputes over the merits of "modernism" and "postmodernism," the hold of unsettling proposals regarding hermeneutics by Richard Rorty, Stanley Fish, and Jacques Derrida on the larger academic community, the historical reading of Roman Catholic scholars like Congar and Rahner regarding the relationship between Tradition and Scripture, ecumenical dialogues between Pentecostals and Roman Catholics, Southern Baptists and Roman Catholics, and Lutherans and Roman Catholics, among multiple other factors, obliged a number of Evangelical scholars in the 1990s to consider new sets of issues not on the intellectual drawing boards in the 1940s and 1950s.[55]

At the end of the century, as Christian Smith tells us, the vast majority

---

53. Jack Rogers and Donald McKim, *The Authority and Interpretation of the Bible: An Historical Approach* (New York: Harper & Row, 1979).

54. A flurry of books and articles appeared. The Council on Biblical Inerrancy sponsored a number of replies to the Rogers and McKim proposal. The present author wrote one as well, *Biblical Authority: A Critique of the Rogers/McKim Proposal* (Grand Rapids: Zondervan, 1982).

55. For a review of many of these issues, consult Charles Colson, *How Now Shall We Live?* (Wheaton, IL: Tyndale House, 1999); Grenz, *A Primer on Postmodernism;* D. A. Carson, *The Gagging of God: Christianity Confronts Pluralism* (Grand Rapids: Zondervan, 1995).

of Evangelical laity continued to believe Scripture to be wholly truthful and an infallible rule for faith and practice. Many Evangelicals remained resolute in their hostility to tradition if defined in their perception of Tridentine terms.

Nonetheless, a number of influential Evangelical academics argued that a stand-alone doctrine of *sola scriptura* made little sense from the perspective of insights gained from "postmodern" hermeneutical theories. Scripture can only be read appropriately in community. A text-based doctrine of *sola scriptura* that excluded the reader's own role and that of his or her community in shaping Scripture's "meaning" and significance is not viable.[56] Still other Evangelical academics found Kevin Vanhoozer's rejoinder to this argument persuasive. On the last page of *The Bible, the Reader and the Morality of Literary Knowledge: Is There a Meaning in This Text?* (1998), Vanhoozer concludes a sophisticated and nuanced analysis and critique of postmodern hermeneutical theories with this considered judgment: "Ultimately, Luther stands for the possibility that the text and its meaning remain independent of the process of interpretation and hence have the ability to transform the reader. Indeed, one reliable indicator of good Protestant hermeneutics is whether it allows reformation. . . . The church should be that community of humbly confident interpreter believers whose consciences, seared and sealed by the Spirit, are captive to the Word, and whose commentaries and communities seek progressively to embody the meaning *and* significance of the text."[57] The Bible's authority as a written revelation of God, then, is independent of our fallible attempts to interpret Scripture's contents. Certain forms of a community-based approach to scriptural interpretation force the intrusion of the interpreter's own perspectives into the interpretive process in a manner ruinous to the doctrine of *sola scriptura*. To the detriment of the Bi-

---

56. For the impact of the alleged collapse of Foundationalism on Evangelical faith, see Amos Yong, "The Demise of Foundationalism and the Retention of Truth: What Evangelicals Can Learn from C. S. Peirce," *Christian Scholar's Review* 29:3 (Spring 2000): 563-88. Yong writes: "The problem is that the death of foundationalism appears to have relativized all truth claims, resulting in a debilitation if not paralysis of theological thinking. Because of their insistence on the importance of truth, some evangelicals have continued to reject the validity of the anti-foundationalist critique. . . . I do not think that evangelicals can remain intellectually viable if the former strategy of resistance continues, nor do I think that the latter postliberalism *by itself* is an adequate methodological response, since it in turn poses new dilemmas" (563-64). For a defense of a propositional view of truth, see: Harold A. Netland, *Dissonant Voices: Religious Pluralism and the Question of Truth* (Grand Rapids: Eerdmans, 1991).

57. Kevin Vanhoozer, *The Bible, the Reader, and the Morality of Literary Knowledge: Is There a Meaning in This Text?* (Grand Rapids: Zondervan, 1998), 467.

ble's final authority, the authority of the interpreter's personal perspectives and that of her community's traditions are greatly augmented and largely determine what the biblical texts may mean and their significance (at least for her and her community).

Other Evangelicals, Thomas Oden among them, while acknowledging the final authority of Scripture and defending *sola scriptura,* encouraged Evangelical Christians to consider the "consensual" views of the church fathers regarding faith and practice to help them gain a better understanding of Scripture. A number of Evangelical and Roman Catholic scholars met on occasion to discuss in what ways if any "The Great Tradition" thought to be shared by both groups could serve to help interpret Holy Scripture.[58]

In a word, various Evangelical views of the relation between Scripture and tradition existed in the twentieth century. The doctrine of *sola scriptura,* however, remained the dominant stance of Evangelical Christians throughout the century.

Evangelical Views of Tradition

A. Pietistic, Non-Confessional Evangelicalism and Fundamentalism until 1960

In many regards Charles Fuller, an activist evangelist, represents well a pietistic, experiential, non-confessional form of Evangelicalism and Fundamentalism that was attractive to millions of Americans in the first six decades of the twentieth century. Charles Fuller had little interest in "tradition" as an authoritative revelation from God. Nevertheless, he was "traditional" in the sense that he wanted to preach the "old-fashioned" gospel as he believed other faithful men of God had preached it before him. Millions of Americans liked Fuller's approach. During the traumatic days of World War II, one East Coast columnist noted that he believed it "restful to hear an old-fashioned preacher preach old-time religion in the good old-fashioned way."[59] Joel Carpenter proposes that Fuller's interest in upholding an old-

58. Cutsinger, ed., *Reclaiming the Great Tradition.* Robert Webber has written many books in which he encourages Evangelical Christians to use the sources available to them in church traditions in their worship.

59. Carpenter, *Revive Us Again,* 139. Carpenter believes the radio audience of the program may have reached fifteen to twenty million persons as early as 1939. With great insight he analyzes an aspect of the program's appeal: "So what was the appeal of the *Old Fashioned Revival Hour?* Part of its charm must have been its intimacy. The Fullers, Rudy,

fashioned gospel was associated with his desire to restore a "mythic" Christian America by inducing a national revival.

Like many other businessmen turned para-church leader, Charles Fuller did not pay much attention to the doctrinal distinctions of particular Protestant denominations. Rather like Torrey Johnson (Youth for Christ) and Dawson Trotman (Navigators), and other younger founders of para-church organizations, he had a burning desire to see persons converted to Christ. Consequently, he preached a simple gospel message in terms that laypersons could comprehend. He wanted people to understand the gospel so that they might be "born again," whatever their denominational affiliation or lack thereof. Experiencing a personal relationship with Christ was far more important than acquiring "head" knowledge of theology and the history of doctrine. The "truthfulness" of the Christian faith could be confirmed by the believer's personal experience of Christ. A favorite chorus in popular pietistic Evangelicalism was "He Lives." It includes these words: "You ask me how I know He lives, He lives within my heart."

Charles Fuller and many other American Fundamentalists and Evangelicals of the 1930s, 1940s, and 1950s had little doubt that they understood what the gospel was. These activist Christians were convinced that what they believed about the gospel and the faith was what the Bible taught, plain and simple.

At the same time, they had the conviction that their basic beliefs were well in line with what some earlier faithful Christians had also believed. Among others, their list of the loyal exponents of the gospel in the history of the Christian churches included Dwight L. Moody, Charles Finney, Charles Spurgeon, Jonathan Edwards, John, Charles and Susannah Wesley, George Whitefield, Menno Simons, John Calvin, Martin Luther, John Wycliffe, and Augustine.

But if the truth be known, many Evangelicals and Fundamentalists were not much inclined to cite their own past stalwarts or reference ancient creeds and Reformation confessions in explicating their faith or justifying its claims. Nonetheless, Evangelical and Fundamentalist children read engrossing books and sat on the floor listening to records on phonographs in which the heroic deeds of missionaries like Adoniram Judson were recounted in a mesmerizing manner. Pastors sometimes added inspirational punch to their sermons by recounting the harsh travails and glorious triumphs of "great" Christian heroes of the past or by rehearsing colorful testimonies of certain well-known

---

and the quartet were like family, and they came into millions of homes at one of the most commonly observed family hours, Sunday evening" (138).

personages to demonstrate the power of the gospel to change lives. In general, however, these Evangelicals and Fundamentalists were quite disposed to by-pass church history in order to talk directly about Christ's birth, miracles, sacrificial death on the cross for sinners, resurrection, and second coming and to tell Bible stories about Old Testament figures like Adam and Eve, Noah, Abraham, and David and New Testament figures like Mary and Joseph, John and Peter, and to trace Paul's evangelistic missionary journeys as recorded in the book of Acts. Moreover, in popular, pietistic Evangelicalism and Fundamentalism, the Apostles' Creed was read on occasion in church services or studied in confirmation classes. Relatively little concern existed, however, to check to see if contemporary Evangelical and Fundamentalist beliefs conformed to the great creeds or liturgies of the past. Any such endeavor seemed somewhat beside the point.

What served as a measure for good preaching and teaching were not the creeds or confessions, but whether or not the preacher or teacher had in fact "rightly divided the Word of Truth" and whether he had "searched the Scriptures" properly before he preached. It also helped if the preacher or teacher was a spellbinding orator, and if possible, entertaining.

In popular, pietistic Evangelicalism and Fundamentalism, it was assumed that most anyone could read the Scriptures for himself and herself and basically understand the essential truths of the gospel. In an article entitled "The Scriptures" published in *The Fundamentals*,[60] A. C. Dixon, for example, spelled out the several ways Christians study the Bible. He indicated that a precondition for "searching" the Scriptures was spiritual discernment: "Every Christian with the Bible in hand is rich whether he knows it or not. Let him search and find hidden treasures. This search implies sight and light. There is need of spiritual discernment: 'The natural man discerneth not the things of God.'" Dixon claimed that any "method of searching is good, though some may be better than others."[61] Whereas the "grasshopper method by which we take a word or subject and jump from one place to another, collating the texts which have the word or subject in them" was not to be despised (Moody had used it with great success and been blessed of God), Dixon preferred "the sectional method": ". . . one begins at a certain place and goes through paragraph, chapter or book, gathering and classifying every thought." Dixon also cited with approval Luther's approach to Bible reading. For Dixon, the purpose of this Bible reading and study were twofold: "1. That we may have right

---

60. A. C. Dixon, "The Scriptures," *The Fundamentals: A Testimony for the Truth*, vol. 5, 72-80.
61. Dixon, "The Scriptures," 77.

thinking about eternal life . . . ; 2. That we may learn of Christ." He concluded with an admonition to his readers: " 'Search the Scriptures' for a vision of the Lord Jesus Christ."[62]

Stirred by the long-standing Protestant conviction that individuals could read and understand Scripture on their own, many Evangelicals and Fundamentalists were moved to engage in tract distribution. In fact, the distribution of "Gospel Tracts" heavily sprinkled with Bible verses became a common practice in Fundamentalist and Evangelical circles. Placing Gideon Bibles in hotel rooms throughout the United States reflected the same conviction that persons on their own could read the Bible and understand it. A weary traveler troubled in soul could seek solace and guidance in Scripture reading. The illuminating power of the Holy Spirit would help the traveler to understand what he or she read in Holy Scripture. This approach to Bible reading eliminated the need to have a cleric or an extensive biblical commentary at hand to provide interpretative guidance.

In many Fundamentalist and Evangelical circles, problems in interpreting difficult passages of the Bible were left to Bible teachers, pastors, and the leaders of various para-church ministries. At Bible camps large audiences thrilled to hear popular Bible teachers unpack the meaning of complex biblical prophecies found in the Book of Revelation, Daniel, or Ezekiel. Many of these Bible teachers argued that they and their audiences were living in the last days and that they could read about the fulfillment of certain biblical passages in daily newspapers.[63] And if the Bible teachers at the camp could not explain a particularly difficult passage, there were always the teachers in Bible colleges or seminaries, or famous pastors who could. The notes of certain versions of the Bible, in particular the Scofield Reference Bible, were especially authoritative for many Fundamentalists. In certain churches a pastor could safely ask the congregation to turn to a specific page number in the Bible to consult specific texts. He knew that nearly everyone in the audience had a Scofield Reference Bible.

Of course, in the Bible schools, colleges, and seminaries of these Fundamentalists and Evangelicals, some professors were very familiar with the history and creeds of the Christian churches. They greatly respected what Christian theologians and Bible scholars had believed and written in the past. Theologically liberal critics might scoff at these teachers as academically "obscurantist" and "anti-intellectual" because they refused to embrace the

---

62. Dixon, "The Scriptures," 77-80.

63. See, for example, articles on biblical prophecy and its relation to current world events of the 1930s as discussed in Arno C. Gabelein's *Our Hope* magazine.

agenda of "modernists" to wed Christianity to the findings of "higher criticism" and "evolution." But in fact a good number of the teachers were not truly anti-intellectual. Their ranks included Merrill Tenney, Carl F. H. Henry, Kenneth Kantzer, Edward Carnell, Gleason Archer, George Eldon Ladd, Roger Nicole, and others who were very well educated having studied at Harvard University or Boston University in the 1940s or early 1950s.[64] These men simply had a different view of what should rule the life of the mind. They believed that the Bible was God's inerrant Word and that "higher criticism" and atheistic forms of Darwinism subverted the Bible's authority. For them, it was an intellectually responsible thing to do to yield one's mind to God's Word and the Lordship of Christ. Interestingly enough, a number of the revivalists who did excoriate the life of the mind and railed at "liberal" and secular educators for putting the nation's young into harm's way, sometimes decided to found their own Bible schools or colleges.

Although differing attitudes and strategies for evangelistic outreach emerged among Evangelicals and Fundamentalists, this circumstance did not cause enormous discomfort for most laypersons and clergy until 1957 (Billy Graham's New York Crusade), with the exception of the hard-hitting disputes spawned by Carl McIntire's criticism of NAE. For example, in the mid-1950s, Billy Graham, the leading "Evangelical" evangelist who followed the principle of "cooperative evangelism," was warmly welcomed at the Word of Life Camp in Schroon Lake, New York, by his longtime friend, Jack Wyrtzen, one of the leading separatistic and Fundamentalist evangelists of the era. After all, it was still thought that the most significant doctrinal chasms that existed were between Evangelicals/Fundamentalists and "modernists," the "neoorthodox," Roman Catholics, and the Orthodox, not between "Bible-believing" Christians. For did not these latter Christians adhere to the "fundamentals" of the faith?

Even those Christians like Harold Ockenga and Carl F. H. Henry who in the 1940s had become more comfortable with the name *Evangelical* and criticized Fundamentalists' fighting and divisive spirit and views of separation, reiterated the fact that they shared with Fundamentalists a commitment to the same fundamental doctrines of the faith, including the final authority of the Bible.

The Bible, then, played a very important role in the thought and lives of pietistic, popular Fundamentalists and Evangelicals in the first six decades of the twentieth century. Formally speaking at least, they gave little heed to the authority of tradition as a divine revelation. Billy Graham's first article in

---

64. Carpenter, *Revive Us Again*, 191.

Christianity Today, entitled "Biblical Authority and Evangelism" (October 1956), highlights just how important the Bible's authority was for Evangelicals. In that article, Mr. Graham explained that his ministry was dramatically changed after he accepted the full authority of Holy Scripture. He wrote: "During the Crusade [Los Angeles, 1949] I discovered the secret that changed my ministry. I stopped trying to prove that the Bible was true. I had settled in my own mind that it was, and this faith was conveyed to the audience. Over and over again I found myself saying 'The Bible says.' I felt as though I were merely a voice through which the Holy Spirit was speaking. Authority created faith. Faith generated response, and hundreds of people were impelled to come to Christ."

For Billy Graham, Charles Fuller, and many other popular evangelists and preachers at mid-century, the supreme authority of the Bible was confirmed to them by the witness of the Holy Spirit and by the way the Bible preached. The Holy Spirit honored the Word of God when it was faithfully preached and thousands upon thousands of people accepted Christ as Lord and Savior. Sophisticated arguments about trying to prove the Bible was God's Word or about matters of biblical interpretation held relatively little interest. It was much more important to preach the Word faithfully, "to see souls won to Christ," to engage in "personal evangelism," to pursue regular personal Bible study, to have a "daily quiet time," to avoid "worldliness," "to keep short accounts with sin" through confession (1 John 1:9), and to be "ready to meet the Lord at any time."

Noticeably ahistorical in outlook and sometimes suspicious of learning, some of the evangelists and pastors of popular and pietistic Evangelicalism/Fundamentalism were not especially concerned to reflect in serious ways about whether or not their own beliefs and standards for personal behavior had a history or a tradition. They assumed that what they believed was taught directly in Holy Scripture. Their beliefs had essentially escaped being influenced by developments in doctrine, historical or social conditioning or any factor that could have subverted them from representing what the Bible taught. If they referenced *tradition* in any positive sense they did so to lend credence to their contention that their own beliefs represented what certain "Bible-believing" Christians of the past had believed before them. For Charles Fuller, this meant using an expression like "The Old Fashioned Revival Hour." They were generally not concerned by the role their own traditions played in influencing their Christian beliefs and ideals for Christian living.

Academic Evangelicals of our day may be tempted to criticize or look down on these earlier pietistic, popular evangelists, pastors, and laity for the simplicity of their faith and for the alleged naiveté of their understanding of biblical interpretation and hermeneutics, including their belief in proposi-tional revelation.[65] But this reaction would not be especially generous and could be a touch elitist. On occasion a number of popular Bible expositors and evangelists did teach and preach things that revealed a serious lack of un-derstanding of Christian doctrine. On occasion, they interpreted the Bible in ways that can still shock. And yet, most Evangelicals of today undoubtedly recognize in the preaching of a Charles Fuller, a Torrey Johnson, a Dawson Trotman, and a Billy Graham and other evangelists the basic message of Christ's gospel. As they said quite simply, Christ came into the world to die on the cross for lost sinners. By his substitutionary death on the cross, Christ paid the penalty for our sins. Those persons who receive Christ as Lord and Savior will have eternal life. We are saved not by our works but by grace alone through faith alone in Christ alone. Although described as the "old-fashioned gospel," this message that gave so much solace to Americans at mid-century should not be dismissed in a reductionist fashion as solely the product of nineteenth-century American "revivalistic" preaching. Most Evangelicals would concur that it contains the essential elements of what the Bible does in fact teach about how we might be saved. Moreover, if a comparison is made of the relatively short list of basic (fundamental) Christian beliefs these ear-lier Evangelicals and Fundamentalists upheld with the relatively short list of beliefs that Tertullian, an early church father, stipulated every Christian must believe (see his various formulations of the rule of faith), the similarities are quite striking. Even if they did not pay much attention to the church fathers or to church history and the history of doctrine, many of these Evangelicals and Fundamentalists affirmed beliefs about the Christian faith that did re-flect biblical teaching and were in line with basic Christian truths found in the early Christian rules of faith.

---

65. See Nancy Tatom Ammerman, *Bible Believers: Fundamentalists in the Modern World* (New Brunswick, NJ: Rutgers University Press, 1987). Ammerman in her criticism remains quite respectful of the community of Fundamentalists she studies. By contrast, Kathleen C. Boone's *The Bible Tells Them So: The Discourse of Protestant Fundamentalism* (Albany: State University of New York Press, 1989) contains a number of sharp criticisms of the ways Fundamentalists read Scripture. She writes: "Finally, even if the Bible were inerrant, we have seen that inerrancy is ultimately incidental to the way fundamentalist authority is actually constituted. Although it is perceived by fundamentalists themselves to be vital for authority, biblical inerrancy becomes in actual practice a political tool whereby one's questions or objections can be deferred to the text" (111). Boone acknowledges the in-fluence of Stanley Fish and Michel Foucault as significant in shaping her own views of text and power. Her own religious convictions are not specified in the study.

B. *"Confessional Evangelicalism"* (1920-2000)

If we conclude our story at this juncture, we will have left several chapters untold. As the Evangelical movement broadened during and after World War II (the post–World War II Evangelical Resurgence, 1945-1958), it began to attract and sometimes repel Christians whose perspectives were not totally identical with those of pietistic Evangelicals and Fundamentalists regarding issues related to traditions and confessions. Whereas pietistic Evangelicalism often seemed quite ahistorical in orientation and ambivalent if not hostile to creeds and confessions, many conservative Protestants who shared a number of the basic beliefs with these Evangelicals and Fundamentalists did view their own confessions, those of the Protestant Reformation and a number of the early creeds, as having great authority. Not only did creeds and confessions provide authoritative summary statements regarding the essential doctrines of the Christian faith, they also provided useful standards which if abandoned could make persons prey to heresy. David Scaer has described the Lutheran position on confessions in this fashion: "Lutheran theology is derived from Holy Scripture, but it is also normed or regulated by the ancient, catholic creeds and the Lutheran Confessions from the sixteenth century. . . . The first task of the Lutheran theologian is to test the Confessions and to accept them as his confession of faith after comparing them to the biblical documents."[66]

These conservative Christians were often uncomfortable in being identified too closely with certain streams of the Evangelical or Fundamentalist movement. According to D. G. Hart, during the 1930s and 1940s, they included members of the Orthodox Presbyterian Church, the Christian Reformed Church, Missouri Synod Lutherans, and some ethnic Anabaptists.[67] They warily viewed these other "Evangelicals" and Fundamentalists as Christians who had weak or unformed ecclesiologies, who did not sufficiently respect the Lord's ordinances or sacraments, who reduced conversion to making a decision for Christ, who seemed ready sometimes to elevate the authority of religious experience over the Bible's final authority, who looked with ambivalence or hostility upon creeds and confessions, and who still hoped to restore a "Christian America" through revivalism.

Nonetheless, confessional Evangelicals sometimes came into close con-

66. David Scaer, "How Do Lutheran Theologians Approach the Doing of Theology Today?" in *Doing Theology in Today's World: Essays in Honor of Kenneth S. Kantzer,* ed. John D. Woodbridge and Thomas E. McComiskey (Grand Rapids: Zondervan, 1991), 197.

67. D. G. Hart, *Defending the Faith: J. Gresham Machen and the Crisis of Conservative Protestantism in Modern America* (Baltimore: The Johns Hopkins University Press, 1994), 170.

tact with northern and western Evangelicalism and Fundamentalism and Pentecostalism especially in the wake of the creation of the NAE. The Christian Reformed Church, for example, has as its standards the Belgic Confession, the Heidelberg Catechism, and the Canons of Dort. Yet it joined the National Association of Evangelicals as a charter member. Clarence Bouma of Calvin Theological Seminary became an early officer of the NAE.[68] In this way, the denomination came into closer contact with Fundamentalists, Evangelicals, and Pentecostals until it withdrew its membership.[69]

Even earlier, J. Gresham Machen, known as a confessional Presbyterian, had come into close contact with the larger Fundamentalist and Evangelical movement. Interestingly enough, Machen is frequently singled out as the leading intellectual of the Fundamentalist movement in the Twenties and Thirties, and this despite the fact that he viewed his struggle with Protestant Liberalism much more as a battle to uphold the historic Evangelical faith than as an initiative to bolster Fundamentalism. For good reason, D. G. Hart, Machen's recent biographer, portrays the Princetonian as a "traditionalist," who along with his colleagues at Westminster Theological Seminary (after 1929) and members of the Orthodox Presbyterian Church (after 1936) wanted to uphold the Standards of the Westminster Confession of Faith.[70] Fundamentalists, too, recognized that Machen was not fully one with them regarding eschatology, ecclesiology, standards for personal conduct, his opposition to Prohibition, and a number of other issues. The "insider" historian of Fundamentalism, George Dollar, characterized Machen not as a Fundamentalist but as an "Orthodox ally."

Nonetheless, in *Christianity and Liberalism*, Machen, the "traditionalist," upheld many of the same basic beliefs as those of Fundamentalists. Regarding biblical inerrancy he wrote: "It [the plenary inspiration of the Bible] supposes

---

68. Carpenter, *Revive Us Again*, 157.

69. The CRC officially became a member of NAE in 1943 and withdrew its membership in 1951. In 1951 the CRC sent a letter to Dr. Fowler, President of the NAE, that included the following discussion of the CRC creed: "The Christian Reformed Church is a close-knit denomination with a very specific creed and a practice based upon and in harmony with this creed. Membership in the National Association of Evangelicals, loosely organized and without a well-defined program of action, easily does lead and in the past has led to embarrassment and difficulty. It was felt that the testimony the Christian Reformed Church is called to bring in this day and in this world is in danger of being weakened by continued membership in the National Association of Evangelicals" (Acts of Synod, June 1954, at Calvin College Auditorium, Grand Rapids, Michigan [Grand Rapids: Christian Reformed Publishing House, 1954], 175 [Suppl. 11] as cited in D. Min. Paper by Melvin J. Jonkman, Trinity Evangelical Divinity School, 1996).

70. Hart, *Defending the Faith*, 165.

that the Holy Spirit so informed the minds of the Biblical writers that they were kept from falling into the errors that mar all other books. The Bible might contain an account of a genuine revelation of God and yet not contain a true account. But according to the doctrine of inspiration, the account is as a matter of fact a true account; the Bible is an 'infallible rule of faith and practice.'" Moreover, he demonstrated a very generous attitude towards conservative Christians other than orthodox Presbyterians. He observed that he could cooperate with "premillennialists" even though they pursued a "false method of interpreting Scripture": "Certainly, then, from our point of view, their error, serious though it may be, is not deadly error; and Christian fellowship, with loyalty not only to the Bible but to the great creeds of the Church, can still unite us with them."[71] He could fellowship with Arminians even though their theology represents a "serious impoverishment of the Scripture doctrine of divine grace." Even though he rejected the Anglican view of ministry, he could "regard the Anglican Church as a genuine and very noble member in the body of Christ." In sum, Machen believed that "true evangelical fellowship is possible between those who hold, with regard to some exceedingly important matters, sharply opposing views."[72]

As a "traditionalist," Machen even acknowledged that Roman Catholics and Evangelicals did share a common heritage in the early Christian creeds: "Far more serious still is the division between the Church of Rome and evangelical Protestantism in all its forms. Yet how great is the common heritage which unites the Roman Catholic church, with its maintenance of the authority of Holy Scripture and with its acceptance of the great early creeds, to devout Protestants today! We would not indeed obscure the difference which divides us from Rome. The gulf is indeed profound. But profound as it is, it seems almost trifling compared to the abyss which stands between us and many ministers of our own Church." Machen went on to indicate that the "Church of Rome may represent a perversion of the Christian religion; but naturalistic liberalism is not Christianity at all."[73] How different was Machen's attitude towards Roman Catholicism from that of T. W. Medhurst, who had written in The Fundamentals.

In the confessional wing of the "Evangelical" movement, great appreciation existed for the creeds and confessions but also for the thought of specific Protestant Reformers. The latter were perceived to be men of God who had

71. J. Gresham Machen, *Christianity and Liberalism* (Grand Rapids: Eerdmans, 1923), 49.

72. Machen, *Christianity and Liberalism*, 51-52.

73. Machen, *Christianity and Liberalism*, 52.

recovered the gospel of Jesus Christ. Although the Protestant Reformers did not have the prerogatives of a papal monarch, their writings nonetheless possessed great authority and circulated widely among confessional Christians. What Luther or Calvin thought and taught became benchmarks of orthodoxy for some of the faithful. If Luther or Calvin indicated something was the case, then the position should be considered very carefully. Both men were esteemed as having understood the Evangelical faith in accordance with God's Word.

At schools like Westminster Theological Seminary and Calvin Theological Seminary, faculty and students attended carefully to the study of Calvin's works and various Reformed confessions or standards. Although non-Calvinist students sometimes complained that teachers were forcing Reformed thought upon them, most students and faculty members were generally disposed to locate their beliefs under the rubric "The Reformed Tradition."[74] In certain Reformed denominations, pastors were required to subscribe to the appropriate Reformed confessions.

As "traditionalists," many confessionalists did not feel comfortable participating in the wide-ranging coalition of conservative churches that constituted the National Association of Evangelicals. Hart observes that Westminster Theological Seminary, despite its academic stature, "remained on the sidelines of the post–World War II evangelical resurgence because of its close ties to the Orthodox Presbyterian Church."[75] For that matter, many confessional Lutheran bodies wanted to keep at arm's length from Evangelicals and Fundamentalists as well.

Not only did Reformed and Lutheran Christians take creeds and confessions very seriously, but Methodists did so as well. Methodists, historically known as "Evangelicals," encouraged a greater appreciation for tradition in the larger world of pietistic and popular American Evangelicalism. This interest in tradition went back to John Wesley himself. Albert Outler, a leading Methodist historian, has argued that John Wesley held a "quadrilateral" view of authority in which Scripture was conjoined to three other authorities — tradition, experience, and reason.[76] Nonetheless, Wesley believed Scripture sat in judgment over the other authorities and was a defender of *sola*

---

74. Hart writes: "Methodists, who comprised roughly 20 percent of the study body, thought Westminster professors presented Calvinism too belligerently. Meanwhile, premillennialists, who outnumbered other views four to one by one estimate, complained that faculty too readily denounced dispensationalism" (*Defending the Faith*, 162-63).

75. Hart, *Defending the Faith*, 161.

76. Albert Outler, "The Wesleyan Quadrilateral — in John Wesley," *Wesleyan Theological Journal* 20 (1985): 16-17.

scriptura. Wesley wrote: "In the year 1729, I began not only to read, but to study the Bible as the one, and the only standard of truth, and the only model of pure religion."[77] At the same time Wesley greatly appreciated tradition and evidenced very high regard for the Thirty-Nine Articles of the Anglican Church — the church from which he broke ranks only with great reluctance.

For Outler, Wesley's quadrilateral approach to doing theology held out many benefits. In 1985, he wrote that "if we are to accept our responsibility for seeking *intellecta* for our faith, in any other fashion than a 'theological system' or, alternatively, a juridical statement of 'doctrinal standards,' then this method of a conjoint recourse to the fourfold guidelines of Scripture, tradition, reason and experience, may hold more promise for an evangelical and ecumenical future than we have realized as yet."[78]

Whether they were Reformed in theology, or Methodist, or Lutheran, the confessionalists believed that the creeds and confessions they affirmed were valid only to the extent they reflected the teaching of the Bible. This was a centuries' old Protestant assumption. It was spelled out clearly in a number of the Reformation confessions the confessionalists embraced. For example, Article 2 of the *Epitome of the Articles* of *The Formula of Concord* (1576; 1584) indicates that no writing including creeds is equal to Holy Scripture, "but are all to be esteemed inferior to them, so that they be not otherwise received than in the rank of witnesses, to show what doctrine was taught after the Apostles' times. . . ." Article 2 notes that Lutherans do embrace the "brief and explicit confessions, which contained the unanimous consent of the Catholic Christian faith, and the confession of the orthodox and true Church (such as are the APOSTLES', the NICENE, and the ATHANASIAN CREEDS). . . ." Article 7 of The Irish Articles of Religion (1615) reads: "All and every [of] the Articles contained in the *Nicene Creed*, the *Creed of Athanasius*, and that which is commonly called the *Apostles' Creed*, ought firmly to be received and believed, for they may be proved by most certain warrant of holy Scripture." Article 10 of *The Westminster Confession of Faith* (1647) made it clear that the Holy Spirit speaking in Scripture sat in judgment of earlier creeds and councils and human opinions: "The Supreme Judge, by which all controversies of religion are to be determined, and all decrees of councils, opinions of ancient writers, doc-

---

77. Colin Williams writes: "Wesley must be placed with the Reformers in his principle of *sola scriptura* in the sense that scripture is the final authority in matters of faith and practice: not in the sense that tradition and experience have no value, but in the sense that these further sources of insight must be congruous with the revelation recorded in scripture" (quoted in Allan Coppedge, "How Wesleyans Do Theology," in *Doing Theology in Today's World*, 279).

78. Outler, "The Wesleyan Quadrilateral," 16-17.

trines of men, and private spirits, are to be examined, and in whose sentence we are to rest, can be no other but the Holy Spirit speaking in the scripture."[79]

Just as Chemnitz had argued, many confessionalists believed there was a true "Evangelical tradition" that was expressed in certain select creeds of the early church and in their own particular confessions — statements that witnessed to what the Scripture taught. Whereas many popular, pietistic Evangelicals paid little attention to the creeds and confessions, these Evangelicals appreciated the "witness" the confessions made to a biblically-based Evangelical faith. They also believed that the creeds and confessions could serve as rules with which orthodoxy could be sorted out from heresy.

As the twentieth century wound down, so frustrated were a number of these "traditionalists" or confessionalists with popular, pietistic Evangelicals, that they disavowed the use of the name Evangelical. They felt very discomforted with the alleged non-doctrinal, non-liturgical, "revivalistic," and Arminian emphases of late twentieth-century Evangelicalism. For them, Christian tradition possessed real authority but not of the same kind attributed to it by Trent. Other Christians, by contrast, formed the Alliance of Confessing Evangelicals, hoping to give more confessional and doctrinal ballast to the larger Evangelical world.

Confessionalists often produced serious works in church history and the history of doctrine. Richard Muller's study, *Post-Reformation Reformed Dogmatics Volume 2: Holy Scripture: The Cognitive Foundation of Theology* (1993), provides an excellent illustration of the kind of historical scholarship that supports the confessionalists' perspectives on the Bible's authority as it relates to tradition. Muller urges scholars to situate the Protestant doctrine of Scripture in the context of medieval theology, not solely in terms of the theological debates that surged between Roman Catholics and Protestants in the sixteenth. He writes: "Indeed, it was the assumption of the theologians of the thirteenth and fourteenth centuries that Scripture was the materially sufficient 'source and norm' for all theological formulation, granting the inspiration and resulting authority of the text. The language of these thinkers, although not precisely the meaning and application, looks directly toward the Reformation and particularly toward the Protestant orthodox assumption of a positive biblical *principium* for theological formulation."[80] Muller's interpretation is very much in line with that of Yves Congar whom he cites.

---

79. For the creeds from which these statements are drawn, consult Philip Schaff, ed., *The Creeds of Christendom, Volume III: The Evangelical Protestant Creeds with Translations* (Grand Rapids: Baker, 1969).

80. Muller, *Post-Reformation Reformed Dogmatics*, vol. 2, 30.

Pentecostal Evangelicals

In contradistinction to confessional Evangelicals, Pentecostals early in their history eschewed the making of doctrinal standards. Russell Spittler cites the *Minutes* of the Annual Assembly of some Pentecostals from North Carolina (1906) to make this point: "We hope and trust that no person or body of people will ever use these minutes, or any part of them as articles of faith upon which to establish a sect or denomination."[81] But by 1916, this non-standards approach had to be abandoned. In that year, the Assemblies of God (founded in 1914) was obliged to draw up the "Statement of Fundamental Truths" in an attempt to countermand the non-trinitarian, "Jesus Name" teaching that was spreading in Pentecostal circles.

Donald Dayton has proposed that Pentecostalism is "the most influential Christian movement of our time," its growth has been so explosive throughout the world. The early Pentecostal churches in the United States included the Assemblies of God, the Church of God (Cleveland, Tennessee), the International Pentecostal Holiness Church, the International Church of the Foursquare Gospel, and the Church of God in Christ.

As noted earlier, in the 1920s and 1930s, Pentecostal Christians had ambiguous if not tense relations with Evangelicals, Fundamentalists, and confessionalists owing to their different views of the "full gospel," signs and wonders and the work of the Holy Spirit in the life of the believer (the baptism of the Holy Spirit accompanied by speaking in tongues). But a number of Pentecostals joined NAE at the time of its inception and the New England Fellowship had some Holiness and Pentecostal roots. Pentecostals shared with other conservative Christians the belief that the Bible is an infallible rule for faith and practice and they upheld the doctrine of justification by faith alone.[82] Like other conservative Protestants, they had a profound commit-

---

81. Russell P. Spittler, "Theological Style Among Pentecostals and Charismatics," in *Doing Theology in Today's World,* 291.

82. Regarding Scripture, the Assemblies of God affirm the following position as enunciated in the Statement of Fundamental Truths: "The Scriptures, both the Old and New Testaments, are verbally inspired of God and are the revelation of God to man, the infallible authoritative rule of faith and conduct. . . ." The church also published a statement in 1970 entitled, "The Inerrancy of the Scriptures" where that position was maintained. Not all Pentecostals uphold the doctrine of inerrancy. Concerning Scripture's authority and hermeneutics among Pentecostals, consult Russell Spittler, "Scripture and the Theological Enterprise: View from a Big Canoe," *The Use of the Bible in Theology: Evangelical Options,* ed. Robert K. Johnston (Atlanta: John Knox Press, 1985), 56-77. Regarding justification by faith alone, Article 8, for example, of the Articles of Faith for the International Pentecostal Holiness Church, reads: "We believe, teach, and firmly maintain the scriptural doctrine of

ment to personal holiness and wanted to avoid the temptations of "the world." They were very zealous to take the gospel of Jesus Christ to others in obedience to the Great Commission.

In the first few decades of the century, Pentecostals produced relatively few theological texts. Spittler observes: "The writing of theological books and articles does not rise naturally among classical Pentecostals."[83] By the end of the century, however, they had established seminaries, colleges, and Bible schools, and the thriving Society for Pentecostal Studies had been in existence for thirty years. A number of Pentecostal scholars occupied key positions as professors and administrators in leading Evangelical seminaries. Key doctrinal books for the Pentecostals included Myer Pearlman's very influential *Knowing the Doctrines of the Bible* (1938; 1948) and Ernest Williams, *Systematic Theology* (1953) among others.

A second response to our central question may now be appropriate. As we saw, Evangelical Christians have generally remained critical of "Tradition" if it is defined as an unwritten revelation of God equal in authority to Holy Scripture. At the same time, Evangelicals have been influenced by traditions or have created traditions themselves. In pietistic and popular Evangelicalism, many Christians, inclined towards an ahistorical perspective, often did not sense that their own beliefs and customs could have been conditioned or shaped by "traditions." By contrast many confessional Christians wanted to identify with and norm their beliefs with the confessions of their own churches and with the early Christian creeds. J. Gresham Machen could speak of the gospel "as found in the Bible and in the historic creeds." On occasion Evangelicals could invest certain of their "traditions" (beliefs, customs, practices) with such enormous authority that these "traditions" appeared to take on authority equal to or surpassing the authority of Holy Scripture itself. On other occasions Evangelicals usefully turned to "traditions" (creeds, confessions, the historical beliefs and practices of denominations and churches) as "witnesses" to help them discriminate between orthodoxy and heresy, to guide them in worship, church governance, and other matters of faith and practice. Many Evangelicals from various streams of the movement viewed these "witnesses" (even if they used other words for them) as fallible but very instructive guides in interpreting Scripture.

---

justification by faith alone" (*The International Pentecostal Holiness Church Manual 1997-2001* [Franklin Springs: Life Springs Resources, 1997], 26).

83. Spittler, "Theological Style Among Pentecostals and Charismatics," 291.

Concluding Remarks

On a hot Saturday evening in the summer of 1956, a group of fast-talking teenagers from Brooklyn jostled their way into Pine Pavilion at Word of Life Island camp, located deep in the Adirondack Mountains, Schroon Lake, New York. In what amounted to a large wooden auditorium that overlooked the lake, they squished themselves onto wooden benches along with hundreds of other young people who were also trying to find a seat. The Brooklyn teenagers knew they were in for a real treat. Jack Wyrtzen, the white-haired Fundamentalist youth evangelist with a cheery face, was right in front of them on the stage. He was talking earnestly with a few members of the Word of Life Quartet about last minute program arrangements. The Word of Life radio broadcast was about to go on the air live from the island. The program would blanket the airways especially in the northeastern United States.

At the organ the teenagers could see the young Harry Bolback, whom they greatly admired. They had been to camp the year before and knew Bolback was a very funny man. In addition, he could "really play" the organ and piano. At the moment he was demonstrating his musical virtuosity by warming up for an organ solo for the broadcast. To watch Bolback's feet romp up and down the pedals and his hands fly repeatedly back and forth over the keyboard was a sight you could not forget. From the organ came swelling crescendos of notes. With a little careful reflection, most of the churchgoing teenagers from Brooklyn could discern in the cascade of notes pouring forth from the organ the simple melody of a Christian hymn, now greatly embellished.

The very next day, Sunday, out in Long Beach, California, Rudy Atwood would sit down at a piano. Just like Harry Bolback, he would play in a similar lively style a Christian hymn for Charles Fuller's Old Fashioned Revival Hour, broadcasting from Municipal Auditorium. Fuller's broadcast would blanket the entire United States.

In the 1940s and 1950s from northern New York to Southern California and many places in between and beyond, the gospel message of the Evangelical/Fundamentalist movement went out over the airways in the United States. The movement itself was experiencing the post–World War II Evangelical resurgence that, as Joel Carpenter has argued convincingly, received much of its impetus from the regrouping efforts of conservative Protestants in the 1930s. The conservative Protestants who made up the movement believed that the gospel of Jesus Christ is the answer to our sinful human condition and taught that the Bible is the inerrant Word of God. During the same time frame, confessional Evangelical Protestants, Southern Baptists, and Pentecostals, who shared many of the same beliefs, were also faring well. Members of the national media were generally oblivious to the fact that conservative Protestant-ism was involved in a full-blown cultural comeback after the disastrous fall-out from the Fundamentalist-modernist controversies and the failure of Prohibition.

In the late 1950s, however, painful divisions ensued between Fundamen-talists and New Evangelicals, only to be followed by "Battles for the Bible" in various theatres of the larger Evangelical world. Nonetheless, at the end of the twentieth century, despite its notable weaknesses, divisions, and moral fail-ures, Christian Smith made the bold and controversial claim that the Evan-gelical movement, shunted to the cultural sidelines earlier in the century, had become the most vital Christian tradition in the United States — a claim that many Evangelicals themselves would probably contest.

For Evangelical Christians of the twentieth century the final authority of Holy Scripture *(sola scriptura)* was a non-negotiable or fundamental doctrine of their movement. Many Evangelicals did not believe that this doctrine was a license for interpretations of Scripture that could simply follow the personal whims and fancy of the individual interpreters, even though they were only too aware of frustrating examples of this kind of interpretation. Rather, for Evangelicals, as J. I. Packer has indicated, the Holy Spirit illuminates the be-liever "to understand how it [Scripture] touches us" and what the Holy Spirit "brings home to our hearts [is] demonstrably in line with the credal, confes-sional, and catechetical dogmas of the evangelical communions to which the Bible students belong." But in all this, Evangelicals realized that, whereas the Bible is infallible, their interpretations of it are not. Moreover, they viewed the risk of someone interpreting passages of Scripture incorrectly as not suffi-ciently compelling to prohibit the putting of the Bible into the hands of per-sons who may read the Word of God on their own. Most Evangelicals were pleased to hear reports about Gideon Bibles being placed in hotel rooms. Most Evangelicals were thrilled to learn about prisoners being given portions of God's Word. They were also delighted to hear reports of the large numbers of persons who had come to saving faith in Christ through reading the Bible, whether they did this in a hotel room, a cell in a prison, a hospital room, a bar, or a boardroom.

Whether they feel more at home in popular pietistic Evangelicalism or in confessional Evangelicalism, in Pentecostalism or in the charismatic move-ment, or in a church setting that blends emphases from these streams of gos-pel faith, as the new millennium begins the overwhelming majority of Evan-gelicals do profess a belief in *sola scriptura*.[84] Even if they do not always use

84. In *Reinventing American Protestantism,* Donald Miller describes the key distinc-

this exact expression, they will frequently say: "What does the Bible say about this issue?" For these Christian believers, the Bible alone remains the only infallible rule for faith and practice. The Psalmist wrote: "Your word is a lamp to my feet and a light for my path" (Ps. 119:105).

---

tion between a "new paradigm religion" and an "old paradigm religion": "The measure of when a new paradigm religion starts to become an 'old paradigm' religion is when it begins to substitute procedures for guidance by the Holy Spirit, and when it relinquishes the job of ministry to professional clergy rather than claiming this for the entire congregation" (147). The leaders of these churches nonetheless affirm the same basic doctrines of the Evangelical movement at large, despite their great reluctance to be "traditional."

Reading Scripture in the Catholic Tradition

FRANCIS MARTIN

In making this contribution to the dialogue we have undertaken on Scripture and Tradition I am conscious of the need for profound and extended conversation in order to approach a common mind. I consider it a privilege to be a participant in this effort and I am grateful to the Lord for what he has enabled us to accomplish so far. I am sure that all of us have been struck by the intricacy of our conversations, how much unsaid experience and tradition we bring to the task. It is in this light that I am presenting this essay. I want to try to articulate part of what we Catholics bring to any discussion of this topic and to recognize our common need to become more deeply in touch with the thought of past ages as well as learn from each other and from all that has been achieved, though often not without aberration, in modern thought.

In order to accomplish this, I am dividing the essay into two parts. In Part One I wish to begin the process of retrieval by offering my own experience of the Catholic tradition, both personal and vicarious, through the writings of others. Thus, I will share my experience and then reflect upon it in theological categories. Part Two will be dedicated to an investigation into what, both positively and negatively, has taken place in the approach to the Sacred Text. Retrieval is not archeology. We must grasp what is sound in our heritage from the more remote past, assess what has been said in the more recent past, and move forward to a new realization in the future. I offer this as an act of respect and gratitude to those who have been part of this dialogue.

Part One: The Roots of the Catholic Tradition

My Personal Experience

I will begin this presentation with a brief biographical sketch. As I have reflected on my own experience within the Catholic tradition, it has become clear to me that many facets of the Catholic approach to Scripture are not well articulated but taken for granted, as it were, and in need of some explanation. It is for this reason that I begin with an account of my own experience, which harbors several facets not readily available in the post–Vatican II church. I am inspired to do this by the approach taken by Professor Packer in his account of reading Scripture in the Evangelical tradition.

I was brought up in a family that prayed the rosary every night and prepared for Sunday Mass early on Sunday morning by reading the Scripture passages that were to be read out in church. I don't remember any real accent on Scripture in my Catholic education, though I do remember a vague sense that it was "dangerous" to go off on one's own and read the Bible since that could lead you into error: it was safer to leave that to the experts and follow the teaching of the church. Then, at the age of twenty, I entered the Cistercian Monastery in Spencer, Massachusetts, where I spent fifteen happy years (three of them in Rome doing graduate studies), and was plunged into a world that, while it was very much a part of the twentieth century in regard to technology, had changed but little spiritually in over eight hundred years.

The day, which began at 2:00 AM and ended at 7:00 PM, was structured around eight periods of common prayer, all in Latin, the backbone of which was the Psalter sung or recited in such a way that the whole of the 150 psalms were prayed in the period of a week, with many of these being repeated several times in the week. The psalms were sung in the context of antiphons, readings from Scripture, and prayers which were composed in such a way that the ordinary days repeated themselves and the great feast days had special components. In addition there was a daily Eucharistic Liturgy, also sung in its entirety. The church and monastery in which this prayer took place, after we had helped to build it, was a place of beauty and spiritual peace. The music, the Gregorian chant, sung by a group of monks considered to be among the most skilled in the country, was a constant education in the interpretation of Scripture. Let me explain.

The basic principle of Gregorian chant is that it should be "a carpet for the words of Scripture to walk upon and thus enter your soul"; it is a musical exegesis of the sacred text composed in an atmosphere of prayer and fasting. Even as I write these words I can hear the Entrance Antiphon for Easter morning with its calm and powerful 4th mode melody carrying one into the world of the Mystery: "I have risen and am still with you," as the purposely double meaning of the Vetus Latina renders Psalm 139 (138):18. The antiphon goes on to allude to other verses: "You placed your hand upon me, your knowledge has become marvelous" (vv. 5-6). That is, "You have claimed me from the dead and revealed to all the world the inner depths of the mystery hidden for ages and now revealed in me, your Son." This psalm, an intimate dialogue of wonder at the creating power of God, passed through the soul of Christ and has become a sacrament giving access to his inner life. But there is more: the grace animating the psalmist made of his song an anticipation of the surge of joy that coursed through the heart of Christ as he was raised from the dead. The real subject of the psalm is Christ; the psalmist is an anticipatory participation in that mystery of God's plan which is known now in its fulfillment. In order for the words of this psalm to unfold in this way, there must be song, that is, there must be community, people together to make this song. They are gathered on Easter morning and sing what had been sung for centuries at this moment. Our song makes us one with those who sang this song before us. We are bound together by the living Christ who sings his song in us on earth and in them in heaven. It is because of this mystery, the Christ in us, the hope and fulfillment of glory, that time is no longer a neutral reality but rather something that, once caught up in the life of the Body — the Christ — becomes eternal.

Other moments occur to me. The Offertory hymn which celebrated Moses' prayer to God in Exodus 32:11-14. "Moses prayed in the sight of the Lord: 'Why Lord, are you angry with your people? . . . Remember Abraham, Isaac, and Jacob, your servants to whom you swore by yourself. . . .' And the Lord repented from the evil he had spoken against his people." Once again Christ is praying in us. Moses, an anticipated partial realization of Christ, stepped into the breach, preferring to be blotted out of the book of Life rather than renounce solidarity with his/God's people (Exod. 32:31). Now Christ, exercising his eternal priesthood, is always living to make intercession for us (Heb. 7:25) and joins us to himself in this prayer through the words of Moses. Christ's heavenly prayer still has an historical dimension in the prayer of his Body, the church.

In the monastic liturgy the Books of Samuel and Kings are read throughout the summer, that time "after Pentecost" which symbolizes the life of the church, in the heat of the battle, looking to the heroes of the past whose lives are an example for us. Foremost among these, of course, is David since Jesus, the new David, is the one Shepherd who feeds the flock of God (Ezek. 34:23-24). On hot Saturday afternoons, after a day of work, we met for First Sunday

Vespers in the church and at the *Magnificat* sang David's generous words of love and forgiveness: "Saul and Jonathan beloved and lovely! In life and death they were not divided. . . . The arrow of Jonathan never turned back. . . . I grieve for you my brother, Jonathan . . . your love to me was wonderful, passing the love of women" (2 Sam. 1:22-27). Here is tenderness and pardon, the heart of Christ portrayed for us, not only in this magnanimous grieving for both Saul his persecutor and Jonathan his friend, but even more in David's weeping over Absalom his rebellious and treacherous son: "Absalom, my son, my son Absalom, who would grant to me that I might die instead of you! O Absalom my son!" (2 Sam. 18:33). In this latter song, the melody even carries the sound of David's weeping — Christ weeping over us — and teaches us what it means to continue on earth the prayer of forgiveness of Christ himself. Finally, on a Sunday, as we approached the Lord at Communion, we sang the dialogue between Jesus and the woman taken in adultery, the confrontation of *Misericordia* and *miseria,* to quote Augustine's memorable phrase: "Has no one condemned you woman? No one Lord. Nor do I condemn you — go in peace and do not sin anymore." Once again, the melody, oscillating between calm majestic love and fearful hope, brings us into the action as participants experiencing the love of Christ even as we express it and respond with the same tremulous expectancy.

Reflections on This Experience in a More Common Context

The Liturgy

This world in which I lived and learned, I now see upon reflection, taught me several basic things about Scripture and Tradition. First, I learned that the native home of Scripture is the Liturgy. Even the monastic practice of *lectio divina* (private contact with the Sacred Text for several hours a day) is a continuation of the communal prayer which is basically the singing of the biblical text in a setting that repeated itself year after year drawing the cyclic time of the cosmos into the eternal dimension of the Resurrection.[1] Usually I read

---

1. In *Fides et Ratio,* Pope John Paul II accented the importance of time, that is history, in the Christian dispensation: "God's Revelation is therefore immersed in time and history. Jesus Christ took flesh in the 'fullness of time' (*Gal* 4:4); and two thousand years later, I feel bound to restate forcefully that 'in Christianity time has a fundamental importance.' It is within time that the whole work of creation and salvation comes to light; and it emerges clearly above all that, with the Incarnation of the Son of God, our life is even now a foretaste of the fulfilment of time which is to come (cf. *Heb* 1:2)" (Par. 11).

the Bible in the Vulgate translation, since this made it easier to catch all the multiple allusions to the Text in the writings of the Latin Fathers. I began reading the Greek Fathers as well, and this exposure gave me a sense of the delight they mediated to us from their own contact with the Sacred Text. Henri de Lubac, whom I discovered after about three years in the monastery and who is an abundant source of understanding of the Fathers, said this of their attitude toward the Bible:

> Scripture is not only divinely guaranteed, it is divinely true. The Spirit did not only dictate it; he is, as it were, contained in it. He inhabits it. His breath perpetually animates it. The Scripture is "made fruitful by a miracle of the Holy Spirit." It is "full of the Spirit."[2]

The Spiritual Sense, or Spiritual Understanding

Knowing that Christ was somehow contained in the events mediated to us in the Old Testament was not so much the result of study as it was of experience at the Liturgy. For nearly the whole of Tradition it is axiomatic that the events of the Old Testament share in some mysterious manner in the Christ event. To recognize the anticipations of the Christ event in the events present to us in the Old Testament narrative is to appreciate the *spiritual sense* of the Old Testament. It is obvious in the examples I have given above that this sense of the Text was presupposed in the manner in which the Liturgy, with its nearly two thousand year history, prayed the Old Testament. The other name given to the spiritual sense is the "allegorical" sense which, for tradition, meant exactly the same thing, though this latter term particularly covered many extravagant interpretations.[3] There are two senses which derive from the meaning of the Old Testament once it has been sublated into the Christ event.[4]

---

2. Henri de Lubac, *Exégèse Médiéval: Les Quatres Sens de l'Écriture* (Théologie, 41), Part I (Paris: Aubier, 1959), 129. The texts quoted in the text are from Anselm, *De concord.* 3,6 (*PL* 157, 528B) and Origen, *De Princ.* 4,1,7, respectively. I am indebted for this reference to the unpublished dissertation of Marcellino D'Ambrosio, "Henri de Lubac and the Recovery of the Traditional Hermeneutic" (Catholic University of America, 1991), 147-48.

3. For a balanced view of this question see Henri de Lubac, *Sources of Revelation*, trans. Luke O'Neil (New York: Herder & Herder, 1968).

4. The process I am referring to is aptly portrayed in this description of sublation given by Bernard Lonergan: "What sublates goes beyond what is sublated, introduces something new and distinct, yet so far from interfering with the sublated or destroying it, on the contrary needs it, includes it, preserves all its proper features and properties, and carries them forward to a fuller realization within a richer context." Bernard Lonergan, *Method in Theology* (New York: Herder & Herder, 1972), 241.

These are the "tropological" sense which derives from the Greek term *tropos* ("way of acting"), and the "anagogical" sense which, deriving from the Greek term *anagoge* ("ascent"), refers to the eschatological dimension. It is important to realize that, for the ancients, these four senses — the literal, the allegorical/spiritual, the tropological, and the anagogical — are not four meanings of the words, but four dimensions of the *event* which is being mediated by the words: the words are important because they are a privileged means of mediating the realities. As St. Augustine expresses it: "It is in the event itself, and not only in the text, that we must seek the mystery."[5]

That such was the way to read Scripture was more than obvious to me because of the environment in which I first contacted the Sacred Text, impregnated as it was by the whole outlook of Tradition. I have since tried to render a more reflexive account of what I learned almost by "osmosis." Allow me to explain.[6]

Much modern philosophy has moved away from the mental abstractions and fascination with practical reason that characterized the Enlightenment to a deeper understanding of the concrete. By "the concrete" here I mean the actually and uniquely existing *individuum* as distinct from the particular which is but one instance of a class. Such a move is in the direction of biblical thought since it is in the direction of giving primacy to that revelation of Being that has taken place in history.[7] The prime analogate of this revelation of Being is Jesus on the cross as he is engaged in giving his life to the Father in an act of love because all the saving acts of God participate in this act, not only notionally but also in the order of being.[8] There is a relation in being between an act of God in the OT and God's act in Christ. Jesus' act of love on the cross establishes a new order of being, both proleptically, in creation and the covenant, and eschatologically, in the final consummation when the plan of the

---

5. "*In ipso facto, non solum in dicto, mysterium requirere debemus.*" Augustine, *On Psalm 68* (PL 36, 858).

6. In what follows I am dependent upon material published in my article, "Israel as the Bride of Yhwh," *Anthropotes* 9 (2000).

7. For an excellent treatment of this point see Martin Bieler, "The Future of the Philosophy of Being," *Communio* 26 (1999): 455-85.

8. While this is not the place to enter into a discussion of this point, it is important to note that the foremost proponent of the spiritual sense of Scripture in our time, Henri de Lubac, insisted that the "allegorical" or spiritual sense is found in the *events:* "Précisons d'ailleurs aussitôt que cette allégorie à decouvrir, on ne la trouvera pas à proprement parler dans le texte, mais dans les réalités dont le texte parle; non pas dans l'histoire en tant que récit, mais dans l'histoire en tant qu'événement." Henri de Lubac, *Exégèse Médiévale*, 493. This whole passage, with its patristic quotes, is well worth reading.

Father to bring all things under Christ as Head (Eph. 1:10) will be completely realized.

We are dealing here with the metaphysical notion of participation. Gregory Rocca, paraphrasing Cornelio Fabro, states: "[P]articipation is especially the ontology of analogy and analogy is the epistemology and semantics of participation."[9] Participation is usually divided into predicamental and transcendental. In predicamental participation two realities are said to participate in the same notion: one may be the exemplar of the other. In transcendental participation one reality (God) possesses something *totaliter* ("Whatever is totally something does not participate in it but is essentially the same as it"),[10] while another reality shares in that something but not essentially. Here there is efficient causality in addition to exemplar causality. Participation in this case involves a dependence in being between the first reality and the second. As the phrase cited above indicates, this second type of participation is the "ontology of analogy," allowing God's being to be correctly though inadequately spoken of on the basis of those perfections in creatures which participate, through God's efficient causality, in something of which he is the ineffable exemplar.

In the light of the Incarnation a new dimension of reality is made available to humanity. I would wish to call this "economic participation." Just as transcendental participation is an ontological reality now seen because of the revelation of creation, so economic participation is an ontological reality because of covenant. The covenant relation is itself based upon and expressive of acts of God in time, in history, and, as, we have seen, these events participate in a proleptic manner in the mystery of the Incarnation, especially its own high point in time, the death and resurrection of Jesus. There is thus an economic participation in which all God's acts in human history are related to the supreme act, the cross, which realizes and is, *totaliter,* the economic action of God, the exemplar and instrumental efficient cause of all the other acts.[11] It is for this reason that, already within the OT itself, there is a relating of successive acts of God as realizations of the same plan even as Israel "looked for a new David, a new Exodus, a new covenant, a new city of God:

9. Gregory Rocca, "Analogy as Judgment and Faith in God's Incomprehensibility: A Study in the Theological Epistemology of Thomas Aquinas" (Ph.D. diss., Catholic University of America, 1989; Ann Arbor, MI: UMI Dissertation Services, 1994), 537. Rocca is condensing the thought of Cornelio Fabro, *Participation et Causalité selon S. Thomas d'Aquin* (Louvain: Publications Universitaires de Louvain, 1961), 634-40.

10. Thomas Aquinas, *Sententiae libri Metaphysicorum* 1.10.154.

11. Some of this is treated by Hans Urs Von Balthasar in *A Theology of History* (1963; San Francisco: Ignatius, 1994).

the old had thus become a type of the new and important as pointing forward to it."[12] Economic participation includes, however, not only event, but also relation. The new covenant in the blood of Christ confers an infinite and eternal concreteness, so to speak, upon the reality of relation and grounds what may be called a metaphysics of relation.[13]

It is upon this basis for the spiritual sense of Scripture that we can point to one characteristic of reading Scripture in the Catholic tradition, namely that it is concentrated on the *acts* of God rather than on the words of Scripture which bear these acts to us. It is for this reason that the home of Scripture, the place where it is most actualized, is found in communal and sacramental worship. This also gives Catholic thinking its instinctive analogical way of thinking: it is concentrated upon what I have been calling the economic participation of all God's present saving acts in the prime analogate of these acts, namely Christ's act of love on the cross and his permanent state in glory as fixed in that act.

In the time before the fourteenth century's move to nominalism, an era we can only imagine but not experience again — except partially in the kind of life context I described above — the accent was placed upon understanding the *reality* mediated by the words more than on the words themselves. This is the work of the Holy Spirit, bringing the mind and spirit of the reader into contact with the divine realities. As a movement of grace, such a way of approaching Scripture is very fruitful and it grounds further reflection. Theology, therefore, is a matter of perceiving the relation between *realities* by the use of reason enlightened by faith but not of drawing conclusions from texts.[14] The greatness of the fathers of the church consisted in their graced ability to speak of divine realities with which they were in personal contact under the guidance of the authoritative words of Scripture to which they were submitted. It suffices to trace the dogmatic conflicts of the early church, Nestorianism, Arianism, Monophysitism, and the rest, to appreciate the manner in which these mystics, men in touch with the Mystery, argued from Scripture. Tradition, in the Catholic understanding, is precisely this life-giving activity of the Holy Spirit, moving in the whole Body of Christ, served

12. Gerhard von Rad, *Old Testament Theology,* trans. D. M. G. Stalker, vol. 2 of *The Theology of Israel's Prophetic Traditions* (New York: Harper & Row, 1965), 323.

13. In addition to the article by Bieler mentioned above, see also David Schindler, "God and the End of Intelligence: Knowledge as Relationship," *Communio* 26:3 (1999): 510-40.

14. "Yet it must always be remembered that the assent to these other truths, the various material objects of faith, presupposes the formal object as providing the authenticating force for the assent" (Brian J. Shanley, "Sacra Doctrina and Disclosure," *The Thomist* 61:2 [1997]: 163-88, at 174-75 with a citation from *ST* 2-2,1,1c).

and guided by the prophetic action of the magisterium, by which the realities of God and his saving grace continue to be the light and life of the people of God. This process is described well in the Constitution on Divine Revelation of Vatican II:

> This tradition which comes from the apostles develops in the Church with the help of the Holy Spirit. For there is a growth in the understanding of the realities and the words [note both terms] which have been handed down. This happens through the contemplation and study made by believers who treasure these things in their hearts (cf. Lk 2:19, 51), through the intimate understanding of the spiritual things they experience, and through the preaching of those who have received through episcopal succession the sure gift of truth. (*Dei Verbum* #8)[15]

Tradition, as everyone agrees, is not the same as custom, nor is every habitual understanding of the text the work of the Holy Spirit. We Catholics have to acknowledge that we do not always see the difference. The text just cited indicates one way in which the whole body of believers, through contemplation, study, intimate understanding and experience, as well as by accredited preachers, can use the inspired text as a corrective to what passes for tradition but is not really so. They do this in the force of the divine realities transmitted to them. As Martin Luther said: "The one who does not understand the realities cannot draw the meaning out of the words."[16]

Presence

Sometime early in the fifth century, Pope St. Leo I told his congregation:

> All those things which the Son of God both did and taught for the reconciliation of the world, we not only know in the account of things now past, but we also experience in the power of works which are present.[17]

That he intended by this to refer not only to the sacraments of the church but also to the reading of the Scriptures is evident from his oft-repeated notion that the Gospel text, when received by faith, *makes present* that which it

---

15. For a discussion of this text see Alessandro Magglioni, "Magisterial Teaching on Experience in the Twentieth Century: From the Modernist Crisis to the Second Vatican Council," *Communio* 13:2 (1996): 225-43.

16. From the frontispiece of Part II of Hans Georg Gadamer, *Truth and Method*, trans. Joel Weinsheimer and Donald Marshall (New York: Seabury, 1989).

17. *On the Passion*, 12 (*SC* 74, 82).

speaks about.[18] Leo's teaching, splendid in its clarity, does but sum up nearly five hundred years of thinking about how the events in the life of Christ continue to have their effect in the life of the church. I have tried, in my account of the monastic liturgy in which I was formed, to show how this is a matter of experience in such a setting, and is one more aspect of the Catholic intuition concerning the *res* mediated by the Sacred Text. The Gospels themselves indicate how they effect such a presence. Allow me to give some examples.[19]

In the New Testament passages which explicitly link Jesus' transformed human state with his power to touch and change us now, there are apparently insignificant details which show us how the Gospel writers presume that the power of their narrative will make the Lord present to us. For instance, in his account of the storm at sea, Mark records the words of the frightened disciples, who had taken Jesus "as he was, into the boat" (Mark 4:36): "Master, doesn't it matter to you that we are going under?" (Mark 4:38). Matthew, recounting the same incident, first remarks that Jesus entered the boat, "and his disciples *followed him*" as disciples always have and will (Matt. 8:23). When the storm arose, these disciples pray to Jesus: "*Lord, save* (us), we are going under" (Matt. 8:25). Matthew is most probably putting words from the liturgical prayer of his community on the lips of the disciples, thus establishing a continuity between the original disciples and all those who follow Jesus now and receive help from him.

Another example of liturgical, specifically baptismal, overtones is probably found in the phrase "your faith has healed/saved you" (Matt. 9:22 par.; Mark 9:52/Luke 18:42; 7:50; 17:19) since it juxtaposes *pistis* and *sozein* in a way found elsewhere in the NT.[20] In the same way, Mark tells us that the enlightened blind man (a type of all who receive spiritual sight from Jesus) became a disciple as we still do today: "and he *followed* him on the *way* [the ancient name for Christianity]" (Mark 10:52). An attentive reader will find many examples of this mode of procedure and will, if he or she will ponder the text, be drawn into its mysterious movement and the call to discipleship that Jesus, by the Holy Spirit, still proffers in and through the text.

18. *On the Resurrection*, 1 (*SC* 74, 123); *On the Epiphany*, 5 (*SC* 22 bis, 254); *On the Passion*, 5 and 18 (*SC* 74, 41; 112). For the references to these citations, see Dom Marie-Bernard de Soos, *Le Mystère Liturgique d'après saint Léon le Grand* (Mimeograph Thesis presented to the Faculty of Toulouse on June 10, 1955).

19. For a more complete treatment of this subject consult the study from which these few lines are taken with the permission of the publisher: Francis Martin, "St. Matthew's Spiritual Understanding of the Healing of the Centurion's Boy," *Communio* 25 (1998): 161-77.

20. See also Acts 14:9; 3:16; 16:31; Rom. 1:17; 10:10, etc.

Such an understanding of presence is also found in the ability of our predecessors to identify their lives with the narratives in the Scriptures, realizing that, while the narrative is completed the story still goes on. An article by Eric Auerbach is perhaps the most adequate study of the mentality that intuitively grasped the open quality of biblical events and understood how their relation to God made them a source of living and understanding one's own history.[21] The term most often used to express this understanding is *figura,* a word preferred in the West to *typus,* also understood and used, because this latter "remained an imported lifeless sign" while the former continued to grow and exploit its roots in both popular and rhetorical language.[22]

Figural interpretation of Scripture differs from symbolic interpretation in that figural interpretation establishes a connection between two events or persons, while a symbolic interpretation, popular from the time of the Reformation, connects the former historical reality with an idea, or a mystical or ethical system.[23] Figure sees events as related to one another because of their relationship to God. Symbol sees events as significant because they are expressions of a meaning. History is still in progress, and thus it is still possible to understand one's self and one's future by connecting the events in the life of the church and one's own life to the events of the past. This view of reality is well articulated by Auerbach:

> Figural prophecy implies the interpretation of one worldly event through another; the first signifies the second, the second fulfills the first. Both remain historical events; yet both, looked at in this way, have something provisional and incomplete about them; they point to one another and both point to something in the future, something still to come, which will be the actual, real, and definitive event. . . . Thus history, with all its concrete force, remains forever a figure, cloaked and needful of interpretation. . . . [T]he event is enacted according to an ideal model which is a prototype situated in the future and thus far only promised.[24]

The aspect not sufficiently accented in the above description is the important distinction between the Old and New Testaments which Augustine once described in this way: "The Old Testament is the promise in figure

21. Erich Auerbach, "Figura," in *Scenes from the Drama of European Literature* (Gloucester, MA: Peter Smith, 1973), 11-76.

22. Auerbach, "Figura," 48-49.

23. Auerbach, "Figura," 54-55. This same point was made in regard to the Old Testament by G. von Rad in his treatment of "Typology" in Volume II of *Old Testament Theology.*

24. Auerbach, "Figura," 58-59.

(promissio figurata), the New is the promise understood in the Spirit (spiritualiter intellecta)."[25] The aspect which is highlighted is the notion that what we now experience is a participation in being of what once was in promise, is now present in icon, and will be fully present in glory. This is the meaning of the rhythm expressed in Hebrews 10:1: "For the law had a sketch (skian) of the good things to come, and not the image itself (autēn tēn eikona) of the realities. . . ." The law only possessed a shadow or sketch, we possess the realities but "in icon," that is, we possess them but not according to their proper mode of existence, but rather in another mode, in signs and symbols, until we are with Christ in heaven. This understanding of the Hebrews text was already expressed by Ambrose, who spoke of "shadow," "image," and "truth."[26] This view of history is the common denominator between Sacred Text and Sacrament, particularly the Eucharist. These fulfill the events of the Old Testament in the act by which Christ makes himself present "in icon," even as he anticipates the fullness of his presence "in truth."

A Hermeneutics of Trust

The theologian who has made the most of this beautiful expression — a "hermeneutics of trust" — is Anthony Thiselton, who contrasts it with a "hermeneutics of suspicion" about which I will speak later.[27] A hermeneutics of trust is founded in faith and operates on the implicit epistemological presupposition that the mind of the reader can participate in the mind of the author by sharing his intention. We must bear in mind, however, that the intention of the author is not a psychological reality, what the author is "trying to say," but rather an ontological matter, what the mind of the author intends as he communicates to his audience.[28] Once again we are in the presence of the notion that the Sacred Text is mediating reality to us and not merely words. Here as well the thought of Henri de Lubac comes to our aid. As early as 1938 he wrote in Catholicisme:[29]

---

25. Augustine, Sermon 4,8.

26. "Primum igitur umbra praecessit, secuta est imago, erit veritas. Umbra in lege, imago vero in evangelio, veritas in caelestibus." Ambrose, On Psalm 43 (Corpus Scriptorum Ecclesiasticorum Latinorum, 64,204).

27. Anthony C. Thiselton, New Horizons in Hermeneutics: The Theory and Practice of Transforming Biblical Reading (Grand Rapids: Zondervan, 1992).

28. See D. C. Dennett, "Intentionality," in The Cambridge Dictionary of Philosophy, ed. R. Audi, 381 (Cambridge: University of Cambridge Press, 1995).

29. Henri de Lubac, Les aspects sociaux de Dogme chrétien (Paris: Cerf, 1938, 1941), 119. Translation is from Ignace de La Potterie, "The Spiritual Sense of Scripture," Communio

God acts *within* history, God reveals himself *within* history. Even more, God inserts himself *within* history, thus granting it a "religious consecration" which forces us to take it seriously. *Historical* realities have a *depth;* they are to be understood *spiritually: historika pneumatikôs* . . . and on the other hand, *spiritual* realities appear in the movement of becoming; they are to be understood *historically: pneumatika historikôs.* . . . The Bible, which contains revelation, thus also contains, in a certain way, the *history* of the world.

We can readily see that the spiritual understanding of *historika,* and the awareness of the presence of Christ in and through the *historika* as these are transmitted to us in the Scriptures requires that the act of faith knowledge involved in reading the Sacred Text terminate, not in the words, but, to repeat the expression of Augustine, *in ipso facto.* We can go even further. Faith rests, not only in the *factum,* but in God, the First Truth itself. This is why Aquinas can say: "Faith adheres to all the articles of faith because of one reason *(medium),* namely because of the First Truth proposed to us in the Scriptures understood rightly according to the teaching of the Church *(secundum doctrinam Ecclesiae).*"[30]

I consider it a singular grace of God that for fifteen years, I experienced, through the Scriptures, the Liturgy, and the Fathers, the fact that my mind was borne to communicate in the saving acts of God through these sacred words and gestures. I knew that I was in touch with Reality through these instruments of mediation. I thus knew the living center of the Catholic tradition before I had the inestimable privilege of studying Scripture according to modern methods, of seeing where this tradition had not grown where it should have grown, where it contained exaggerations, and of learning how to use the tools of historical research in order to penetrate more deeply into the Mystery contained in these precious instruments of Tradition. I would like to reflect now on that experience and the challenge that it presents to us today.

23:4 (1996): 738-56, at 743; emphasis is in the text. For a discussion of this aspect of biblical narrative from the point of view of the "openness of the event," see Francis Martin, "Historical Criticism and New Testament Teaching on the Imitation of Christ," *Anthropotes* 6 (1990): 261-87.

30. Thomas Aquinas, *Summa Theologiae* 2-2,5,3c and ad 2. It may be helpful to quote here another principle, also enunciated by St. Thomas, since it is a wonderful example of the authority Aquinas gives to "the Scriptures understood rightly according to the teaching of the Church," and to the complete lack of conflict he sees in this principle and the following: "Our faith rests on the revelation made to the Prophets and Apostles who wrote the canonical books, not on a revelation, if such there be, made to any other teacher" (1,1,8, ad 2).

Part Two: The Challenge of Retrieval

After eight formative years in the monastery I was sent to live in the central house of the Order in Rome in order to do graduate work in Sacred Scripture. The basic monastic routine was retained there. After acquiring a Licentiate in theology (basically Thomistic theology), I began my studies at the Pontifical Biblical Institute and received the degree of Licentiate in Sacred Scripture two years later. Ten years later I returned to Rome and began work on the degree of Doctor in Sacred Scripture. After two years I went to live at the Ecole Biblique et Archéologique Française in Jerusalem where I continued my own work and eventually taught as well, receiving the doctoral degree in 1978. The time of my biblical studies was a delight to me. I was trained under some of the best minds in the church at that time and I learned, once again by "instinct," that the historical methods were not enemies but friends of genuine biblical learning. Nevertheless, I began to see that the methods themselves derived from philosophical principles and presuppositions that, if not critically assessed and corrected, could deflect the faith direction of one's thinking.

At that time I began a philosophical pilgrimage, concentrating mostly on the philosophy of knowledge, the philosophy of history, and literary theory in order to begin a process of retrieval, substantiating what I knew of the power of the Catholic Tradition while moving that Tradition forward in the light of the truth discovered in the Protestant Tradition and by thinkers as diverse as Bultmann and Barth, Heidegger, Husserl and Gadamer, Sokolowski, Schmitz and Derrida. In the last twelve years, my study of feminist hermeneutics gave me a very acute sense of the need to elaborate a faith hermeneutics that was adequate to the importance of the problems being raised in Feminist and Liberationist Theologies.[31] Along the way, especially in the last fifteen years, I have discovered or rediscovered some "fellow travelers" on this pilgrimage among both Protestants and Catholics. I cannot name them all, but among them most prominently are de Lubac, von Balthasar, historical exegetes such as Brown, Fitzmyer, and many of the authors who contribute to commentary series such as the Evangelical series, the Word Biblical Commentary, as well as literary investigators such as my friend Luis Alonso Schökel, Meir Sternberg, and Michael Fishbane.

I would like now to elaborate some of the factors that must be present in a retrieval of the Catholic Tradition of reading Scripture, a retrieval that consists in a deeper penetration and further advancement of that Tradition with the help of all that is true in the other Christian Traditions as well as the authentic

---

31. Much of the result of this work can be found in *The Feminist Question: Feminist Theology in the Light of Christian Tradition* (Grand Rapids: Eerdmans, 1994).

advances in philosophical understanding that have been achieved in recent centuries. First, there must be a greater popular faith familiarity with the message and the power of the Sacred Text. Professor Packer's contribution to this dialogue describes the kind of Evangelical reading of Scripture that Catholics must acquire even as they, hopefully, learn to experience once again the Liturgy as a matrix of spiritual understanding of the Bible. Second, what is valid in the "turn to the subject" that characterizes modern thought must be modified and corrected in the light of a "turn to the person" with all that implies for the understanding of communication and the interpersonal nature of truth. Finally, historical research must be moved from historicism to a genuine understanding of the interiority of history and the meta-anthropological (not only metaphysical) foundation of a philosophy of being.[32]

I would like now to sketch in a few brief lines some elements of how this retrieval can be effected. I can only claim for these the nature of guidelines in the undertaking of this daunting task, which will engage the energies of all who wish to recover a way of reading Scripture that is Catholic in the ancient sense of the term. I will consider in reverse order three components of the Catholic Tradition I treated previously.

A Hermeneutics of Trust

The Present Situation

The story of the movement from a hermeneutics of trust, that is, an interpretative theory that was realistic epistemologically and still in touch with a Christian plausibility structure culturally, to a hermeneutics of suspicion has been told often enough.[33] The first trust to be eroded was trust in God. William of Ockham, whose nominalism succeeded in reducing theology to words about the utterly Unknowable, succeeded as well in placing man before a God whose will was supreme but whose truth was unattainable to the point of being arbitrary:

> Theology which now closes in upon itself, must become fideistic and can ultimately only be practical. And the Franciscan image of God — love beyond

---

32. By the expression "turn to the person" I mean the theological retrieval that has accepted all that is sound in the philosophical epistemology and anthropology of the last few centuries but has moved it from the subjectivism and individualism which characterized it into a metaphysics of relation or what may also be called a "meta-anthropology."

33. I have traced this story in *The Feminist Question*, chapter two, "The Isolation of Theology." The reader is invited to consult that work and the literature given there.

the limits of knowledge — must therefore degenerate into an image of fear (which is no longer even that of the Old Testament) since this God of pure freedom might always posit what is contrary [to the world and its cosmic and moral structure as we know it].[34]

The next trust to be weakened was trust in what was handed down by the church and by society. This occurred in the Renaissance with its independent and critical access to documents, its reliance on the findings of "modern science" (especially physics, history, and geography), and the resulting divergence between a sophisticated understanding of the world and history and the worldview of the Bible. The intrinsic intelligibility of the universe and of man's place in it became rather an independent intelligibility which had no need of revelation. Modern atheism arose when, because of a misguided understanding of "philosophy," religion appeared to need physics to establish its fundamental principle, that is, the existence of God, but physics did not need religion to return the favor. As Michael Buckley puts it: "Atheism came out of a turn in the road in the development and autonomy of physics."[35]

Along with the nominalism of the period, which had invaded Catholic thought, and the critical mindset of the Renaissance, came the Protestant Reformation and the ensuing debates concerning the authority of Scripture. The whole cultural world which had borne the Sacred Text (the world which I attempted to describe in Part One) became no longer an atmosphere but rather an object, something to be looked at from a distance. The most prominent word to be found on both sides of the debates of the time was *certitudo*. At length, in order to find refuge in a turbulent sea of countercharges, the Socinians searched for an unassailable and permanent place to stand: "They looked for a new, clear and generally understandable way of clarifying the word and will of God, and in so doing came upon that authority which was a rising star on the horizon of the century: reason."[36]

Finally, trust was lost in the ability of our senses to bring reality's witness to itself into our consciousness, and with this any ability to account for the mystery of human communication. The isolated subject, trapped in a world

---

34. Hans Urs von Balthasar, *The Glory of the Lord: A Theological Aesthetics, Volume V: The Realm of Metaphysics in the Modern Age,* trans. Oliver Davies, Andrew Louth, Brian McNeil, John Saward, Rowan Williams (San Francisco: Ignatius, 1991), 50.

35. Michael Buckley, "The Newtonian Settlement and the Origins of Atheism," in *Physics, Philosophy, and Theology: A Common Quest for Understanding,* ed. W. Stoeger, R. Russell, G. Coyne (Vatican City State: Vatican Observatory, 1988), 81-102, at 96.

36. Klaus Scholder, *The Birth of Modern Critical Theology: Origins and Problems of Biblical Criticism in the Seventeenth Century,* trans. John Bowden (London: SCM, 1990), 38.

of uncertain impressions, must have recourse to the immediate presence of individual consciousness (Descartes) and finally to the structures of that consciousness as it confronted an alien and rigidly determined cosmic system. Immanuel Kant's description of the isolated subject which must be determinative in the act of knowing bears eloquent witness to the penultimate stage in the journey toward a complete hermeneutics of suspicion:

> We have now not merely explored the territory of pure understanding, and carefully surveyed every part of it, but have also measured its extent, and assigned to everything in it its rightful place. This domain is an island, enclosed by nature itself with unalterable limits. It is the land of truth — enchanting name! — surrounded by a wide and stormy ocean, the native home of illusion, where many a fog bank and many a swiftly melting iceberg give the deceptive appearance of farther shores, deluding the adventurous seafarer even anew with empty hopes, and engaging him in enterprises which he can never abandon and yet is unable to carry to completion.[37]

The ultimate stage in the journey is arrived at in the postmodern suspicion of language itself which, rather than being an instrument of intersubjective communication, becomes the tool of power. While acknowledging the validity of this insight into the abuse of language, it must be borne in mind that an abuse is essentially the distortion of something that is being used in a way that is contrary to its nature. In the field of hermeneutics, suspicion becomes the way in which structures of power hidden in language are identified and unmasked. Where these are present, they must be understood for what they are, but this very unmasking presupposes that language is for the communication of truth and for the creation of community, not for the establishment of domination. A thoroughgoing socio-critical hermeneutics destroys, even while it uses, language as a means of communication.[38]

Retrieval

The Catholic way of reading Scripture must be genuinely *Catholic*, that is, it must be in living contact with the traditional reading of Scripture in the

---

37. Immanuel Kant, *Critique of Pure Reason*, trans. Norman Kemp Smith (New York: St. Martin's Press, 1929), 257.

38. Thiselton, *New Horizons*, 379: "*Socio-critical hermeneutics* may be defined as an approach to texts (or to traditions and institutions) which seeks to penetrate beneath their surface-function *to expose their role as instruments of power, domination, or social manipulation*" (emphasis in text).

church and also move that experiential understanding of the past into the present by integrating all that is true in the various Christian and philosophical traditions that have arisen in recent centuries. This, as I have said, is not a matter of a static juxtaposition but of a dynamic move forward. In this instance, I would suggest that a hermeneutics of trust must incorporate what is true in a critical hermeneutics in order to achieve what can be called a hermeneutics of disclosure. The topic is obviously vast; I wish here only to indicate some directions of the effort in order to show how a hermeneutics of disclosure can be achieved. I will rely on the chapter in Robert Sokolowski's *Eucharistic Presence: A Study in the Theology of Disclosure* in which he discusses the nature of the theology of disclosure.

The primary contribution of the theology of disclosure, particularly as it is relevant to a retrieval of the Catholic reading of Scripture, is that, as the application of the basic insights of phenomenology it manages to bypass the "egocentric predicament" created by the successive developments of a hermeneutics of suspicion. Since I wish to apply the method to the two issues of "presence" and "spiritual sense," I will content myself here with some lines from Sokolowski's discussion.

> [According to modernity] Ideas exist in the self-enclosed mind and they are immediately present to it. Ideas come between us and things. We have to get around them and outwit them if we are to reach the things themselves. To do so, we form hypotheses and build models in our minds, and we try to determine, by experiment, which of these hypotheses and models are false and which can be at least provisionally confirmed. In this way we hope to get beyond appearances to the things themselves, to the things that always remain absent and hidden from us.
>
> The suspicion of appearance in modernity has made manifestation the central issue in the philosophy of the last five centuries. Appearances are the metaphysical problem of modernity.
>
> The literary and philosophical movements called structuralism and deconstructionism claim that words and images refer only to other words and images: there are only texts that refer to other texts, codes that become reinterpreted into other codes; there is no center, nothing beyond the merely apparent to which our words, images, and consciousness can be related.[39]

Earlier forms of this dilemma act as a sort of "virus" in both Catholic and Protestant exegesis when they uncritically accept the unexpressed premises of

---

39. Robert Sokolowski, *Eucharistic Presence: A Study in the Theology of Disclosure* (Washington, D.C.: Catholic University of America Press, 1993), ch. 13, "The Theology of Disclosure."

the historical critical method. A genuine retrieval of the Tradition will respect the results which can be achieved by the method while critically moving from its twofold deficiency of making the mind the norm of reality ("critical" studies) and of contenting itself with the analysis of words ("textuality"), what may be called "verbal-centricity." An appreciation of what is meant by "intentionality" in the phenomenological view can enable us to account for the faith experience of Christians (even exegetes!) when they approach the Sacred Text in faith and come into contact with God and the divine realities of salvation. As Sokolowski says in another context:

> One of phenomenology's greatest contributions is to have broken out of the egocentric predicament, to have checkmated the Cartesian doctrine. Phenomenology shows that the mind is a public thing, that it acts and manifests itself out in the open, not just inside its own confines. . . . By discussing intentionality, phenomenology helps us reclaim a public sense of thinking, reasoning, and perception. It helps us reassume our human condition as agents of truth.[40]

This brief look at the contribution of phenomenology to the movement from the hermeneutics of suspicion to the hermeneutics of disclosure, shows us how the retrieval of the sense of presence and of the spiritual understanding of the Text can take place. I will give now just a few lines indicating some of the work to be done to effect a retrieval.

Presence

Commenting on 2 Timothy 3:16, Aquinas asks why only the Scriptures should be considered divinely inspired since, according to Ambrose, "anything true, by no matter whom said, is from the Holy Spirit." His response is that God works in two ways, one that is immediate and this pertains to him alone, such as is the case with miracles, and one that is mediate, that is through the mediation of lesser causes, as is the case with natural operations. He then says: "And thus in man God instructs the intellect both immediately through the sacred letters and mediately through other writings."[41]

---

40. Robert Sokolowski, *Introduction to Phenomenology* (New York: Cambridge University Press, 1999), 12.

41. *In 2 Tim 3*, lect. 3 in Thomas Aquinas, *Super Epistulas S. Pauli Lectura.* Volume 2 §812 (Rome: Marietti, 1953). For a complete discussion of this issue, and other texts of Aquinas, see Francis Martin, "Sacra Doctrina and the Authority of Its Sacra Scriptura in St. Thomas Aquinas" (forthcoming).

What Aquinas refers to as the "immediate" instruction given by God through the sacred letters, is precisely what I have been referring to as "presence," and what St. Leo intended by his phrase, "power of works which are present." In a Catholic perspective, the primary locus of this presence is, as I have pointed out, the Liturgy. This is the principle behind this statement of Vatican II:

> The Church has always venerated the Divine Scriptures as it has venerated the Body of the Lord, in that it never ceases, above all in the sacred liturgy, to take and distribute to the faithful from the one table the word of God and the Body of Christ. (*Dei Verbum* #21)

This statement is an invitation and a challenge to Catholics today to make that principle a reality by the way in which the liturgy is celebrated and in which the word is preached. But there is another dimension to retrieving the awareness of presence and continuity that must be attended to. Protestantism was born in the age of what philosophy calls "the turn to the subject" with its greater appreciation of the reality of the person, his or her dignity and rights. The danger latent in that move has been treated above in the discussion of the hermeneutics of suspicion. But there is another, and very important aspect of this that affects the reading of Scripture and must figure in a retrieval and enhancement of the Catholic approach to the Bible.

The "turn to the subject" must become the "turn to the person." The person must experience the "public" character of revelation and of his own mind in a deeply interior and personal reading of the Scriptures. It is time for Catholics, under the aegis of the Evangelical example (and of the Protestant example in general), to retrieve the monastic practice of *lectio divina* and make it once again, and in a much more widespread way, one of the backbones of lay piety.[42] There must be a *personal* reading of Scripture, with its concomitant experience of the presence of God and the efficacy of the mysteries of Christ as they are mediated by the Sacred Text. There is much work to be done here, but the thirst of Catholics for this type of reading is evidenced by the number of ecumenical Bible studies taking place all over the world and the way in which Catholics are profiting by the Evangelical charism for the simple and direct teaching of the Scriptures.

---

42. There has been a resurgence of interest in *lectio divina* for the laity. Among the works which have propounded this see Divo Barsotti, *La Parola e lo Spirito: Saggio sull'esegesi spirituale, Nuova Collana Liturgica 4* (Milano: Edizioni O.R., 1971); Salvatore A. Panimolle, ed., *Ascolto della Parola e Preghiera: La "Lectio Divina," Teologia Sapienziale 2* (Vatican City: Libreria Editrice Vaticana, 1987).

The Spiritual Sense

As I tried to point out at the beginning of this essay, the "spiritual sense" of the Sacred Text is really the spiritual understanding of the events mediated by the text, along with all the words of prayer, praise, explanation etc. that derive from these events. All is concentrated in Christ, the prime analogate in whose act of love on the cross all the other acts of salvation find their source and meaning.

The primary work of retrieval in this regard has already been accomplished through the historical work of de Lubac and others. The fact of the spiritual understanding of the Scriptures has been established. What remains to be done, however, is an enormous task. The philosophy of history is, at its root, the philosophy of human action, and the philosophical task of understanding the properly human mode of existence, that of a spiritual/material *person* whose proper existence is freedom in time, has yet to be explored. The philosopher who has done most in this regard is Maurice Blondel.[43] As this is undertaken, an entirely new anthropology and meta-anthropology will emerge as the philosophical expression of what the Scriptures teach as an unwritten text, namely the gathering of human act and time into Christ, already present in "shadow" and "image" and existing as "truth" ready to be made manifest in the fullness of time. The theologian who has done the most in this regard is undoubtedly Hans Urs von Balthasar.[44]

Because the Catholic reading of Scripture is founded on event, it is close to Liturgy and is also, instinctively, a development of the understanding of the *res* and not merely the *verba*. Admittedly this is disconcerting to Protestants, especially those whose epistemology is still tinged with the hermeneutics of suspicion (this holds as well for Catholics), when there is a question of the relation between Scripture and Tradition, particularly in the matter of the development of doctrine. A retrieval of this Catholic instinct requires dialogue with the Protestant, and again primarily the Evangelical, instinct for the uniqueness of the scriptural expression of divine truth. The meeting point

43. For an initial study of his thought see Peter Henrici, "The One Who Went Unnamed: Maurice Blondel in the Encyclical *Fides et Ratio*," *Communio* 26:3 (1999): 609-21. Also, Karol Wojtyla, "A Letter from Pope John Paul II to Bishop Bernard Panafieu, February 19, 1993," *Communio* 20 (1993): 721-23. This letter marks the centenary of the publication of Blondel's *L'Action*.

44. See once again the article by Bieler, "The Future of the Philosophy of Being" to whom I also owe the expression "meta-anthropological" in the sense of a philosophy and theology of being that, going beyond meta-*physics* is an understanding of being that is based on *human* being.

will be found in a mutual deepening of the understanding of the interpersonal nature of truth, and in a common experience of the trinitarian source of revelation which is communicated by Jesus Christ as the revealer of the Father and thus, in Johannine terms, is himself the Way, the Truth, and the Life.

Conclusion

I have tried to establish two things. First, the Catholic manner of reading Scripture is basically a contact with the Sacred Text as it mediates divine realities. It views revelation as an act of God by which he manifests and communicates *himself* and a knowledge of his plan of salvation (see *Dei Verbum* #2,6). It finds its primary home in the communal celebration of the Liturgy and in the continuation of that celebration in personal *lectio divina*. Theology is discourse on the realities mediated by Scripture undertaken under the direction and authority of this same Scripture as understood by the whole community of believers, and with respectful submission to the prophetic guidance and safeguards of the lawful leaders of the community.

Second, there is much work to be done in order to effect an authentic retrieval of this way of reading Scipture. This retrieval cannot be accomplished without a reverent docility to what the Holy Spirit has taught other Christian Communions, particularly in regard to the personal, Spirit-guided reading of Scripture and the need for preaching the word. There must be as well a serious, critical, and new appreciation of what is true in the philosophical acquisitions of recent centuries: these affect our minds and must be looked at squarely and competently. Our efforts in this group, Evangelicals and Catholics Together, form an important step in the retrieval I have tried to describe.